CENTERING FAMILIES OF COLOR

FAMILIES, LAW, AND SOCIETY SERIES

General Editors: Nancy E. Dowd and Robin A. Lenhardt

Centering Families of Color

A Reimagination of Family Law

Edited by

R. A. Lenhardt *and* Nancy E. Dowd

New York University Press

New York

NEW YORK UNIVERSITY PRESS
New York
www.nyupress.org

Library of Congress Cataloging-in-Publication Data
Names: Lenhardt, Robin A., editor. | Dowd, Nancy E., 1949–   editor.
Title: Centering families of color : a reimagination of family law /
edited by R.A. Lenhardt and Nancy E. Dowd.
Description: New York : New York University Press, 2026. | Series: Families, law, and society |
Includes bibliographical references and index.
Identifiers: LCCN 2025024117 (print) | LCCN 2025024118 (ebook) | ISBN 9781479833320
(hardback) | ISBN 9781479842025 (paperback) | ISBN 9781479833337 (ebook) | ISBN
9781479833344 (ebook other)
Subjects: LCSH: Domestic relations. | African American families—Social aspects. |
African American families—Social conditions—History. | African American children—
Legal status, laws, etc. | Families, Black—Social aspects. | Children, Black—
Legal status, laws, etc.
Classification: LCC KF505 .C46 2026 (print) | LCC KF505 (ebook) |
DDC 346.7301/508996073—dc23/eng/20250519
LC record available at https://lccn.loc.gov/2025024117
LC ebook record available at https://lccn.loc.gov/2025024118

This book is printed on acid-free paper, and its binding materials are chosen for strength and durability. We strive to use environmentally responsible suppliers and materials to the greatest extent possible in publishing our books.

The manufacturer's authorized representative in the EU for product safety is Mare Nostrum Group B.V., Mauritskade 21D, 1091 GC Amsterdam, The Netherlands. Email: gpsr@mare-nostrum.co.uk.

Manufactured in the United States of America

10 9 8 7 6 5 4 3 2 1

Also available as an ebook

CONTENTS

Introduction

Reframing

R. A. LENHARDT AND NANCY E. DOWD

Standing from the perspective of families of color is essential to engage in equality and social justice for all families. This lens exposes structural flaws and deliberate subordination, as well as systemic needs. Just as significantly, the history and experiences, as well as the daily practices, of families of color offer powerful developmental models and examples of leadership and community activism for the benefit of children and families. If all families and all children are to be equal, the insights and realities of the most marginalized are critical to address the toxic consequences for the privileged as well.

This analysis, generated from the perspective of families of color, could change the law to an agent of equality. If we were to seriously engage in the constitutional component of recognizing and implementing equality for families of color, it would require not only coming to grips with the absence of families of color in the constitutional pantheon of cases trumpeting family values but also denouncing the harms done in the name of the Constitution to families of color.

The valorization of family as pivotal and sacred, embodying relationships and principles older than the Constitution but central to its purpose, has not extended to families of color. To the contrary, law's honoring of family has incorporated racial lines integral to the subordination of families of color. Racial hierarchy as integral to colonization was ratified in the blatant endorsement of slavery and exclusion of the enslaved as persons in Article I of the Constitution.[1] Hierarchy was confirmed in the infamous *Dred Scott* opinion of 1857, finding that persons of African heritage *whether slave or free* were not intended ever to be part of "We the People" and thus had no rights.[2] Neither Dred Scott nor his emancipated wife could protect his family, could save his daughters from separation from their parents, or claim the right to be heard in court, because none of them were people, none were human. The Reconstruction Amendments, a second founding designed to *include* African Americans as part of the people were quickly eviscerated. Racial hierarchy reemerged, and the embrace of inequality and disregard for personhood and family was "redeemed" in *Plessey v. Ferguson*, ushering in unprecedented, comprehensive discrimination and violence under Jim Crow.[3] Not until *Brown v. Board of Education*, just seventy years ago, were the Reconstruction Amendments exhumed and revived.[4]

And yet *Brown's* radicalism is still unrealized. *Brown* by its terms mandated comprehensive equality, to repair the harms of comprehensive segregation. Comprehensive equality by its terms meant the equality of families of color. It heralded potentially a new role for law, to serve as defender and protector of families of color under a regime of equality, rather than oppression. Yet equality has been resisted, challenged, and ignored, while inequality has persisted, hidden behind colorblindness or blamed on its victims. *Brown* itself most recently has been recast as prohibiting virtually all race-conscious policies, ironically preventing efforts to redress the inequalities of our current context to achieve racial equality.[5] This reinscribes inequalities by refusing to acknowledge that they exist.

Inequalities exist. They are rampant. Every economic indicator exposes wide differences between families of color and white families: in average income, rate of employment, wealth accumulation, and the rate of poverty.[6] Children of color, who constitute slightly over half of all children, are the most vulnerable of family members. They have an extraordinarily high level of poverty, and on a range of indicators—birth weight, pre-K education, reading and math proficiency, earning an associate degree or higher, steady employment after completing school, to name just a few—can only count on, on average, less than half the support structure of white children, which translates into less than half the opportunity structure of white children.[7] These measurable factors do not capture the impact of cultural and developmental challenges from the microaggressions and macroaggressions of conscious and unconscious racism. Invisibility and marginalization characterize the treatment of families of color in constitutional law.

Much of the intersection of families and law happens outside of constitutional law. Family law, broadly construed to mean families' interactions with multiple domains of law to fulfill their nurturing role (for example, education, health care, economic support), has been no more inclusive and supportive of families of color than has constitutional law and has arguably been more harmful. Invisibility is present as well as active harm and negative interaction. Were we to rewrite or recast families of color as the focus of family law, we would be required to expose the ways in which the law has ratified racial hierarchy while ignoring the impact of inequality. Family law would need to be transformed in order to be inclusive of families of color and to be committed to their well-being. We would reframe family law not only to be responsive to critique, such as the failure and skewed reach of conventional family law doctrines and structure (excluding families of color), but also to incorporate those structures (or the lack of them) that families rely on and need to support the care and nurture of all family members. At the same time, we would recognize and support the affirmative model of families of color, while also casting off for good the deficit model and inhumanity of our current pervasive assumptions about families of color.

In this book, we aim to begin the project of recasting the treatment of, and promoting the affirmative models of, families of color. This is a project on race, family, and inequality in service to multiracial democratic family equality. Originating in the wake of George Floyd's murder at the hands of Minneapolis police and the ongoing effects of COVID-19 on people of color, the need for this book has only increased with the inequities that persist and the unabated violence that continues. The need to call out structural inequality is ever more apparent in areas as diverse as incarceration, health care, and housing, among others.

This volume presents a critical perspective to reorient the law as it affects families to consider all legal structures that impact families and to incorporate and critically examine the standpoint and experiences of families of color. This volume expands the story of social justice reform by identifying and giving voice to the powerful role of families of color and in particular women of color. It is essential to maintain this perspective, rather than slipping back into a view of law and society that privileges white families while obscuring the subordination of families of color. Our framing of structural inequality has been incomplete. It fails to center families, especially those of color, in both the diagnoses and solutions for change. We aim to play a role in solving this problem. This book looks to close the gap by centering families of color in current debates of structural inequity and its impact. It imagines families as change agents for racial justice and substantive equality in the twenty-first century.

In contrast to the conventional treatment of families of color, which marginalizes their role socially and politically, this volume centers them as families and as mothers, fathers, and children to expose their active role in social change as well as to expose families of color as affirmative, resilient models amid a context of structural and cultural subordination. Their experience and advocacy have been critical to strategies for social justice and reform. The common threads in this collection by outstanding scholars include historical connections as well as contemporary challenges; resilient family models challenging stereotypes and ongoing deficit models; and the identification of systems and structures that embed family hierarchies instead of equitable family support.

Reams of data tell us that families of color have faced disproportionate, unique challenges that continue to bedevil individual, familial, and community success. Too often, however, those very data are used to feed a dialogue of inhumanity, devaluation, and inequality. To the contrary, as the chapters in this volume identify, families of color exemplify healthy and strong models of resilience and resistance, models of liberty, equality, and activism.

* * *

We begin with a critical historical focus, as our current context of the remarkable record of families of color, together with their disproportionate challenges, is rooted in enslavement, toxic racism, and constructed racial hierarchy. Peggy Cooper Davis provides essential framing of the impact of enslavement on family rights and individual personhood, coupled with the radical ideas of freedom, liberty, and equality of the second founding. The realization of those goals remains elusive, while the structural and cultural challenges of enslavement persist along with the record of resistance. The scope of familial rights necessary to freedom, as she outlines, goes far beyond the conventional private realm of family life to the public support of families, particularly with respect to education but other systems as well. Jessica Dixon Weaver's chapter focusing on Black families after Reconstruction underscores the enormity of reconstructing family and community after the Civil War and the modern parallels reflecting the vestiges of still-unresolved inequalities and racial violence. Her recounting of the Memphis Massacre links the undermining of Reconstruction's freedom promise to contemporary echoes of violence and structural inequality. Serena Mayeri takes us to the more recent history of Black women's leadership in the 1960s and 1970s to reform family law and protect the integrity of their families.

The second group of chapters focus on mothers and fathers, challenging the prevailing deficit model of parenting within families of color. Anita Gonzalez uses a different lens to understand and paint a picture of women-headed families in Washington, DC, exposing the survival and thriving practices to sustain family. This includes a description of a performance project, Zora on My Mind, telling the story of Eloise Nash Nichols as a means to understand the construction and lived reality of Black women's lives. Marketa Burnett elaborates on the developmental model of Black families grounded in resilience and resistance and their lessons for thriving. The challenges of Black fatherhood are underscored in the chapter by Derek Griffith et al., identifying with an intersectional lens the persistence of negative tropes of Black fathers even within programs purportedly designed to increase their role in Black families. Essential to the success of Black fathers is a holistic understanding of the context in which they function and the overwhelmingly negative cultural scripts about Black men.

The final group of chapters identify systems that are essential to a reframed idea of family law grounded in the equality of all families, as these systems (and others) are part of the actual family law structure of all families but particularly and negatively impact families of color. Structural inequality is fed by the inadequacy or lack of structural support, the skewed nature of support provided, and the undermining of families by particular systems. Solangel Maldonado targets the foster care system's failure to recruit and support families of color as foster parents to the disproportionate numbers of Black and Brown children in the foster care system. By no means an apologist for the system, she targets a clear mandate that remains unfulfilled: the robust recruitment of diverse families that could serve to maximize best developmental outcomes for children of color who end up in foster care. She asks us to imagine a country in which the law supported and empowered extended family members and fictive kin to care for children The health-care system is the focus of the chapter by Yael Zakai Cannon. Cannon articulates and applies the lens of health justice as a means to health equity to combat the physical and mental harms of structural inequality and intersectional inequalities. Aziza Ahmed and Jason Jackson expose the operation of the health-care system during the pandemic and its disproportionate impact on families of color and, in particular, on essential workers and their families. The invisibility and disregard for the health, well-being, and realities of family and household link to family exceptionalism, rendering family private and unsupported in ways that disproportionately harmed families of color during COVID.

Maxine Eicher offers a comprehensive global picture of the lack of family supports in the US system, a structural lack that hits hardest on families with the greatest needs. This lack of support includes rigid work/family policies, inadequate and expensive child care, meager benefits to ensure adequate income support, and persisting unwillingness to reduce child poverty. She links this to ongoing racist justifications ultimately grounded in the lack of valuing of children of color. Priscilla A. Ocen and Michelle S. Jacobs critique the egregious family law system of incarceration. Ocen identifies "prison family law," the sets of policies and practices that govern and largely undermine family relationships with those who are incarcerated. Jacobs focuses in particular on incarcerated women and their treatment, a horrific and stark reminder of the most extreme end of a continuum that begins outside prison walls. Jacobs identifies the systems that fail women and are linked to why they are incarcerated, as well as their treatment as mothers and the treatment of their children. Under the present system, their families and roles as family members are destroyed. If they are to be respected, a radical change in the carceral system is unavoidable. This systemic structural perspective includes a final overview by Clare Huntington, arguing that significant structural and cultural change is essential but questioning whether it is possible and whether some incremental progress should be viewed positively or does little more than represent an inadequate Band-Aid that hides the critical needs of all families exemplified by focusing on families of color.

These diverse chapters provide a starting point to expand and continue to bring the perspectives and realities of families of color to the center of family law and policy, to achieve the principles of equality, freedom, and justice.

NOTES

1 US Constitution, Article I, Section 2, paragraph 3 (1787).

2 Dred Scott v. Sandford, 60 U.S. (19 How.) 393 (1857).

3 Plessy v. Ferguson, 163 U.S. 537 (1896).

4 Brown v. Board of Education, 347 U.S. 483 (1954).

5 Students for Fair Admissions v. Harvard, 600 U.S. 181 (2023).

6 Andre M. Perry, Hannah Stephens, and Manann Donoghoe, "Black Wealth Is Increasing but So Is the Racial Wealth Gap," Brookings, January 9, 2024, www.brookings.edu; The Neighborhood Finance Guy, "2024 Economic State of Black Struggle and Its Long-Term Effects on Black Wealth," February 15, 2024, https://theneighborhoodfinanceguy.com.

7 Annie E. Casey Foundation, 2024 Race for Results: Building a Pathway to Opportunity for All Children (Annie E. Casey Foundation, January 10, 2024), www.aecf.org; Heller School for Social Policy and Management, Brandeis, "New Data Show Severe Racial and Ethnic Inequities in Child Opportunity In and Between U.S. Metros," March 14, 2024, https://heller.brandeis.edu.

1

Family and the Meaning of Freedom

PEGGY COOPER DAVIS

The critical race theorist Patricia Williams teaches that whereas contract or commercial law focuses primarily on the protection of ownership and control, constitutional law is (or should be) more centrally focused on the protection of human autonomy, dignity, and liberty.[1] The story of the Black family in the United States is a story of Black people's persistent struggle against the control of slavers who had contracted and bartered to own them. It is also a story of the constitutionalization for all people within the jurisdiction of the United States of rights to the autonomy, dignity, and liberty that Black people were denied under the regime of human chattel slavery.

Slavery is by definition the commodification of human beings. Under the laws of slavery, people were owned and could be controlled by their owners. They were property subject to owners' needs or whims rather than constitutional subjects.

Under the laws and practices of slavery in the United States, commodification disrupted human development by denying family. In a state of freedom, families form, and those families choose ways of nurturing children. Within the framework of family nurturance, children develop chosen ways of being. In slavery in the United States, family formation was inhibited, and family nurturance was disrupted. The possibilities of autonomy, of chosen alliances and of chosen values, were foreclosed, as the enslaved being was treated in practice and in law as property and a tool of an owner. In slavery, the enforced tie to an owner superseded instinctive or chosen ties to actual or fictive kin.

Antislavery struggle in the United States was a struggle against the cycles of commodification that were attempted across generations of enslaved people. It was a struggle for family and nascent autonomy rather than ownership and lifelong control. When that struggle was won on battlefields of the US Civil War, the nation reconstructed its Constitution to prohibit human commodification. The reconstructed Constitution guarantees human and family autonomy, and, in turn, it enables social and political affiliation. People can no longer be the possessions of masters. Adult people are self-governing subjects as a matter of constitutional and human right. Children are no longer the property of masters. Children are sons, daughters, and members of extended families with chosen values and chosen ways of being. In sum, the US Constitution was substantially reconstructed by the Civil War Amendments to enable the formation of free families and the nurturance of free personhood within those families.

A full analysis of the antislavery ideology on which the reconstructed Constitution was based reveals that it is properly understood to protect these things:

- *Market agency* and a corresponding right to produce and exchange goods and services
- *Political personhood* and a corresponding right to education and civic participation
- *Human dignity* and a corresponding right of public accommodation
- *Family recognition* and corresponding rights of familial choice

These things were assured because appreciation of each of them had been deepened in the fiery light cast by human chattel slavery's atrocities. I review each of them and consider how understanding their value in the wake of slavery has affected—and how it should affect—our national commitment to human freedom and human rights. As a legal scholar, I take the measure of those effects by examining their manifestations in our constitutional jurisprudence. Each has been reflected in our jurisprudence, although none has received the recognition that it arguably deserves. The last of them—family recognition—is foundational to those listed above it, both in terms of human sensibilities and in terms of democratic theory.

Market Agency

The forcible appropriation of labor is perhaps the most conspicuous aspect of slavery. Chattel slavery on cotton, sugar, tobacco, and rice plantations made the brutality of enforced and unrewarded labor painfully manifest. Men, women, and children were worked to their physical capacities and replaced by the purchase of fresh bodies when they were exhausted, dead, or rebellious. And the prerogative of a slave "master" was little qualified when enslaved people served in less conspicuously punishing capacities than agricultural labor. Lunsford Lane was an enslaved person who did not labor in the fields but in homes and offices. Yet, he lamented poignantly in his narrative of life as an enslaved person that to be another's property was "to know . . . that I was never to consult my own will, but was, while I lived, to be entirely under the control of another."[2]

African American participation in the Civil War was aptly and famously described by W. E. B. Du Bois as a labor strike. It was not, of course, the beginning of rebellion against the slave system. As Caitlin Rosenthal reminds us in her eloquent and scholarly analysis of enslavers' ledger books, it was the culminating step after countless acts of rebellion. Enslaved people naturally "defied planters' efforts to reduce them to columns of capital and units of output." They displayed a beautiful humanity as they "shared information and buil[t] families." Moreover, in defiance of systems designed to extinguish their moral and social existence, leaving only their controlled labor, enslaved people did as free workers do under exploitive conditions. "They slowed the pace of work, took supplies, and shared resources."[3] With the outbreak of hostilities between the slaveholding and free states, everyday resistance swelled to merge with an all-out war that would put an end to the slave system. When the nation was reconstructed after that war, the Thirteenth Amendment was explicit in its prohibition of involuntary labor. This history suggests that the right to withhold and to bargain for one's labor is both an aspect of the freedom guaranteed by the Thirteenth Amendment's prohibition of slavery and other involuntary servitude, as well as an aspect of the Fourteenth Amendment's protection of liberty.

Laborers' rights have had some support in US constitutional jurisprudence. But that support has been limited, and protection of workers' rights has been more the result of legislated measures than of constitutional entitlement. Indeed, protection of workers is so little imagined as a matter of constitutional right that government agencies dedicated to worker protection make little mention of the Constitution.

When the federal Department of Labor or the Equal Employment Opportunity Commission lists workers' civil rights, it tracks federal legislation, without reference to the Thirteenth or Fourteenth Amendment. The same is true of the National Labor Relations Board and the Occupational Safety and Health Administration. As the constitutional and labor scholar Luke Norris has observed, workers in the United States must infer an unwritten set of constitutional rights that have elided judicial recognition and been too often balanced by solicitude toward employers' rights.[4]

Political Personhood

An understanding of political personhood in the United States begins with Dred Scott, his wife, and their two daughters, all of whom were enslaved. Dred Scott sued to establish his freedom and that of his family on the ground that they had been taken by their owner to free territory. The US Supreme Court pronounced their fate in notoriously shocking terms.[5] Not only were Scott and his family not freed by their travels to free territory, but according to the Court, they—and their kind—were political nonentities, having no right to sue in the courts of the United States, having indeed *no* rights that "White men," and hence the nation, were bound to respect. The Supreme Court consigned Dred Scott to statelessness because the majority justices could not imagine that people of African descent were included—or even thought of—when "we the people" set out to form a more perfect union. People of African descent were said to have existed in the minds of the Founders as inferior beings, useful as labor power and fully subject to the will of their betters.

The Civil War and the Reconstruction Amendments overruled the Court's decision in *Dred Scott.* The Thirteenth Amendment forbade enslavement or involuntary servitude (except as punishment for crime), and the Fourteenth Amendment conferred citizenship, with attendant privileges and immunities, as a right of birth on US soil. Neither of these amendments set out the meaning of free citizenship or defined its privileges in any detail. It is safe, however, to say that at minimum, a free citizen is a member of the political community—a person not subject to the Scott family's decreed status of statelessness and political impotence.

The US Supreme Court held in 1875 that women had no constitutional right to vote, thus denying women the most basic right of participatory government. But the Court acknowledged that women, as citizens, were nonetheless *members of the nation.*[6] This is the baseline status that all free citizens hold. They are members of the nation. When ratification of the Fourteenth Amendment made people of African descent citizens, they, too, became members of the nation—members of the US political community. The Court has struggled to define the rights and attributes of members of the US political community. Indeed, it took an additional constitutional amendment to guarantee female members of the political community the right to vote, and it has been argued persuasively that the drafters of the Fourteenth and Fifteenth Amendments did not intend to give competent citizens a right to hold office.[7] It can be seen that acceptance of women and people of color as members of the political family casts revealing light on the nation's willingness—and its obligation—to grant political efficacy to all of its people.

Public Accommodation

Categorical separation is usually hierarchical, and as such, it stigmatizes some and glorifies others. Racial segregation in the United States has carried obvious messages of inferiority and superiority. Segregation by sexual orientation carries the same implications. As the work of the philosopher Jeremy Waldron suggests, the mark of inferiority carried by race segregation in the United States threatens the ability of parents of an ostracized group to nurture their children to a sense of worthiness, of agency, of social comfort, and of civic belonging. Waldron quotes Lyndon Johnson's retort to critics of the 1964 Civil Rights Act and its protections against discrimination in public places. Johnson reportedly said, "A man has a right not to be insulted in front of his children."[8] Respect for the dignity of each member of a community forbids group-based exclusions and refusals, because those exclusions and refusals carry implications of caste and hierarchy. They imply that one group is more or less worthy than another and therefore more or less welcome as a participant in economic and social life. They deny adults the dignity of recognition as respected fellow beings, and they inhibit their children's sense of belonging and squelch their ambition for social engagement as they mature.

The national government and most (but not all) state governments in the United States have enacted legislation against categorical, identity-based denials of access to public accommodation. The Supreme Court has not, however, recognized public accommodation as a fundamental right, and it has bowed in the face of public accommodation denials to gay and lesbian people when those denials were said to have been premised on religious conviction.[9] Justices have signaled that protections against race-based denials of public accommodation are not vulnerable in the face of religious opposition, but the Court's deference to religiously based denials of accommodation is cause for concern: It suggests a failure to appreciate the personal and family harms that the stigma of exclusion causes, not only to individuals but also to family units seeking to nurture a sense of dignity and civic belonging.

Family Recognition

Scholars of slavery have noted that enslaved people were most fundamentally marked by the inability to form, claim, or maintain family. This characteristic, aptly called "natal alienation," exacerbated the negation caused by the statelessness of being a political nonentity. It was even greater than the insult of being physically segregated or excluded from public life. Natal alienation meant that one was property *rather than progeny.* As property, one was subject to the will and to the financial or personal interests of an owner rather than guided and encouraged by parental nurture.

The human spirit resists commodification and is nourished by affection. Bonds of affection held and nurtured free families as the brutal grip of human ownership was broken by resistance and emancipation. Formerly enslaved people enacted their freedom by forming or holding to *chosen* family and fictive allegiances. It is fitting, in light of this history, that the reconstructed Constitution has been held to recognize, however tenuously, rights of choice in marriage, regardless of race and regardless of gender.

* * *

This book speaks to scars left by a history of human commodification. It speaks to the effects of denying human beings market agency, of denying them a place and a stake in the polity, of denying them access in public spheres, and of denying recognition to their chosen families. But most of all it speaks to the will, the love, and the creativity that enabled Black families to endure despite enslavement and that enable us now to thrive, regardless of lingering stigma and structural abuse.

NOTES

1 Patricia J. Williams, *The Miracle of the Black Leg: Notes on Race, Human Bodies, and the Spirit of the Law* (New Press, 2024).

2 Peggy Cooper Davis, *Neglected Stories: The Constitution and Family Values* (Hill and Wang, 1997), 136.

3 Caitlin Rosenthal, *Accounting for Slavery: Masters and Management* (Harvard University Press, 2018), 4.

4 Shaun Richman, "The Right to Organize at Work Deserves Constitutional Protection," *Vox*, September 2, 2017, www.vox.com/.

5 Dred Scott v. Sandford, 60 U.S. 393 (1856).

6 Minor v. Happersett, 88 U.S. 162 (1875).

7 Alfred Avins, "The Right to Hold Public Office and the Fourteenth and Fifteenth Amendments: The Original Understanding," *University of Kansas Law Review* 15 (1967): 287–306.

8 Jeremy Waldron, *The Harm in Hate Speech (Oliver Wendell Holmes Lectures)* (Harvard University Press, 2014), 83–84.

9 303 Creative LLC v. Elenis, 600 U.S. 570 (2023).

2

Elusive Freedom

African American Families in the Reconstruction Era

JESSICA DIXON WEAVER

The 1863 Emancipation Proclamation freed approximately four million enslaved persons.[1] The Proclamation only reached, however, enslaved persons in Confederate states. The Thirteenth Amendment had to be ratified in 1865 to legally abolish slavery across the United States and all its territories. The freedom of African Americans came only after the loss of 750,000 soldiers in the Civil War, and Southern slave owners were reluctant to give them their liberty.[2] The Reconstruction era after the Civil War was filled with hope, uncertainty, and new beginnings for Blacks, who had mostly lived lives punctuated by violence, fear, backbreaking hard work, hunger, and trauma. The idea of freedom was exhilarating, documented by celebrations of joy and hope for a self-determined future.

Albert Harris and his wife experienced both the joy of freedom and the terror of violence targeted at newly freed Black citizens. Born and raised together in Virginia during the early nineteenth century, they were married while enslaved but were "carried away from each other" until the Civil War.[3] They reunited in Memphis, Tennessee, probably by happenstance, where Albert worked as a shoemaker. The Memphis Massacre occurred in 1866. A white mob ran through the streets of Memphis for three days at the beginning of May, terrorizing the Black community. Fifty-three-year-old Albert and his wife were held at gunpoint and robbed of their life savings. Albert's shotgun was stolen from him, but his life and home were spared. Others were not so fortunate. At the end of this southern "outrage," forty-six Black people were killed, seventy-five were wounded, and five females were raped.[4] There were one hundred robberies, ninety-one houses and cabins were burned, and all four

Black churches and twelve schoolhouses were destroyed. The damages totaled $130,981, which is the modern-day equivalent of over $3 million.

The destruction and destabilization of Black communities and families during and after the Reconstruction era is an underexplored part of the history of the United States. Though the Memphis Massacre is the first documented destruction of a Black community, there were over one hundred Southern outrages after the Civil War.[5] "Outrage" was the term used to describe massive deadly attacks on Black communities, typically by organized white groups like the Ku Klux Klan. History is rife with instances when police officers and citizens killed Black people, while governing officials—who knew about the violence—stepped aside, did nothing, or initiated and assisted in the slaughter. Most of the well-known incidents have been the subjects of movies or popular documentaries, such as *Rosewood* and *Dreamland: The Burning of Black Wall Street*.[6] The catalyst for the attacks on Black freedom was often job or housing competition between the white working class and newly freed Black people. There were also fears, often generated by newspapers, about Black people revolting against white people and killing them. At the root of the annihilation of multiple Black communities was the suppression of the full embodiment of Black freedom. While some of the tactics have changed, there are parallels between the racial attacks during Reconstruction and the impact of contemporary structural racism.

This chapter recounts the new lives that were built by freed persons in Memphis, Tennessee. When the Union secured the South, it utilized the Freedmen's Bureau to supervise and manage all matters affecting formerly enslaved people.[7] The Freedmen's Bureau functioned as a government social service agency that provided freed people with food, clothing, medical attention, employment, support for education, and help with military claims of Black men who fought in the Civil War with the Union. Even though the Bureau was in place for four years after the end of the Civil War, it struggled to safeguard the rights of the free Black community. Securing justice for freed people was a priority of the Bureau because "many [new] laws in southern states restricted the rights and legal status of freed people."[8]

On May 30, 1865, Major General Oliver Otis Howard, who was appointed the commissioner of the Freedmen's Bureau by President Andrew Johnson, issued orders to his assistant commissioners on the conditions for solemnizing former slave marriages.[9] The assistant commissioners were authorized to designate officers who had to keep a record of marriages of persons of color, and ministers were required to report on the marriages they performed.

Within a year of the Bureau's marriage registrations with the US government and the state of Tennessee, the Bureau documented the first Southern outrage, dubbed as the Memphis Riots of 1866. "The Memphis Riots and Massacre" also were documented by the US House of Representatives in the first session of the thirty-ninth Congress.[10] This outrage resulted in the destruction of the Memphis Black community at the hands of a white community mob, led by the police and sanctioned by the mayor.

The Memphis riots were notable because they happened on the eve of the passage of the Fourteenth Amendment to the US Constitution. This amendment was intended to protect the rights of emancipated slaves as citizens and to ensure that the government would not take their lives, property, or freedom without a fair trial or legal process, critical to protecting them against racist violence and bigoted state laws. In 1866, the thirty-ninth US Congress grappled with how legislation could support freed people. How and whether the government could protect Black families from violent atrocities, annihilation of their communities, and the stripping away of life's basic necessities are still in question today.

Emancipation and Black Family Status

Even though marriages between enslaved persons were not legal, slave owners often consented to marriage between enslaved couples who built families and passed on traditions from West Africa. Marriage was a means of uniting families and establishing social order throughout Africa centuries before the transatlantic slave trade ever began. It was not a new concept to enslaved persons. The essential difference between white families and enslaved families was the concept of the kinship family.[11] The kinship family system in Africa was derived from blood ties, marriage, or adoption.[12] This West African tradition continued in North America due to the constant separations between parents and children, spouses, and siblings. Children integrated into new enslaved families in the communities where they were sold, and often adults remarried and formed new families after being separated from their first or second families.

Both the struggle and ability to maintain family ties among enslaved persons was controlled by the economy and shifts within slaveholders' family. Members of enslaved families were auctioned off or forced to separate because of the demand for cotton, slaveholders' debts and wills, avoidance of intrafamily turmoil caused by white male infidelities with enslaved women, and punishments for enslaved persons who defied their owner or ran away. A key catalyst for the abolition movement was the negative impact of slavery on the family.

The experiences of children separated from their parents and other family members, as well as spouses sold away from each other, were relayed by the narratives of well-known formerly enslaved persons such as Frederick Douglass, William Brown, and Harriet Jacobs. Douglass was separated from his mother shortly after birth and only saw his mother when she walked twelve miles to sleep next to him at night.[13] William Brown recounted how his mother had seven children, none by the same father, and was told that his father was a white relative of his owner.[14] He witnessed many horrors of the slave trade, including a young woman jumping overboard and drowning herself because she was taken from her husband and child, a man being severely whipped because he walked six miles without permission to visit his wife who was sold away, and a young baby being sold away from his mother because his crying annoyed their master. Harriet Jacobs's narrative painfully tells how she was stalked and sexually assaulted when she was eleven years old.[15]

The length of time that enslaved couples dealt with extralegal complex family dynamics is not widely recognized within sociolegal policy. For over two and a half centuries, enslaved married couples were "precluded from a bundle of privileges: inviolability of their unions, sexual exclusivity, control over their children, the right to spousal recusal before bench and bar, coverture, and comity."[16] An enslaved husband often did not even live on the same land as his wife, and he had no control over his children, who were the property of his wife's owner. It was very common for Black women to be sexually assaulted by white men, and their husbands could not protect them without risking their lives. Hundreds of thousands of biracial children were born as proof of these extramarital activities, and white women often witnessed their children growing up alongside enslaved half siblings. To avoid humiliation, many white wives forced their husbands to sell the enslaved mothers of his children as well as the children. Being sold typically meant permanent separation from a spouse and children, and most enslaved persons remarried and started new families.

The few narratives of enslaved men and women illustrate that almost every person experienced broken relationships because of the institution of slavery. Blood ties were used against enslaved persons by owners, their wives, and other whites to control them or break their spirits. Amid the brutality of enslavement, they loved and found joy within connections that were tenuous and often limited by a timeline outside their control.

During the Civil War, many enslaved couples choose to get married "under the flag." This phrase was used to refer to remarriage ceremonies that "were officiated by military officers and army chaplains literally below flags flying above or nearby."[17] This act redefined the intimate relationships of enslaved persons by ostensibly ridding the African family of Southern state rules. This type of marriage in Union-controlled areas became sought after by enslaved couples—leading to a type of de facto freedom for fugitives. Federal engagement in marriage making was initiated by enslaved persons seeking refuge behind Union lines.

The mere emancipation of enslaved persons did not legitimize their family relationships in every state. In fact, the right to marry in many jurisdictions was created by curative legislation enacted at the end of the Civil War. Tennessee passed the Act of 1866, which "ratified de facto slave marriages and legitimized the children of those relationships."[18] For separated families, freedom allowed them to search for their spouses and/or children.[19] Many couples, parents, and children were reunited. Other couples in Southern states who had lived together for years were happy to legally marry and register their unions with the state and document them with the federal government. Thousands of Black couples were legally married for the first time, experiencing perhaps the first act of citizenship since being freed. Over one hundred documented couples in Memphis, Tennessee, experienced the new citizenship right of legal marriage in 1865 through marriage certificates granted through the Freedmen's Bureau and the state. However, this new privilege did not protect the formerly enslaved population of Memphis from the wrath they encountered in May 1866.

Exercising Citizenship Rights: The Intersection of Law and Violence

After the enslaved population of Black people was freed, they were not provided a roadmap of where to go or what to do, nor were they given much money, land, or other goods to create a life for themselves. Ironically, the US government paid slave owners large amounts of money for the enlistment of enslaved men and women who had been drafted into the Union army. There are letters that document officers paying specific landowners amounts ranging from $200 to $1,200 for named enslaved persons who had enlisted in the Union army. The amount paid was based on an index that afforded funds due based on the number of years left in servitude or whether they were a slave for life. From a modern-day perspective, reparations were paid to the Southern planters and owners of enslaved people—rather than to the enslaved persons themselves.

The fate of the formerly enslaved—how they would live from day to day and how they would be treated by former slave owners and other whites in their community—was precarious at best. Some Blacks enjoyed a period of true freedom—in which they could vote, hold government offices, purchase property, start businesses, marry, and build a life for their families. Others were relegated back to slave-like conditions through sharecropping and apprenticeships of their children. It is unclear how many Blacks were able to fully savor their first taste of freedom; however, what is clear is that freedom was elusive and short-lived in most of the South. Terrorist attacks on Black liberty began shortly after the Thirteenth Amendment was ratified on December 6, 1865. These attacks, often characterized as "race riots," were ignited by false narratives based on unproven allegations by whites. The false stories all centered on physical aggression of Black men against whites, and all proved to have deadly consequences.

Over one hundred Black freedmen towns were attacked and destroyed by white people during the Reconstruction and Redemption eras, often with the assistance of the police and organized ex-Confederate soldiers such as the Red Shirts and the Ku Klux Klan. The stories of all these mass massacres have not been told collectively.[20] The most famous one, however, the Tulsa Race Riot, which destroyed "Black Wall Street," is well documented and has been the basis for a civil lawsuit for reparations.[21] Some of the known outbreaks of extralegal violence meted out against Black self-sustained communities include the Atlanta riots of 1906, the Chicago riots of 1919, the 1923 Rosewood Massacre in Florida, and the Elaine Massacre that occurred in Arkansas in 1919. More than half the riots started in order to break up a Black political meeting or keep Blacks from voting, and a third of the recorded massacres occurred shortly before an election.[22] The term "riot" was used by many white newspapers to describe the violence in a way that ascribed the outbreaks as uprisings by Blacks who stepped out of their social and political place to challenge white authority. The term "massacre" more aptly explained what occurred—a purposeful slaughter of Black men, women, and children—typically incited by a normal, everyday action of a Black person.

The Civil Rights Act (CRA) of 1866 was enacted by Congress on April 9, 1866, and the purpose was to protect formerly enslaved persons from unfettered violence meted out by whites because of their race and status. It defined citizenship and affirmed that all citizens were equally protected by the law. It was vetoed twice by President Andrew Johnson, but the second time, it was passed to support the Thirteenth Amendment, enacted in 1865. A two-thirds majority in both the Senate and the House of Representatives overrode the presidential veto and enabled it to become law.

The CRA of 1866 aimed to integrate Blacks into the United States after the Civil War by defining US citizenship and the rights that accompanied it. It also established that it was unlawful for any person to deprive a citizen of their rights based on race, color, or the prior condition of slavery or involuntary servitude. It was the nation's first federal civil right law. Much of the language of the CRA of 1866 was mirrored within the language of the Fourteenth Amendment. The Memphis "race riot" or "race massacre" occurred during the middle of the congressional battles about the Fourteenth Amendment, and the fact that the CRA of 1866 provided no protection or recourse for newly emancipated Black persons further supported its passage. The Fourteenth Amendment was necessary because there had to be a constitutional law to which states were bound that upheld the rights and privileges of formerly enslaved persons.

The meaning of the Equal Protection and Due Process Clauses has taken years to develop, and many scholars note how far away interpretations have strayed from the clauses' true intent. It is important to note the ways in which the federal governing body grappled with accountability of white law enforcement and political leaders, ultimately failing to penalize anyone for their criminal acts. There was no repayment to the Black community for their losses—the homes, schools, churches, stores, and personal property destroyed or stolen. The elusiveness of freedom after emancipation was both clear and challenging for the future of the United States.

A Tale of Two Cities: The Memphis "Race Riot" of 1866 and the Memphis Massacre

The first federally documented "race riot" in the United States was in Memphis, Tennessee, on May 1, 1866. The narrative of what exactly happened depends on who tells the story. It is a tale of two different incidents—one started by angry, offended whites and another begun by disgruntled, uprising Blacks. How this Southern outrage began depends on the author of the investigative reports. There were at least three different investigations by various members of the US government and an investigation conducted by *The New York Times*. The first government investigation was initiated by the department of Tennessee via the superintendent of the Freedmen's Bureau for the district of Memphis, led by Brevet Brigadier General B. P. Runkle. Another committee, led by Major General Clinton B. Fisk, had instituted a commission, a special committee of the US House of Representatives. These two government reports ultimately resulted in a majority and minority report. Interestingly, the congressional transcript reflects the tensions between the two committees, as well as concerns regarding the publishing and distribution of the testimony. These tensions displayed the fragmented sides of a political debate about belonging and citizenship in the US. As one politician stated,

> Why, sir, there was no riot in Memphis, notwithstanding the terms of the resolution which was referred to us. There was no riot, and it is an abuse of language to say so when the civil authorities of a city of sixty thousand

inhabitants conspired together to murder in open day unoffending citizens of the United States. . . . This subject does possess some political and public significance. The great question now before the country is whether the people of the eleven States lately in rebellion are yet in a fit condition to be intrusted with a share in the government of the country. The *animus* and the spirit of the people enter into the inquiry. The details of this report and testimony go to that very spirit and that very *animus* of the leading people of the city of Memphis. I do not wonder that the gentleman from Kentucky [Mr. Shanklin] likes to shield his friends. I do not wonder that peculiar means have been used—I do not refer to the amiable gentleman, the chairman of the Committee on Printing [Mr. Laflin] to prevent this report from getting before the country at all.[23]

Following the Civil War, the political propaganda of the Rebels, or the Confederate army and their Southern supporters, was that the country was in a moment of radicalism versus liberty. In 1876, the Rebels proclaimed that the clash after the Civil War ended was between a "Monarchy vs. Republican Government."[24] Fear was generated by threats of future occurrences, which included guns and "ammunition being shipped to negroes all over the South, for the purpose of murdering white men, women and children, and carrying those States for [congressional candidates] Hayes and Wheeler."[25] The "outrages" had a different meaning within the Rebel political propaganda, which defined them as "wholesale massacres of white people in the South," with assertions that "for a negro in the South [to declare] his intention to vote the Democratic ticket [a vote for the former slaveholding Confederacy], his life must pay the forfeit."[26] It was clear that the central issue behind this propaganda was whether the formerly enslaved were full citizens with the right to vote.

A further investigation of witnesses from the minority report set forth that the spark of the Memphis "riot" was that two boys, one white and one Black, got into a fight but were parted by two policemen. The Black boy was much larger than the white boy and was "severely pounding" him. There were some Black soldiers who were near the fighting boys, and the soldiers were allegedly drunk and "very indignant at the police for parting them." These Black soldiers then allegedly attacked the policemen, killing one and wounding the other. The wounded policeman retreated and was reinforced by several other police officers who attempted to arrest the Black troops. The Black soldiers gathered reinforcements, allegedly numbering in the hundreds, and were able to repeatedly repulse the whites. This alarmed the entire city, and "nearly every white man who had any arms at his command rallied to support the authorities in quelling the negro mob." White citizens were afraid and had allegedly been aroused by a Black man who had told his former slave master that the Blacks "were going to rise up and murder every rebel in Memphis."[27] This version of events purports that Blacks drove through the streets and shot white men, with twelve or fifteen of being killed and wounded.

A different version of the events began with a false claim that was perpetuated by the police that a Black Union soldier had shot a policeman. In truth, the evidence collected by the Freedmen's Bureau revealed that that a white police officer accidentally shot another white police officer in a scuffle with Black Union soldiers. The situation in Memphis between Blacks and whites had been volatile for months before the riot. A *New York Times* investigation also revealed that there was a general feeling of hostility between the two races. The Irish-heritage Memphis police force was angry at Black Union soldiers who, since the war's end, were able to congregate in public and carry their own weapons. In addition, hotel workers, mechanics, and other white laborers came into competition with newly freed Blacks for the same jobs.

The real, underlying cause of the riots was much deeper, however. A letter dated May 23, 1866, from Benjamin P. Runkle to Brig. Gen. Jemel C. B. Fish, a chief superintendent for the Freedmen's Bureau, revealed that for months before the riots, local Memphis newspapers had been raising false claims that "the negroes were all going to rise before Christmas."[28] Runkle documented that the police and laborers were led to believe the teachings of the newspapers—that Blacks were inferior beings and had no equal right to compete with them.

This clash of local government, law enforcement, and the white laboring class with Black Union soldiers resulted in a white-supremacist mob. Memphis City Recorder John C. Creighton incited people, urging them to arm themselves and to "kill every negro and drive the last one from the city."[29] John Park, the mayor of Memphis, lost—or gave—control of his city to the white mob, failing to suppress the riot and restore peace.

The "reign of terror" worked to keep Black people from telling the authorities who had harmed their family members.[30] After it was over, no one was arrested for any of the crimes committed over those three days. Congressional testimony of the criminal court judge revealed that there were not enough white people in Memphis who were willing to bring the perpetrators to justice.

Hate Crimes and Trauma

Law enforcement along with regular townsfolk pillaged the Black community, raping at least five women and stealing money and valuables from people who had previously never been paid for a lifetime of work. They shot Black women and children in their beds and burned down houses, schools, and churches, sending survivors running for their lives. At the end of the third day, there were forty-eight people dead, forty-six Blacks and two whites. The terrorizing of Black communities was a massive hate crime that left many Black families in disarray. The full extent of the impact that these incidents had on freed people is unknown beyond the documentation of the congressional testimony. The record shows that this trauma affected the mental health of some of the women and men and caused marital and family separations. For those who were shot and wounded, it probably caused some permanent physical disabilities that plagued them for the rest of their lives, impacting their ability to work and earn a living.

Sexual assault and deadly violence were often used during and after slavery to exert control over enslaved women and men. The rapes and murders that occurred over the three-day period were documented by the Freedmen's Bureau, and in most cases, the perpetrators were known to the victims. Black women and girls made six to eight allegations of rape. Lucy Tibbs was raped and witnessed the murder of three people, including her brother. She stated that she was "ravished." Harriet Merriweather was raped by four men simultaneously and was noted to sometimes be "a little deranged since then." Her husband, whom she had just married months before the riot, left her. Harriet Armour, also married, was raped by two men. Her husband also "went away." It was reported that Mrs. Bloom, the wife of barber Reub Bloom, was "ravished." Frances Thompson testified that she was raped by four men and that Lucy Smith, a sixteen-year-old, was choked and raped by three men. Thompson stated that all the men were Irish and that they drew their weapons and threated to kill the women "if they didn't let them have their way." Smith was left close to death—her throat was swollen for two weeks, and she could not speak. Thompson and Smith testified before Congress about what happened to them—becoming the first Black women to speak out about sexual assault at the federal level.[31]

There was no protection against rape during slavery because "the actual or attempted rape of an enslaved woman was an offense neither recognized nor punished by law."[32] Rape was a negligible injury to an enslaved woman because she was not considered human and was also stereotyped as lascivious and carnal, always willing to engage in sexual relations. Enslaved women were considered stock for breeding, but some were purchased for the purpose of sexual exploitation—to be concubines.[33] "Rape, like lynching and murder, served as a tool of psychological and physical intimidation that expressed white male domination and buttressed white supremacy."[34] The congressional committee's declaration that Black women had a right to legal protection against racial and sexual violence was a radical departure from the cultural norm of white men dominating enslaved women and young girls.

Many of the married couples witnessed the murder of their spouse. Emma Lane witnessed her husband, Richard, and two-year-old daughter shot by men who broke into their house. She said her daughter "looked as though she had been dipped in a tub of blood." Sarah Long witnessed her husband killed by a mob. Shadrach Garrett was shot and killed, leaving behind his wife and children. As mentioned earlier, Albert Harris was shot and found in the street by his wife before he died, but his wife was unable to comfort him when he took his last breath because she would have been killed. Mr. Shedd was lying sick in his bed when he was pulled up and shot dead, leaving behind a wife, daughter, and two others who depended on him. Parents also witnessed their children killed or shot. Jason and Jane Sneed, a married couple, witnessed their daughter being shot and killed.

Of the couples, several were physically harmed and experienced financial losses. Some lost their homes to fire, and others witnessed their spouses or children get shot or beaten. Primus Lane and his wife, along with his friend Mason and his wife, were all robbed. The Lanes' family home was burned down, but he and his wife survived. Mary Walker recounts seeing her husband, Joseph, shot. Maria Marshall's husband, Joe, was also shot. His home was burglarized, and his relatives' bar was burned down. As he was trying to extinguish the fire, he was shot in the leg.

Sixteen-year-old Rachel Hatcher was shot and burned by a white mob. She was known to be remarkably intelligent and was a teacher of younger students. She was deliberately shot after going into a neighbor's burning house to save some of the things from being destroyed. After being threatened by several men with loaded weapons who surrounded the burning home, she made the decision to run out of the burning home, facing a mob firing squad. They killed her and also blew off the arm of a child who was trying to escape the fire. This same mob burned another woman's house and allowed her to go back inside to get some of her belongings. She brought out some items along with her son from the house. The mob then shoved her son back inside the house while the house was burning and burned the items that she had retrieved.

The impact of these violent physical encounters on the freed women and men in Memphis was perhaps greater than similar instances that occurred when they were enslaved. The vulnerability of women to the sexual advances of white men remained unchanged, while the reaction of the men in their lives arguably worsened. During slavery, enslaved men often had to endure witnessing the abuse of their wives and children while powerless to do anything to protect them. Enduring the pain and indignity associated with the public physical assault of their families and their own bodies was difficult for many men to bear, as they could offer no defense without certain death. With freedom, they could leave their wives and move on even though they were legally still married and together.

How Black men and women endured the psychological damage of both experiencing and witnessing violent encounters against themselves and loved ones is captured in some of the congressional testimony. Hannah Robinson recounted how her daughter was sick but getting better at the time of the "riots." Twenty men broke into her home and demanded the guns in the home. They went to the bed where her daughter was lying and broke down the bed so that her daughter was squashed down. This frightened her daughter so much that she did not get over her sickness and died. Mary Black described how her home was set on fire while she, her child, and an older woman were inside. When asked if she had made any effort to get her and her daughter out the burning home, she replied that she was so scared that she could do nothing. She also witnessed one man get repeatedly shot and killed, along with four other dead bodies that remained unburied in the street for several days. After Lavinia Goddell was forced to leave her husband in the street as he lay dying, she expressed that she was so badly distraught that he was killed that she did not notice who the other people were around her. This mental toll has been recently labeled as "Black fatigue," a cycle perpetuated by centuries-old racist systems.[35] Generations of oppressively inequitable life experiences and outcomes caused by unmitigated systemic racism yields intergenerational stress and trauma, which in turn causes inherited racist disparities in health.[36] Terror attacks like the Memphis Massacre also instilled fear in other Black towns where Black people sought equal work, better education for their children, a home of their own, and economic success. The indiscriminate violent acts and murder of Black people for daring to live as equal citizens was a critical tool used by whites to maintain political, social, and economic control.

The law was of no use to the freedmen and their families. On the same day as the Memphis Massacre, the secretary of war ordered the power of the Freedmen's Bureau's court system to be stripped away. Ironically, the local judges, who were now supposed to mete out justice for the freedmen who had been hurt in the riots, were the same people who had committed the violent acts.[37] The *Report on Memphis Riots and Massacres*—which condemned the violence—was submitted to the US House of Representatives on July 18, 1866, just six weeks after congressional endorsement of the Fourteenth Amendment. Even if the amendment had passed before the massacre, it would have done little to prevent the bloodshed that occurred. The end of Reconstruction and the removal of federal troops from the South made the potential for this sort of racist violence worse.

This brutality had one purpose: quashing the freedom of recently emancipated Blacks.[38] White police, local officials, and citizens used brutality and death to deliver a message: *Stay in your place. You may be free, but you have no rights. You may be emancipated, but you have no individual or collective agency.*

Conclusion: Modern-Day Destruction of Black Family Assets and Members

The elusiveness of freedom after emancipation was both clear and challenging for the future of the United States. Black families faced challenges and often experienced destruction of their homes and personal property as well as the harm or death of family members by white mobs and police violence sanctioned by the law. Some of the couples who were registered with the Freedmen's Bureau and married after the Civil War were victims of violence shortly thereafter. Even though they were able to take advantage of the right to marry, some spouses were raped, maimed, murdered, or driven off their land during attacks on the Black community. "In the postwar period, urban riots were the most visible sign of the efforts by white southerners to stamp down [B]lack political mobilization and prevent economic independence."[39]

The Memphis Massacre and similar terroristic actions across the South during the time the Freedman's Bureau was a federal presence made the case for why the Fourteenth Amendment was necessary. Constant assaults on the new freedom exercised by the formerly enslaved ultimately meant that they could not pursue life, liberty, and property without fear, and there was certainly no due process procedure in place to protect them or their property. After the Memphis Massacre was over, no one was charged with any wrongdoing, and there was no expectation that anyone would be, not even by the local judge. In theory, the Act of 1866, which ratified slave marriages and legitimized enslaved children, also granted equal rights to freed persons of color in Tennessee. This act included "full and equal benefits of all laws and proceedings for the security of person and estate."[40] This act was passed after the Memphis Massacre, arguably to address the massive dereliction of duty by state actors who led citizens in the killing of formerly enslaved Black people and the destruction of their property.[41]

Freedom as a concept is as much a tangible right—such as the right to marry and the right to vote—as is it a mindset. It is the ability to conceive of a life plan for your family and actually execute that plan to establish a home, earn a living, and provide a way for your children to enjoy life and the fruits of the family's labor for generations to come. The Memphis Massacre and subsequent massacres throughout Reconstruction were designed to take the tangible rights of Black families and leave a fearful impression that took away the hope of freedom. The inability to imagine a life free from terror and violence essentially cages the mentality of a people and keeps them from being physically and legally free. "Between the end of Reconstruction in 1877 and 1950 white antiBlack race riots, mob violence, and lynchings set the tone for strict segregation laws during the Jim Crow era. . . . This gave discriminatory laws their power to intimidate, discourage, and reverse Black success."[42]

Though it may not seem like race massacres still occur, the mass destruction of Black families remains prevalent in similar and different ways. One hundred years after the Memphis Massacre and other race "riots" occurred across the country, 128 cities experienced another set of large, destructive riots attributed to the exasperated experiences and protests of Black Americans. These riots mostly occurred in African American neighborhoods, often referred to as "ghettos." The Kerner Commission, a group appointed by President Lyndon B. Johnson in 1967, was charged with determining the cause of 164 civil disorders and developing a plan to prevent them from happening again.[43] The commission issued a report that set forth several basic reasons for the racial disorders, including pervasive discrimination and segregation in education, housing, and employment, resulting in continued exclusion of Black people from economic progress and "a backlog of frustrated hopes as a result of unfulfilled expectations generated from passage of judicial and legislative victories of the Civil Rights Movement."[44]

The Kerner Report was controversial because it concluded that the root cause for these riots was white racism.[45] This was the first time that a president acknowledged and identified institutional racism and the role it played in creating and maintaining the disenfranchisement present in poor, urban Black communities. The report identified critical areas of inequality, including housing, education, employment, police-community relations, and welfare. Unfortunately, the findings of the report did not result in specific, targeted solutions to address these areas. In fact, a review of the final report indicated that "participants were deeply disturbed by the inclination of some governmental bodies to respond to [B]lack needs with repression rather than reform. America cannot be a just society if repression is substitute for redressing the inequalities of our society."[46]

More violence ensued after the Kerner findings were released; Martin Luther King Jr. was assassinated less than two months later. Major civil rights legislation—the Civil Rights Act of 1964, the Voting Rights Act of 1965, and the Civil Rights Act of 1968 prohibiting housing discrimination—was passed within a relatively short period. However, this legislation was necessary because the protections offered through the Fourteenth Amendment had still not been realized by most of the descendants of the formerly enslaved in the United States. These laws were not passed in response to the Kerner Report but rather due to massive nonviolent protests and global exposure of the violence and injustices perpetrated against Black people.

Fifty years after the Kerner Report, many disparities in the same areas persist. The connections between emancipation, anger over Black economic advancement, and state violence against the Black community during Reconstruction are still present today. This white rage is illustrated by the deliberate destruction of Black lives through a variety of means, including mass incarceration, the school-to-prison pipeline, underfunded public schools, the disproportionate removal of children from Black families, the influx of drugs in certain Black communities, and the killing of young, unarmed Black men and women. This web of withholding and snatching away opportunities from African Americans operates in the same way that the race massacres did. The physical, emotional, and financial toll of the damage is generational and ongoing.

While the Fourteenth Amendment was intended to protect Black people from state violence, state legislatures quickly passed laws to keep the caste system in place so that the Black community remained at the bottom. Formerly enslaved people insisted on simultaneous establishment of schools and churches during and after the Civil War for support and future sustenance.[47] When massacres occurred, these foundational institutions were destroyed. Recent Supreme Court jurisprudence, such as the overturning of Roe v. Wade and the near end of affirmative action, call into question whether the Due Process and Equal Protection Clauses of the Fourteenth Amendment will be reinterpreted to eliminate any meaningful safeguards for the liberty of the people it was intended to help.

The painful truth is that freedom, wealth, and power for whites has been built on the inhumane treatment of African American families throughout history. A lack of community and a safe place to rest and be nourished prevented formerly enslaved people from securing life, liberty, and property. Freedom is elusive for Black families because there are still laws and policies in place that limit or prevent access to the things that would allow Black communities to flourish: ownership of property and land, inclusive quality education, unabridged access to the franchise, and living wages.

NOTES

1 J. David Hacker, "From '20 and Odd' to 10 Million: The Growth of the Slave Population in the United States," *Slavery and Abolition* 41, no. 4 (2020): 840–55.

2 Henry Louis Gates Jr., *The Stony Road: Reconstruction, White Supremacy, and the Rise of Jim Crow* (Penguin Books, 2020), 16.

3 G. S. Shanklin, *Memphis Riots and Massacres*, Views of the Minority, Report No. 101, 39th Congress, 1st sess. (July 25, 1866). The term "carried away from each other" denotes that one of them was sold and forced to move to a different town or city with a new owner.

4 Shanklin, *Memphis Riots and Massacres*.

5 William A. Darity and A. Kirsten Mullen, *The Black Reparations Project: A Handbook for Racial Justice* (University of California Press, 2023), 213–16, appendix A.

6 John Singleton, dir., *Rosewood* (Warner Brothers, 1997), www.amazon.com; Salima Koroma, *Dreamland: The Burning of Black Wall Street* (Springhill Entertainment, 2021), www.cnn.com.

7 Elaine C. Everly, "Marriage Registers of Freedmen," *Prologue: The Journal of the National Archives*, Fall 1973, 150–54.

8 Records of the Field Offices for the State of Tennessee, Bureau of Refugees, Freedmen, and Abandoned Lands, 1865–1872, M 1911, Congress and National Archives and Records Administration, 2005.

9 Reginald Washington, "Sealing the Sacred Bonds of Holy Matrimony Freedmen's Bureau Marriage Records," *Prologue Magazine* 37 (Spring 2005): 1.

10 E. B. Washburne, *Memphis Riots and Massacres*, Report No. 101, 39th Cong., 1st sess. (July 25, 1986).

11 Herbert G. Gutman, *The Black Family in Slavery and Freedom, 1750–1925* (Knopf Doubleday, 1976), 211–13.

12 Akosua Adoma Perbi, *A History of Indigenous Slavery in Ghana from the 15th to the 19th Century* (Sub-Saharan, 2004), 111.

13 Frederick Douglass, *Narrative of the Life of Frederick Douglass—An American Slave*, ed. Benjamin Quarles (Harvard University Press, 1845), 25.

14 William Wells Brown, *Narrative of William W. Brown, A Fugitive Slave* (Anti-Slavery Office, 1847), 2.

15 Jacobs Harriet, *Incidents in the Life of a Slave Girl* (Washington Square, 2003), 35–38.

16 Tera W. Hunter, *Bound in Wedlock: Slave and Free Black Marriage in the Nineteenth Century* (Harvard University Press, 2017), 84.

17 Hunter, *Bound in Wedlock*, 121.

18 Darling C. Goring, "The History of Slave Marriage in the United States," *John Marshall Law Review* 39 (2006): 315–16.

19 Deborah Gray White, *Ar'n't I a Woman? Female Slaves in the Plantation South* (Norton, 1995), 170–71.

20 The documentation of these outrages is within the Freedmen's Bureau and other archival records, most of which must be painstakingly searched by county and state. See William A. Blair, *The Record of Murders and Outrages: Racial Violence and the Fight over Truth at the Dawn of Reconstruction* (University of North Carolina Press, 2021), 1–5. Other local records have been destroyed, and the memory of these events has only been passed down orally among Black family members.

21 David K. Li, "Survivors of 1921 Tulsa Race Massacre File Lawsuit Seeking 'Relief,' Victims Fund," *NBC News*, September 2, 2020, www.nbcnews.com.

22 Thomas Craemer, Trevor Smith, Brianna Harrison, Trevon D. Logan, Wesley Bellamy, and William A. Darity Jr, "Wealth Implications of Slavery and Racial Discrimination for African American Descendants of the Enslaved," in *The Black Reparations Project: A Handbook for Racial Justice*, ed. William A. Darity Jr., A. Kirsten Mullen, and Lucas Hubbard (University of California Press, 2023), 47.

23 Cong. Globe, 39th Cong., 1st Sess. 4266 (1866).

24 *Southern Outrages: Atrocities as They Passed Through the Hopper: Facts for the American People to Read: Brutal Outrages upon Frances Thomas [sic]: 1866 vs. 1876* (Eureka, 1876), 24, https://archive.org.

25 *Southern Outrages*, 26.

26 *Southern Outrages*, 26; Farrell Evans, "The 1868 Louisiana Massacre That Reversed Reconstruction-Era Gains," January 23, 2024, www.history.com; Lorraine Boissoneault, "The Deadliest Massacre in Reconstruction-Era Louisiana Happened 150 Years Ago: In September 1868, Southern White Democrats Hunted Down Around 200 African-Americans in an Effort to Suppress Voter Turnout," *Smithsonian Magazine*, September 28, 2018; Marsha J. Tyson Darling, "A Right Deferred: African American Voter Suppression After Reconstruction," Gilder Lehrman Institute of American History, Summer 2018, www.gilderlehrman.org.

27 *Southern Outrages*, preface, iii–iv.

28 Records of the Assistant Commissioner for the State of Tennessee Bureau of Refugees, Freedman, and Abandoned Lands, 1865–1869, National Archives Microfilm Publication M999, roll 34.

29 Washburne, *Memphis Riots and Massacres*, 23–24.

30 Ross A. Webb, "The Past Is Never Dead; It's Not Even Past: Benjamin P. Runkle and the Freedmen's Bureau in Kentucky 1866–1870," *Register of the Kentucky Historical Society* 84, no. 4 (1986): 343–60.

31 Crystal N. Feimster, *Southern Horrors: Women and the Politics of Rape and Lynching* (Harvard University Press, 2009), 44.

32 Saidiya V. Hartman, *Scenes of Subjection: Terror, Slavery, and Self-Making in Nineteenth Century American* (Norton, 2022), 137.

33 Peggy Cooper Davis, *Neglected Stories: The Constitution and Family Values* (Hill and Wang, 1997), 174; Maurie D. McInnis, *Slaves Waiting for Sale: Abolitionist Art and the American Slave Trade* (University of Chicago Press, 2011), 139.

34 Danielle L. McGuire, "'It Was Like All of Us Had Been Raped': Sexual Violence, Community Mobilization, and the African American Freedom Struggle," *Journal of American History* 91 (December 2004): 906–31.

35 Mary-Frances Winters, *Black Fatigue: How Racism Erodes the Mind, Body, and Spirit* (Berrett-Koehler, 2020), 4–5.

36 Winters, *Black Fatigue.*

37 Bernice B. Donald and Pablo J. Davis, "To This Tribunal the Freedmen Has Turned: The Freedmen's Bureau's Judicial Powers and the Origin of the Fourteenth Amendment," *Louisiana Law Review* 79, no. 1 (2018): 34–35.

38 Jessica Dixon Weaver, "Juneteenth Shows Why Black Freedom Remains Elusive," *Washington Post*, June 19, 2020, www.washingtonpost.com.

39 Feimster, *Southern Horrors*, 43.

40 Act of May 26, 1866, Sec. 5, 1866 Tenn. Laws.

41 Craemer et al., "Wealth Implications of Slavery," 49.

42 Craemer et al., "Wealth Implications of Slavery," 49.

43 *The Kerner Report Revisited: Final Report and Background Papers* (University of Illinois, Institute of Government and Public Affairs, June 1970), 9.

44 *Kerner Report Revisited*, 10.

45 Susan T. Gooden and Samuel L. Myers Jr., "The Kerner Commission Report Fifty Years Later: Revisiting the American Dream," *Journal of the Social Sciences* 4, no. 6 (2018): 1–17.

46 *Kerner Report Revisited*, 4–5.

47 Rita Roberts, *I Can't Wait to Call You My Wife: African American Letters of Love and Family in the Civil War Era* (Chronicle Books, 2022), 269.

3

Family Pioneers

Black Feminist Leadership in Twentieth-Century Legal Transformations

SERENA MAYERI

Today, it should seem unremarkable to recognize Black feminists at the forefront of thought, community activism, and legal advocacy for family integrity, reproductive justice, and equal citizenship. From family regulation in the name of child welfare to the criminalization of poverty and parenthood, from antiviolence and anticarceral activism to reproductive freedom, from equal employment opportunity to voting rights and democracy defense, Black feminist intellectual leadership is indisputable.[1]

The precursors to this theorizing, organizing, litigating, and strategizing are less well-known, however, at least to legal scholars. This chapter examines the 1960s and 1970s, a time when people of color—Black women and feminists in particular—led an array of efforts to transform the law of the family. Their leadership took many forms and reflected varied visions of the relationship between family structure, gender, race, poverty, and economic justice. Family pioneers came from all walks of life. Some held prominent positions as lawyers, elected officials, administrators, and policy makers, the first generation to wield this kind of influence. Others engaged in local community activism, legislative lobbying, or litigation in state and federal courts. Some deliberately set out to change the law; others found themselves fighting to defend the integrity of their own families or to keep a job that would allow them to survive. Some took radical positions that challenged fundamental features of US political economy; others sought to reform existing law along liberal egalitarian lines. Some challenged social and sexual conventions, while others sought to redefine respectability and responsible citizenship.

Drawing on my own and others' research, this chapter explores the contours of Black leadership in a range of law reform efforts during two pivotal decades of transformation in US family life. The chapter focuses on several overlapping areas: efforts to make marriage more internally gender egalitarian; campaigns to open employment opportunities and jury service to women; challenges to discrimination based on marital and birth status; welfare rights activism and litigation; and other advocacy for what Black feminists would later name reproductive justice. My aim in considering these efforts together is to identify patterns and commonalities but also to highlight diversity and disagreement over matters of substance and strategy. It is to recognize the underappreciated role of Black pioneers in the transformation of family and equality law. And it is to suggest that the successes and failures of these efforts shed light on the persistence of structural racial and economic inequality in modern US law and life.

Employment Opportunity, Equal Citizenship, and Egalitarian Marriage

The 1965 Moynihan Report, *The Negro Family: The Case for National Action*, drew criticism for denigrating Black families with its assertion that "matriarchal family structure" created a "tangle of pathology."[2] It also reflected a midcentury liberal consensus—shared by many civil rights leaders—that restoration of Black men to their proper role as heads of households was a prerequisite for racial progress. According to this approach, poor Black families could prosper only if they strove for patriarchal marital families in which husbands and fathers served as breadwinners while wives and mothers tended the home. Its adherents saw Black women's superior educational attainment and role as primary breadwinners as a problem to be solved by renewed focus on Black male job training and employment. The alternative, they warned, was poverty, juvenile delinquency, welfare dependency, and social disorder that would impede advances toward racial equality.[3]

Equal Employment Opportunity

Feminists of all races countered Moynihan's diagnosis and prescription by insisting that equal employment opportunity for women—especially

Black women—and egalitarian partnerships between men and women would better address racial and economic inequality. Pauli Murray, a pioneering civil rights activist, lawyer, and feminist and an early critic of the Moynihan Report, wrote in 1965, "It is bitterly ironic that Negro women should be impliedly censured for their efforts to overcome a handicap not of their making and for trying to meet the standards of the country as a whole." Murray worried that "the Negro males may be pitted against the Negro females in a highly competitive instead of cooperative endeavor." A Washington, DC, job-training center director articulated a typical policy of concern to feminists: "We're not encouraging women. We're trying to reestablish the male as head of the house."[4]

The Moynihan Report cast a long shadow over family policy in the following decades, but it also galvanized feminist activism, including Murray's.[5] By 1965, Murray already placed Black women—often at the margins of male-dominated racial justice advocacy and predominantly white women's organizations—at the center of feminist legal and constitutional strategy.[6] Murray's influential 1962 memo for the President's Commission on the Status of Women (PCSW) outlined a Fourteenth Amendment strategy that became a blueprint for two decades of feminist constitutional advocacy, modeled on the National Association for the Advancement of Colored People (NAACP) Legal Defense Fund's successful campaign against racial segregation.[7] Murray hoped that litigation under the Equal Protection Clause would bridge two divides that threatened feminist unity: disagreement over the Equal Rights Amendment (ERA) and its effects on sex-specific protective labor legislation, and fissures over the relationship between equality for women and Black civil rights in light of an opportunistic alliance between white National Woman's Party members and segregationists in Congress.[8]

Murray also authored an influential memo that helped to secure the inclusion of "sex" in Title VII of the Civil Rights Act of 1964.[9] Some white and female proponents framed the sex amendment as a question of equity for "white Christian women of United States origin," who otherwise would be left unprotected by legislation that banned discrimination based on race, color, religion, and national origin. Some civil rights supporters worried that the inclusion of sex might sink the whole civil rights bill, given that the segregationist Rep. Howard Smith (D-VA) had introduced the sex amendment. To counter this skepticism, Murray emphasized the imperative to fight sex discrimination in employment so as to achieve genuine racial and economic justice.[10]

Murray's memo stressed Black women's family responsibilities as a reason to fight *for* their access to job opportunities: Without the sex amendment, Murray insisted, the Black women who shouldered disproportionately the burdens of financial support and caregiving could not ensure their families' sustenance. "In a more sharply defined struggle than is apparent in any other social group in the United States, [the Black woman] is literally engaged in a battle for sheer survival," Murray wrote.[11] She "had trouble finding a mate, remains single longer and in higher incidence, bears more children, is in the labor market longer, has less education, earns less, is widowed earlier and carries a heavier economic burden as a family head than her white counterpart."[12] Because a Black woman "must be prepared to support herself and others for a considerable period of her life . . . if civil rights legislation is to be effective, it must of necessity include protection against discrimination in employment by reason of sex," Murray argued.[13]

Historians credit Murray's widely distributed missive with helping to save Title VII's sex amendment when it was in danger of failing in the Senate.[14] After the Equal Employment Opportunity Commission (EEOC) initially dithered about enforcing the provision, Murray, Aileen Hernandez, Dorothy Height, and other Black women led efforts to hold government officials to account. As Height and the economist Caroline Ware wrote in 1966, it would "profit [Black women and their families] little to be no longer blocked because of race but barred by sex from effective employment and citizen participation."[15]

Equal Citizenship

Feminists like Murray also placed Black women at the center of efforts to win the right to jury service regardless of sex or race, essential both to Black defendants' right to be tried by a jury of their peers and to effective prosecution of white defendants accused of anti-Black violence.[16] In 1965, Gardenia White and other Black women plaintiffs challenged the de jure exclusion of women and the de facto bar on Black men from the all-white, all-male jury that acquitted the white men suspected of murdering the civil rights activist Viola Liuzzo. When a three-judge federal district court accepted Murray's and fellow ACLU leader Dorothy Kenyon's argument that Alabama's jury service prohibition discriminated against women in violation of the Equal Protection Clause, the state declined to appeal—a signal feminist victory that also meant *White v. Crook* would not become a "women's *Brown v. Board*," as Murray had hoped.[17]

Constitutional challenges to jury service exemptions and exclusions "spotlight[ed] how racial discrimination intersected with the paternalistic assumptions about gender and family roles that stunted women's participation in public life."[18] The US Supreme Court had ruled in *Hoyt v. Florida* (1961) that women's position "at the center of home and family life" justified their exemption from jury service.[19] Disregarding *White v. Crook*, the Mississippi Supreme Court upheld the state's total exclusion of women from juries in 1966 on the ground that the "legislature has the right to exclude women so they may continue their service as mothers, wives, and homemakers, and also to protect them . . . from the filth, obscenity, and noxious atmosphere that so often pervades a courtroom during a jury trial."[20]

Lillie Willis's lesser-known case showcased how ideas about the "protection" of women "provided a rhetorical cover for a legal regime that kept Black and white women in their respective places and reinforced white male dominance" in public and private life.[21] Willis, a local leader in the Mississippi Freedom Democratic Party, was arrested and charged with perjury, forgery, and other crimes when she helped her elderly, nonliterate mother register to vote in Sharkey County in 1965. She had also "been active in seeing that the children of plantation workers and displaced farm hands enrolled in formerly all-white schools in Mississippi."[22] Twenty-eight-year-old Eleanor Holmes Norton, a Murray protégé, helped draft a brief challenging the exclusion of Black men and all women from Sharkey County, Mississippi's jury pool.

The Mississippi legislature repealed its jury exclusion law in 1968, and the Willis case never produced a federal court decision. But the Willis family paid dearly for their multigenerational activism. Lillie Willis's thirteen-year-old daughter, Jennie, lost her right eye to gunfire when she stepped onto the porch of her family home on Thanksgiving Day 1966. Lillie Willis and her lawyers suspected the bullet was meant for her, though Jennie herself was a civil rights activist, having tried to register for seventh grade at an all-white local elementary school weeks before.[23]

Egalitarian Marriage

Leading Black feminist professionals also promoted gender-egalitarian marriage in response to Moynihan's prescription for a restoration of male household headship. Eleanor Holmes Norton became an especially vocal proponent in the early 1970s. Later a long-serving delegate to Congress from the District of Columbia (1991–), Norton's early professional career focused on free speech, racial justice, and feminist objectives, including jury service and workplace equality for women and people of color. After a stint at the American Civil Liberties Union (ACLU), Norton served as the chair of the New York City Human Rights Commission (1970–77) and later of the EEOC (1977–81), taught at Georgetown University Law Center (1982–), coauthored one of the first sex discrimination casebooks (published in 1974), and cofounded the National Black Feminist Organization (1973).

A mother of two, Holmes Norton touted her marriage to fellow attorney Edward Norton as an equal partnership that exemplified an ideal family structure. In 1971, she declared, "My husband is the answer to a woman's dream—a strong, completely secure male, unthreatened by women who want to improve themselves outside the home."[24] Indeed, Norton and other Black feminist lawyers, including Patricia Roberts Harris—former Howard Law School dean and later secretary of housing and urban development during the Jimmy Carter administration— promoted Black couples' egalitarian relationships as a model to which white families should aspire. In 1971, Harris responded to echoes of the Moynihan Report when she said, "Despite assertions to the contrary, Black women did not make Black men second-class citizens. Whites did that." She continued, "Black women have a life experience of equality with men to protect, and it is one to be proud of."[25] Norton said in 1970 that Black women "already ha[d] a rough equality which came into existence out of necessity and is now ingrained in the Black lifestyle. . . . That give[s] the Black family very much of a head-start on egalitarian family life."[26]

Instead of Black families trying to emulate the white, middle-class, male-breadwinner/female-homemaker model of marriage, these feminists argued, couples of all races should strive for relationships in which both partners shared wage-earning and caregiving responsibilities.

Norton encouraged Black couples to "pioneer in establishing new male-
female relationships around two careers."[27] She urged, "Let's build an
entirely new kind of family with the recognition that there may be two
people who work, two people who are strong, and nobody has to be dependent."[28] In 1973, the journalist Caroline Bird described Pauli Murray
as hopeful that Black women could enter "egalitarian marriages which
can serve as models for young people of both sexes and races."[29]

This gender-egalitarian model of marriage had deep roots in Black
American thought and practice.[30] It also masked considerable diversity
even among prominent professional women. Not all Black women leaders wore the feminist mantle as assertively and comfortably as Norton
did. Tomiko Brown-Nagin poignantly describes how the civil rights
lawyer, politician, and federal judge Constance Baker Motley carefully
cultivated an image as a devoted wife and mother who did not allow
her tireless work outside the home to overshadow either her husband's
career or her own domestic obligations.[31] For feminists like Murray and
Aileen Hernandez, each of whom briefly married men but formed life
partnerships with women, egalitarian marriage was more political position than personal objective.

Together with Murray's PCSW memo and the Murray/Kenyon brief in
White v. Crook, the Black feminist vision of egalitarian marriage laid conceptual groundwork for Ruth Bader Ginsburg's successful constitutional
litigation campaign, which established government neutrality toward
sex roles within marriage. In cases such as *Frontiero v. Richardson* (1973),
Weinberger v. Wiesenfeld (1975), and *Califano v. Goldfarb* (1977), Ginsburg
and her allies persuaded the Court to declare that husbands and wives,
mothers and fathers, widows and widowers were equally entitled to government benefits available to a breadwinner's dependents or to a surviving parent seeking to care for a child after a wage earner's death.[32] By the
early 1980s, the Court had also invalidated state laws that preferred men
over women as estate administrators, provided alimony only to wives,
established different parental support obligations for sons and daughters,
or declared husbands the "heads and masters" of their households.[33]

This stream of advocacy, radical in its rejection of gendered division
of labor and its linkage of equality based on race and sex, did not directly challenge the legal primacy of marriage or the privatization of dependency within the family.[34] The relative success of these efforts—the

establishment of formal legal equality within marriage and in employment and jury service—may stem in part from their acceptance of those
foundational premises of political economy. By the early 1980s, despite
a successful campaign to derail ratification of the ERA, feminists had
achieved under the Equal Protection Clause much of what Murray and
Ginsburg set out to do.[35]

Roots of Reproductive Justice: Family Status, Work, Poverty, and Welfare Rights

A parallel, less visible stream of legal advocacy and activism during
this period pursued aims consonant with what Black feminists would
eventually name reproductive justice. Women insisted on sexual and
reproductive freedom and the ability to have and raise families, marital
or not, with support rather than interference from the state—what feminists of color in SisterSong later called the right "to maintain personal
bodily autonomy, to have children, not have children, and parent the
children we have in safe and sustainable communities."[36]

Reproductive Freedom

Recent scholarship spotlights Black leadership in fights for abortion rights
and access before and after *Roe*. The historian Sherie Randolph shows
how the Black radical activist and lawyer Florynce "Flo" Kennedy used
her experience representing Black Power advocates to "place the state on
trial and to mobilize support outside the courtroom" in pre-*Roe* abortion
litigation.[37] Felicia Kornbluh details how, in the late 1960s, Black legislators like Rep. Percy Sutton of Harlem were at the forefront of abortion
decriminalization in New York; labor leader Dollie Lowther Robinson
spearheaded a sex equality amendment that would have codified abortion rights in New York's constitution; and Shirley Chisholm championed
reproductive rights and feminist causes more generally.[38] Melissa Murray
highlights how Black women, including Kennedy, Chisholm, Frances Beal,
and Toni Cade, struggled against depictions of birth control and abortion
as racial genocide. They underscored how Black freedom and equality
depended on reproductive freedom broadly construed to include the
resources to access health care, education, child care, adequate housing,

transportation, and other social supports.[39] As the historian Keeanga-Yamahtta Taylor writes, for Black feminists then as now, "reproductive freedom . . . was the most basic element of self-determination in a society where their choices were heavily circumscribed." They therefore "not only took up the immediate questions concerning reproduction but they also raised issues about child care, employment, welfare, and the other material necessities that could help women take care of their children and choose to bring them into the world."[40]

Black and Latina feminists and their allies saw abortion restrictions, including state and federal public funding bans, through this broader lens. Khiara Bridges writes of Black women's activism against the Hyde Amendment—from Cora McRae, who challenged the denial of Medicaid funds for an abortion she needed, to Faye Wattleton, the first Black president of Planned Parenthood and a former nurse who had watched Black women die in a Harlem hospital from botched abortions, to Rep. Yvonne Brathwaite Burke, who explained to her congressional colleagues the devastating impact of forced childbearing on Black women and families.[41] Depriving poor women of abortions and access to affordable birth control also pushed many toward sterilization procedures they would not have voluntarily undergone otherwise, these advocates warned.[42]

Sterilization abuse, which primarily targeted poor women of color in the postwar period and well into the 1970s, loomed large for communities where reproductive control often took the form of coercing women *not* to have children and of failing to provide for those children. Fannie Lou Hamer famously estimated in 1964 that six in ten Black women hospitalized in Sunflower County, Mississippi, left having undergone sterilization, often without their consent or even their knowledge.[43] The Puerto Rican physician and activist Helen Rodríguez-Trias and members of organizations such as the Committee to End Sterilization Abuse (CESA) fought for federal guidelines to protect patients from coercive state-funded sterilization.[44] Mexican American women who survived sterilization abuse in California brought suit against a Los Angeles hospital with the help of the lawyer Antonia Hernández.[45] A lawsuit filed in 1973 on behalf of Minnie and Alice Relf, young Black girls sterilized after their parents signed a "consent" form they could not read, exposed tens of thousands of involuntary procedures performed on mostly Black, Native, and Latina women using federal funds.[46] Niall Ruth Cox's lawsuit exposed a similar sterilization campaign in North Carolina.[47] Although activism and litigation did not eliminate sterilization abuse, they helped to prevent further systemic victimization and laid groundwork for later, ongoing movements for reparations.[48]

Family Status Discrimination, Work, and Welfare

Also part of this broader fight for reproductive justice were campaigns against birth status discrimination, in which Black families again played a leading role. In the late 1960s and 1970s, plaintiffs challenged discrimination against "illegitimate" children and their parents in a series of cases that reached the Supreme Court. The early litigation—challenging suitable home and substitute father laws, unequal provision of welfare benefits, and birth status discrimination in wrongful death statutes, workers' compensation, government benefits, and inheritance laws— was brought almost entirely by Black mothers and their children. They made constitutional claims of discrimination based on race and poverty as well as on birth status; some also brought sexual privacy and sex discrimination claims, as well as claims to reproductive autonomy and family integrity.[49]

Plaintiffs and their advocates variously framed nonmarital sex and parenthood: Some, such as lawyers for the late Louise Levy's children (*Levy v. Louisiana*), presented single mothers as upstanding citizens who worked hard to support families and care for children alone without any assistance from the state. Ms. Levy, her attorney Adolph Levy (no relation) told the court, scraped together enough money to send her children to Catholic school and enjoyed a loving bond with them like any other parent. Why, he asked, should taxpayers support surviving children while tortfeasors escaped "scot-free"? If the Levy children were denied recovery for their mother's wrongful death, "the tortfeasor need reimburse no one. The State must support the tragic victims."[50]

Others, such as Mrs. Sylvester Smith and her attorney Martin Garbus (*King v. Smith*), used emerging sexual privacy precedents to argue that single mothers should not have to remain celibate to receive government benefits and avoid state intrusion on their intimate lives. When asked to confirm or deny her intimate relationship with a family friend, a married father of nine, Smith told a white caseworker that her personal life was none of the state's business and that she had every intention of "going with" whomever she pleased as long as she was young enough to enjoy the company of men.[51] Smith and her family sacrificed for the cause of sexual freedom: Living miles from her children in Selma, where she worked as a short-order cook, she could ill afford to sacrifice the meager welfare benefit that her family lost when she challenged Alabama's "substitute father" law.[52]

Some, like the Philadelphia community activist and city employee Lois Fernandez, fought to redefine responsible parenthood and citizenship. Fernandez, chagrined to find that she could not even obtain a birth certificate for her child born outside of marriage in the late 1960s, insisted that single motherhood should be a source of pride, not shame. With the help of Philadelphia's Women's Law Project and Community Legal Services, Fernandez launched a decade-long and ultimately successful lobbying and litigation campaign to remove birth status discrimination from Pennsylvania laws. Rather than focus solely on her children's innocence, Fernandez emphasized her deliberate decision to become a single parent—and the unfairness of punishing women for nonmarital childbirth. Fernandez's lawyers argued that state inheritance laws that prevented nonmarital children from inheriting from fathers who died intestate aggravated women's economic disadvantage.[53] Outside of court, Fernandez attacked the "sexual double standard that stigmatized unmarried mothers" even as overt discrimination against nonmarital children eased. She fought "the stereotype of mothers of out-of-wedlock children as promiscuous" and declared, "To have a child without a husband was my choice. I made the decision with pride. . . . To give birth is one of the most beautiful experiences I have ever had."[54]

Fernandez's status as a worker, home owner, and taxpaying citizen allowed her to attack demeaning ideas about "unwed mothers" as "lazy welfare chiselers."[55] Plaintiffs in employment discrimination cases, too, sought to redefine responsible parenthood and citizenship to include single mothers who supported and cared for children on their own. Katie Mae Andrews, who sued a Mississippi school district that banned parents of nonmarital children from teaching, presented herself as respectable, churchgoing young woman whose one "mistake"—born of a lack of knowledge about or access to birth control—should not doom her to a life of welfare dependency. The civil rights icon Fannie Lou

Hamer testified that the Black community valorized the choice Andrews and her coplaintiffs made: to keep and raise their nonmarital children and to seek gainful employment and economic mobility. "You always tell us . . . we have got so many kids on the welfare roll, 'Why don't you get up and do something?' And then when we start doing something, 'You don't have any business being that high.'"[56] Mae Bertha Carter, whose family had integrated the Drew school system several years earlier, testified that she would be proud to have Andrews teach her own children.[57] These witnesses made clear that single mothers who raised and supported their children against all odds were heroic figures to be celebrated and emulated, not condemned as immoral, deficient role models for impressionable youth.

Not all of the young women turned away by Drew school district for nonmarital childbearing framed their sexual activity as error, however. Violet Burnett, a teacher's aide who lost her job because of her nonmarital child, remained unapologetic. When the school district's lawyer asked on cross-examination whether Burnett felt "that it's moral or immoral for an unmarried person to have sexual intercourse," she replied, "I feel like as an individual a person can do whatever they want to, they has the freedom to do anything they want to as long as it's not hurting anyone." Asked whether she would recommend nonmarital sex to a teenage pupil, Burnett testified that she would tell young people to conduct their intimate lives however they saw fit. "I would tell her if that's what she wanted, . . . go right ahead." Asked whether she would have another child outside of marriage, Burnett answered that she would not "because taking care of one is hard enough." Plaintiff Lestine Rogers, too, expressed moral neutrality toward nonmarital sex: "I can't say it's right and I can't say it's wrong. Because I think it's left up to you as long as you are not hurting anyone else. I think you should do whatever you feel is right." Asked if she intended to have more children outside of marriage, Rogers replied, "I don't know."[58]

Though the Supreme Court never so much as mentioned race in most of the family status discrimination cases it decided, racial subordination and resistance frequently saturated these conflicts.[59] The plaintiffs in the birth status discrimination cases that reached the Supreme Court in the 1960s and 1970s challenged laws that had a hugely disproportionate impact on poor Black families, often by design. The backdrop to the *Andrews* case, which took place in a town not far from the site of Emmett Till's lynching, included protracted battles over voting rights and school desegregation. Less than two year earlier, in 1971, a white drive-by shooter murdered Joetha Collier, a young Black woman who had helped to integrate the local all-white schools, on her graduation day from Drew High School.[60] All five of the Drew women dismissed because they had "illegitimate" children were Black; the son-in-law of the segregationist Senator James O. Eastland represented the school district; and the young Black civil rights lawyer Charles Victor McTeer and colleagues at the Center for Constitutional Rights called the social psychologist Kenneth Clark—coauthor of the "doll studies" cited in *Brown*—along with Hamer, to testify.

The enforcement of employer rules against nonmarital pregnancy and childbearing frequently ensnared young Black women, who often asserted their reproductive freedom as part of a larger struggle for racial justice. Ilene Devone Drake, a Black teacher in Florala, Alabama, excoriated the white superintendent who invaded her hospital room in the spring of 1973—weeks after *Roe v. Wade*—to urge her not to end a nonmarital pregnancy that he said would cost her her job either way. Drake declared her right to have premarital sex and obtain an abortion if she chose, without interference from her white employer. "Just because his skin is white and mine is Black doesn't mean he should have all the power," she told her school board interrogators.[61]

Drake won her case: The right to privacy, ruled a federal district court, shielded a teacher whose pregnancy would never have been a topic of public conversation but for school officials' interference.[62] She continued to teach in Florala. Katie Mae Andrews, too, prevailed and served for decades as a librarian in the Mississippi public schools. Single mothers and women who became pregnant outside of marriage did not always win their employment discrimination cases: As Regina Austin later described in her classic article "Sapphire Bound!," some courts remained willing to allow employers to impose morals regulations on Black women who did not conform to racialized marital norms.[63] But plaintiffs claiming equal inheritance regardless of their children's birth status or the right to seek paid employment rather than depend on public assistance could frame their constitutional claims as consistent with their children's well-being and, importantly, placed no additional demands on the public fisc.[64] Not so for those who more fundamentally challenged the privatization of dependency.

Welfare Rights and Mandatory Paternity Disclosure

By the early 1970s, feminist welfare rights activists exposed how the state conditioned stingy and stigmatized public assistance on surveillance designed to ensnare mothers who relied on male breadwinners and to punish nonmarital relationships—while trapping women in dead-end jobs whose meager wages and terrible working conditions would never enable financial independence. Leaders like Johnnie Tillmon fought for poor and low-income women's right to care for their children and to seek well-paying, nonexploitative employment without depending on a man or submitting to state intrusions on their most private and intimate relationships. Tillmon, a Black single mother who supported six children by working a backbreaking job in a Los Angeles laundry until a disability made hard physical labor impossible, famously wrote in 1972 that welfare was "like a super-sexist marriage. You trade in a man for *the* man. But you can't divorce him if he treats you bad. He can divorce you, of course, cut you off any time he wants. But in that case, he keeps the kids, not you."[65] Tillmon described this dystopian version of marriage in vivid terms: "*The* man runs everything. In ordinary marriage, sex is supposed to be for your husband. On A.F.D.C. [Aid to Families with Dependent Children] you're not supposed to have any sex at all. You give up control of your own body. It's a condition of aid. . . . *The* man, the welfare system, controls your money. He tells you what to buy, what not to buy, where to buy it, and how much things cost."[66]

As the historian Premilla Nadasen describes, Tillmon and other welfare rights activists developed a feminist theory of work and family: They sought a revaluation of their mothering as productive and essential labor regardless of paternal or other male involvement; access to decent jobs that would afford genuine economic mobility and the prerogative to care for young children without being required to work outside the home; and protection against state interference in their sexual and reproductive lives.[67] Tillmon and her allies fought for a guaranteed minimum income regardless of family structure: "There would be no 'categories'—men, women, children, single, married, kids, no kids—just poor people who need aid."[68]

After "suitable home" and "substitute father" laws faced statutory and administrative barriers, "man in the house" rules and "midnight raids" on welfare recipients persisted. When states conditioned AFDC benefits on mothers' cooperation with paternity determinations, courts ruled—as they had in Mrs. Sylvester Smith's case—that children could not be deprived of benefits because of their parents' conduct. States responded by imposing penalties directly on mothers themselves. For example, a Connecticut law forced mothers who gave birth to nonmarital children to disclose the names of their children's fathers or face a fine for contempt or imprisonment. The law technically applied to married women who had children "found not to be issue of the marriage" and to unmarried mothers irrespective of means—but everyone understood that the law's primary targets were poor single mothers, disproportionately Black women. The Connecticut Civil Liberties Union brought a class-action lawsuit on their behalf in 1973, claiming the law violated the right to privacy, due process, and equal protection.[69]

State officials described mothers who refused to disclose paternity as "recalcitrant," "obstinate," and "primarily concerned with their own welfare" rather than their children's well-being. A federal district court judge wrote approvingly that the statute "operates prophylactically against the adverse differential treatment which the unwed mothers would impose on their children" by "casting [them] into the eternal caverns of illegitimacy" and depriving them of a relationship with their fathers.[70] The plaintiff mothers defended their right to make decisions in their children's best interests: In affidavits, they explained their refusal to disclose paternity in terms of their families' safety and welfare. Rena Roe (a pseudonym) said that her child's father had "threatened her with physical harm if she divulges his name." Mildred Walter explained that she had declined to participate in paternity proceedings because she lived in "fear of this man . . . due to the beatings and physical abuse he inflicted" on her, including during pregnancy. Walter would forgo public assistance rather than "place [her] life and that of [her] child in danger." Other mothers feared that disclosing paternity would destroy good and valuable relationships with their children's fathers or with other potential partners and coparents. Several women noted the unlikelihood of recovering any financial support from the fathers—and even if support was forthcoming, it would benefit the state rather than poor children and their mothers.[71]

The plaintiffs also defended their right to personal and sexual privacy. Sharon Roe (a pseudonym) said, "The question of with whom I have had sexual intercourse is private; I don't feel I should be forced to tell any government agency that." Pressured by a judge to "stop playing games," Rosalyn Carr replied that she did not know the father's name, and even if she did, she "would consider it a gross intrusion of [her] privacy to have to give the name." "Even having to be here," Carr continued, "is a gross intrusion of my privacy." The mothers' attorneys secured expert testimony to establish that incarcerating mothers would be inimical to their children's best interests. In the end, the Supreme Court punted on the constitutional issues presented, sending the case back to the lower courts after a new federal regulation preempted the challenged state law.[72] As in *King v. Smith* and *Andrews v. Drew Municipal Separate School District*, statutory and regulatory resolutions to constitutional claims meant a lack of lasting protection when the political winds shifted.

Conclusion

Though plaintiffs and their lawyers made a range of constitutional arguments in welfare and birth status cases—discrimination based on race, poverty, family status, and sex; sexual privacy and reproductive autonomy among them—they most often prevailed when courts could frame the harm as the "illogical and unjust" punishment of "hapless, innocent children" for their parents' "sins." Employment discrimination claims sometimes succeeded when plaintiffs could show that employers imposed sexual and/or racial double standards. But when poor single mothers resisted state-mandated paternity disclosure on pain of fines or imprisonment, they could not obtain constitutional protection. Black single mothers won, in other words, mostly when they could frame themselves as hardworking (outside the home) and self-sufficient, able to care for and support their children without any help from the state. More fundamental challenges—to a political economy that privatized dependency within the family, to an ethos that shamed and stigmatized nonmarital childbearing perceived to threaten the public fisc—met with defeat.[73]

Those defeats had lasting consequences for law and public policy. For example, when the Personal Responsibility and Work Opportunity Act of 1996 imposed lifetime limits on welfare receipt, encouraged states to enact family caps and child exclusion policies, devoted federal funds to marriage promotion rather than cash assistance to needy families, and mandated maternal cooperation with paternity establishment, no constitutional guardrails stood in the way. Marriage became, at least in theory, more internally gender egalitarian—but marriage increasingly correlated with race, education, and socioeconomic status, its benefits concentrated on those who needed them least. The right to be free from employment discrimination based on race and sex failed to guarantee the social supports necessary for low-income single parents, disproportionately of color, to balance caregiving and wage earning.

Black women, mothers, and feminists formed a vanguard of family pioneers. The selective and partial adoption of their varied prescriptions for legal and social change left in place structural inequalities that survive into the twenty-first century. Recovering the history of these efforts is important in its own right. It gives credit where credit is due: Ironically, valid criticism of white feminist activism for marginalizing women of color and poor women can have the unintended effect of obscuring the integral roles feminists and other activists of color played in influencing legal strategy and the law itself.[74] It also provides a corrective to a body of constitutional family and sex equality law that almost entirely ignores race despite its central role in both the history and current operation of laws that discriminate based on sex and family status.[75] As Robin Lenhardt explains, "kinship has a color," and "family law systems and policies shape notions of race and structure inequality."[76] The law of family, work, poverty, and reproductive justice reflects long-standing, unfinished projects of resistance and reconstruction begun by unsung family pioneers.

NOTES

1 A footnote can hardly do justice to this assertion, so I will simply mention three treasured colleagues—Professors Anita Allen, Regina Austin, and Dorothy Roberts—to whom this chapter is dedicated.

2 Daniel Patrick Moynihan, Office of Policy Planning and Research, US Department of Labor, *The Negro Family: The Case for National Action* (1965).

3 Serena Mayeri, *Reasoning from Race: Feminism, Law, and the Civil Rights Revolution* (Harvard University Press, 2011), chap. 2. I have discussed the politics of the Moynihan Report more fully in Serena Mayeri, "Historicizing the End of Men: The Politics of Reaction(s)," *Boston University Law Review* 93 (2013): 729–44.

4 Quoted in Lee Rainwater and William L. Yancey, *The Moynihan Report and the Politics of Controversy* (MIT Press, 1967), 185. On Murray and postsuffrage women's citizenship, see Serena Mayeri, "After Suffrage: The Unfinished Business of Feminist Legal Advocacy," *Yale Law Journal Forum*, January 20, 2020 (citing sources).

5 Mayeri, "Historicizing the End of Men"; Felicia Kornbluh, *A Woman's Life Is a Human Life: My Mother, Her Neighbor, and the Journey from Reproductive Rights to Reproductive Justice* (Grove, 2023).

6 Mayeri, "After Suffrage," 517–18.

7 Pauli Murray, "A Proposal to Reexamine the Applicability of the Fourteenth Amendment to State Laws and Practices Which Discriminate on the Basis of Sex Per Se 10" (December 1962), Doc. 11-20, folder 62, box 8, PCSW Papers, Schlesinger Library, Radcliffe Institute, Harvard University.

8 Serena Mayeri, "'A Common Fate of Discrimination': Race-Gender Analogies in Legal and Historical Perspective," *Yale Law Journal* 110 (2001):1055–63.

9 Pauli Murray, "Memorandum in Support of Retaining the Amendment to H.R. 7152, Title VII (Equal Employment Opportunity) to Prohibit Discrimination in Employment Because of Sex" (April 14, 1964), 4–5, MC 412, folder 1485, box 85, Pauli Murray Papers, Schlesinger Library, Radcliffe Institute, Harvard University.

10 Serena Mayeri, "Intersectionality and Title VII: A Brief (Pre)-History," *Boston University Law Review* 95 (2015): 713–31.

11 Murray, "Memorandum," 21.

12 Murray, "Memorandum," 20–21.

13 Murray, "Memorandum," 23.

14 Nancy MacLean, *Freedom Is Not Enough: The Opening of the American Workplace* (Harvard University Press, 2006), chap. 3; Mayeri, "Common Fate"; Mayeri, "Intersectionality and Title VII."

15 Dorothy Height and Caroline Ware, "To Fulfill the Rights of Negro Women in Disadvantaged Families: A Statement for the White House Conference, 'To Fulfill These Rights,'" June 1–2, 1966, Catherine East Papers, Schlesinger Library, Radcliffe Institute for Advanced Study, Harvard University; Mayeri, *Reasoning from Race*, 26.

16 On the battle over women's jury service, see Linda K. Kerber, *No Constitutional Right to Be Ladies: Women and the Obligations of Citizenship* (Oxford University Press, 1998); Mayeri, *Reasoning from Race*, chap. 5.

17 Kerber, *No Constitutional Right*; Mayeri, *Reasoning from Race*.

18 Mayeri, "After Suffrage," 521; Mayeri, *Reasoning from Race*, 174–75.

19 Hoyt v. Florida, 368 U.S. 57, 61 (1961).

20 State v. Hall, 187 So.2d 861, 863 (Miss. 1966).

21 Declaration of Serena Mayeri, in Support of Plaintiffs' Motion for Partial Summary Judgment, Jackson Women's Health Org. v. Dobbs, Civil No. 3:18-cv-CWR-FKB (S.D. Miss. Apr. 29, 2021).

22 "Girl, 13, Has Eye Shot Out in Mississippi," *Pittsburgh Courier*, December 10, 1966, 1.

23 I use similar language to describe the Willis case in Mayeri, "After Suffrage," 522; Mayeri, *Reasoning from Race*, 174–75.

24 Quoted in Mayeri, *Reasoning from Race*, 49.

25 Mayeri, *Reasoning from Race*, 48, quoting Ann Scott and Lucy Komisar, *And Justice for All: Federal Equal Opportunity Enforcement Effort Against Sex Discrimination* (NOW, January 1, 1971).

26 Norton predicted that "fortified by her uncommon experience as co-breadwinner in the family, the Black woman can be expected to move . . . into far wider participation in business and in all higher-paying occupations." Eleanor Holmes Norton, "For Black Women, Opportunities Open," *New York Times*, January 10, 1971.

27 Eleanor Holmes Norton, "For Sadie and Maude," *Rutgers Law Review* 25 (1970): 23.

28 Cellestine Ware, "The Black Family and Feminism: A Conversation with Eleanor Holmes Norton," *Ms.* 1, no. 1 (1972): 96.

29 Mayeri, *Reasoning from Race*, 48, quoting Caroline Bird, *Everything a Woman Needs to Know to Get Paid What She's Worth* (David McKay, 1973).

30 Tera Hunter, *Bound in Wedlock: Slave and Free Black Marriage in the Nineteenth Century* (Harvard University Press, 2017); Christina Simmons, *Making Marriage Modern: Women's Sexuality from the Progressive Era to World War II* (Oxford University Press, 2009).

31 Tomiko Brown-Nagin, *Civil Rights Queen: Constance Baker Motley and the Struggle for Equality* (Pantheon Books, 2022).

32 Frontiero v. Richardson, 411 U.S. 677 (1973); Weinberger v. Wiesenfeld, 420 U.S. 636 (1975); Califano v. Goldfarb, 430 U.S. 199 (1977); Serena Mayeri, "Marriage (In)equality and the Historical Legacies of Feminism," *California Law Review Circuit* 6 (2015): 126–36.

33 Reed v. Reed, 404 U.S. 71 (1971); Orr v. Orr, 440 U.S. 268 (1979); Stanton v. Stanton, 421 U.S. 7 (1975); Kirchberg v. Feenstra, 450 U.S. 455 (1981).

34 I explore challenges to the legal primacy of marriage in my forthcoming book, tentatively titled *Marital Privilege: Marriage, Inequality, and the Transformation of American Law* (Yale University Press, 2025).

35 Serena Mayeri, "Constitutional Choices: Legal Feminism and the Historical Dynamics of Change," *California Law Review* 92 (2004): 755–839; Reva B. Siegel, "Constitutional Culture, Social Movement Culture, and Constitutional Change: The Case of the De Facto ERA," *California Law Review* 94 (2006): 1323–1419; Mayeri, "Marriage (In)equality."

36 SisterSong, "Reproductive Justice," accessed April 17, 2025, www.sistersong.net.

37 Sherie Randolph, *Florynce "Flo" Kennedy: The Life of a Black Feminist Radical* (University of North Carolina Press, 2015), 169–70.

38 Kornbluh, *Woman's Life*; Anastasia C. Curwood, *Shirley Chisholm: Champion of Black Feminist Power Politics* (University of North Carolina Press, 2023).

39 Melissa Murray, "Race-ing *Roe*: Reproductive Justice, Racial Justice, and the Battle for *Roe v. Wade*," *Harvard Law Review* 134 (2021): 2044–46.

40 Keeanga-Yamahtta Taylor, "How Black Feminists Defined Abortion Rights," *New Yorker*, February 22, 2022.

41 Khiara Bridges, "Elision and Erasure: Race, Class, and Gender in *Harris v. McRae*," in *Reproductive Rights and Justice Stories*, ed. Melissa Murray, Katherine Shaw, and Reva B. Siegel (Foundation, 2019).

42 Bridges, "Elision and Erasure"; Kornbluh, *Woman's Life*.

43 Keisha M. Blain, *Until I Am Free: Fannie Lou Hamer's Enduring Message to America* (Beacon, 2022).

44 Kornbluh, *Woman's Life*.

45 Maya Manion, "The Story of *Madrigal v. Quilligan*: Coerced Sterilization of Mexican-American Women," in Murray et al., *Reproductive Rights and Justice Stories*.

46 Relf v. Weinberger, 372 F. Supp. 1192 (D.D.C. 1974); Dorothy Roberts, *Killing the Black Body: Race, Reproduction, and the Meaning of Liberty* (Vintage Books, 1997).

47 Melissa Murray, "Abortion, Sterilization, and the Universe of Reproductive Rights," *William and Mary Law Review* 62 (2022): 1599–1638.

48 Linda Villarosa, "The Long Shadow of Eugenics in America," *New York Times Magazine*, June 8, 2022.

49 Melissa Murray, "What's So New About the New Illegitimacy?," *American University Journal of Gender, Social Policy and Law* 20 (2012): 387–436; Serena Mayeri, "Marital Supremacy and the Constitution of the Nonmarital Family," *California Law Review* 103 (2015): 1277–1352; Serena Mayeri, "Intersectionality and the Constitution of Family Status," *Constitutional Commentary* 32 (2017): 377–412.

50 Petitions for Writs of Certiorari and Review to the Court of Appeal, Fourth Circuit, State of Louisiana, at 4, Levy v. State, 193 So.2d 530 (La. 1967) (No. 48518); Mayeri, "Intersectionality and the Constitution," 392.

51 Mayeri, "Marital Supremacy"; Mayeri, "Intersectionality and the Constitution."

52 King v. Smith, 392 U.S. 309 (1968).

53 Serena Mayeri, "Race, Sexual Citizenship, and the Constitution of Nonmarital Motherhood," in *Heterosexual Histories*, ed. Rebecca L. Davis and Michele Mitchell (New York University Press, 2021), 282–83; Mayeri, "Marital Supremacy."

54 Mayeri, "Race, Sexual Citizenship," 283.

55 Mayeri, "Race, Sexual Citizenship," 283.

56 Hamer also emphasized the hypocrisy of punishing young Black women for conduct that their white counterparts engaged in with impunity. Mayeri, "Race, Sexual Citizenship," 284–85.

57 Mayeri, *Reasoning from Race*, chap. 5.

58 Mayeri, "Race, Sexual Citizenship," 285.

59 R. A. Lenhardt, "The Color of Kinship," *Iowa Law Review* 102 (2017): 2071–2107; Mayeri, *Reasoning from Race*, chap. 5; Mayeri, "Intersectionality and the Constitution."

60 For more on the Andrews case, see Mayeri, *Reasoning from Race*, chap. 5. For more on Joetha Collier's murder and its erasure from public memory, see Keisha N. Blain, "They Called Her 'Black Jet,'" *The Atlantic*, April 28, 2022.

61 I discuss this case in detail in Mayeri, *Marital Privilege*, chap. 5.

62 Drake v. Covington County Board of Education, 371 F. Supp. 974 (M.D. Ala. 1973).

63 Regina Austin, "Sapphire Bound!," *Wisconsin Law Review* 1989 (1989): 539–78.

64 Mayeri, "Race, Sexual Citizenship," 290.

65 Johnnie Tillmon, "Welfare Is a Women's Issue," *Ms.* 1, no. 1 (1972): 111.

66 Tillmon, "Welfare Is a Women's Issue," 112. I use similar language to describe Tillmon's critique in Mayeri, "Historicizing the End of Men," 741.

67 Premilla Nadasen, *Welfare Warriors: The Welfare Rights Movement in the United States* (Routledge, 2004); Premilla Nadasen, "Expanding the Boundaries of the Women's Movement: Black Feminism and the Struggle for Welfare Rights," *Feminist Studies* 28, no. 2 (2002): 270–301.

68 Tillmon, "Welfare Is a Women's Issue," 111. On the shortcomings of federal and state law and policy in meeting these demands, see, for example, Khiara M. Bridges, *The Poverty of Privacy Rights* (Stanford University Press, 2017); Kaaryn Gustafson, "Degradation Ceremonies and the Criminalization of Low-Income Women," *University of California Law Review* 3 (2013): 297–358; Angela Onwuachi-Willig, "The Return of the Ring: Welfare Reform's Marriage Cure as the Revival of Post-Bellum Control," *California Law Review* 93 (2005): 1647–96; Felicia Kornbluh and Gwendolyn Mink, *Ensuring Poverty: Welfare Reform in Feminist Perspective* (University of Pennsylvania Press, 2018); Nancy Dowd, *In Defense of Single-Parent Families* (New York University Press, 1999).

69 I use similar language to describe *Roe v. Norton* in Mayeri, "Race, Sexual Citizenship," 291.

70 Doe v. Norton, 356 F. Supp. 202, 206 n.6 (D. Conn. 1973).

71 Mayeri, "Race, Sexual Citizenship," 292.

72 Mayeri, "Race, Sexual Citizenship," 294.

73 Serena Mayeri, "The State of Illegitimacy After the Rights Revolution," in *Intimate States: Gender, Sexuality, and Governance in Modern U.S. History*, ed. Margot Canaday, Nancy F. Cott, and Robert O. Self (University of Chicago Press, 2021); Mayeri, "Race, Sexual Citizenship."

74 Serena Mayeri, "The Intersectional Origins of Modern Feminist Legal Advocacy," *Yale Journal of Law and Feminism* (2023): 6–13; Martha S. Jones, *Vanguard: How Black Women Broke Barriers, Won the Vote, and Insisted on Equality for All* (Basic Books, 2020); Julie Suk, *We the Women: The Unstoppable Mothers of the Equal Rights Amendment* (Skyhorse, 2020).

75 For more, see Mayeri, "Intersectionality and the Constitution."

76 Lenhardt, "Color of Kinship," 2071.

4

"Zora on My Mind"

Placemaking and Prospering in Washington, DC

ANITA GONZALEZ

What does it mean for an African American Black woman to live and
prosper in Washington, DC? This chapter investigates how the discipline of performing arts might intervene in empowering Black women
to embrace their potentiality through positive representations of history
and placemaking. Representative storytelling matters in the struggle for
racial equity because Black women for centuries have been labeled and
characterized in the media as inferior, incapable, and worthless. The
performing arts have the ability to create and disseminate new, positive representations of thriving African Americans. Theatrical stories,
when produced by socially conscientious storytellers and performed in
conversation with Black community members, offer opportunities for
African Americans to embrace positive representations of their experiences. Feeling self-empowerment activates and energizes activism for
social change.

This chapter uses reflective writing methodologies to consider placemaking and representation of African American women during the late
twentieth century. First, I focus on placemaking and survival strategies
of my grandmother Eloise Nash-Nichols. I reimagine her story as a tale
of survival within a segregated society. Even after *Brown v. the Board of
Education* legally integrated schools in Washington, DC, Black populations in general and women in particular continued to work within networks of local community activism in order to prosper and make a place
for their family within an often-antagonistic social system. Grandma
Nash's story illuminates the mechanisms of those processes.

Second, I describe a musical theater performance project based on
Grandma Nash's life story, *Zora on My Mind*. The play questions how

Black women absorb and respond to social expectations about their success or failure within American mythologies. The musical's title references the ethnographer and folklorist Zora Neal Hurston, whose writings elevated Black vernacular culture. Hurston's life experiences were deeply rooted in southern community expressions. She defied expectations of allegiance to Euro-American conventions by celebrating the rich contributions of Black lifestyles. *Zora on My Mind* features four characters: two women (one Black and one white) who attempt to write a character in the spirit of Zora; a protagonist named Key who refuses to comply with someone else's imagination about who she can be; and finally, a Black man concocted by the writers to complement Key. Both the real-life story of Grandma Nash and the imaginary tale of Key point to mechanisms for empowered Black women in the struggle for recognition and prosperity.

Eloise Nash-Nichols

When I was a child, my family would travel monthly from New Jersey to visit my mother's childhood home in Washington, DC. There, we would spend time with my grandmother Eloise Wright Nash-Nichols. She was born in 1909 in Laurens, South Carolina, and at the age of nineteen or twenty years old, she gave birth to my mother and moved to Washington, DC.[1] She was married to a preacher, the Reverend Wesley B. Nash, who later became the presiding elder of the Washington Conference of the African Methodist Episcopal Church. Reverend Nash lived away from my grandmother for sixteen years as she raised my mother, later sent her to prestigious schools like Dunbar and Howard University. The story of my grandmother is a testament to how Black families and women-led households survived in the precarious and segregated world of our nation's capital city.

It is particularly important to recognize structures and strategies that have contributed to the survival of Black families. African Americans are resilient people who continuously adjust to adverse circumstances by establishing networks of support. Too often, white social justice narratives focus on white saviors who rescue African American women from destitution or disenfranchisement. A familiar example would be *The Help*, a 2011 film based on a novel by the white author Kathryn Stockett, who narrates an account of African American women working as domestics for white households in Jackson, Mississippi, during the 1960s. The film depicts the perspective of the white central character, Eugenia "Skeeter" Phelan, who is inspired to write about the injustices facing African American "hired help" in the deep South. The film epitomizes a "white savior" approach to depicting Black lives. While the story is emotionally moving and sheds light on discrimination and inequity, it posits that the solution is white intervention in Black community life. To the contrary, Eloise Wright Nash-Nichols was a very proud and dignified woman. She never spoke of her time performing domestic service work, and, somehow, we knew not to bring it up. Even though my grandmother worked as a domestic, she did not consider her maid activities to be the core component of her survival strategy.

African American families have sustained themselves in Washington, DC, and beyond through community networks and small entrepreneurial businesses. My grandmother ran three businesses in addition to her work as a domestic: a hair parlor, a boardinghouse, and the missionary society. Her beautician business expanded from "doing hair" in her home to later managing a salon—The Hollywood Beauty Shop—at the corner of Second and P Streets in Washington, DC. She also converted her home in Northwest Washington to a boardinghouse, where she supported family members from South Carolina as they made their transition from the rural South to government and other jobs in the urban North. Family legend has it that Nash acquired her home because she was fortunate enough to "hit the number" in local community gambling networks. During the 1930s, she supported her sisters and younger relations from Laurens—Clara Wright and Alma Sue, for example—as they found jobs and established employment networks. Clara was a respected schoolteacher in South Carolina but was forced out and had to come to DC, where the only job available to her was domestic work. Aunt Clara's husband, Mr. Norman, who looked like a white man, worked as a maintenance man for a government agency.

Later in life, Grandma Nash's husband, Reverend Nash, returned to live with her after serving in World War II as a captain in the Army Chaplains Corps in Africa and Europe. Once reunited, the couple managed Waters AME Church in Baltimore and Mount Moriah AME Church in Annapolis, Maryland. Grandma Nash was particularly adept at leading the Women's Missionary Society of the AME Church. She was the district president of the Second Episcopal District of the Washington Conference for two years.[2] This international organization of women supports missionary and educational activities globally. A particular area of focus was missionary activities in South Africa and the organization of national conferences to coordinate efforts across constituencies. Karen Cook Bell describes the historical contexts of Black women's community networks, asserting that "church-affiliated societies such as mutual and benevolent associations played a pivotal role in the economic arena of women's lives."[3] My grandmother willingly contributed her labor and time to community-based organizational efforts that counteract narratives of white support and intervention.

Nash-Nichols, an industrious multitasker, drove ministers on all the road trips for conferences and entertained church dignitaries in her homes with scrumptious meals—all of this while making sure her daughter had the best available education, accoutrements, and connections. Eloise's power reflected her position as the skilled assistant of highly respected men who were spiritual leaders. Her roles in the Missionary Society flowed from her position as First Lady of the churches where her husband pastored. In that position, as the wife of a major AME church minister, Nash-Nichols was a power broker as well as a custodian of the church/Missionary Society finances. She was much loved, admired, and feared. In the final phase of her life, in 1982, my grandmother lost her husband, Reverend Wright Nash, to Alzheimer's disease. Still resilient, my grandmother, at the age of eighty, remarried another minister, the Reverend Howard E. Nichols. He was from Annapolis and supported her as a religious and physical companion until his own death in the 1990s.[4] My strongest memory is the way in which Reverend Nichols honored her matriarchal leadership by referring to my grandmother as "my angel."

Eloise Nash-Nichols's story is not unusual. Black women and their families survive through informal networks of support and resiliency that encourage entrepreneurship as a means of achieving self-sufficiency. Even though Grandma Nash had a husband and a job of sorts working for white employers, she did not rely on employers' beneficence. An ancestral understanding of power prevents African Americans raised under the umbrella of chattel slavery from trusting in, or relying on, white generosity. Consequently, Black women invest in networks of community support and implement strategies that will sustain them when white munificence fails. I think about incidents like the Black washerwomen's strike of 1881 in Atlanta, Georgia, where women refused to wash clothing for white women employers until they received an increased wage.[5] Their successful community organizing models how underclass laborers use entrepreneurial strategies for collective sustenance. Experience with entrepreneurial strategies fuels contemporary ecosystems for Black women to excel at new business development in Washington, DC, and beyond. "According to a 2018 report commissioned by *American Express* there are 2.4 million businesses owned by Black women nationally, and Black women actually have higher shares of business ownership than Black men."[6] While entrepreneurial skills help to establish business enterprises, channeling business operations into successful financial returns is an ongoing challenge because systematic structures prevent access to the lucrative financial markets and marketing ecosystems.

Zora on My Mind

Zora on My Mind is a chamber musical written by Anita Gonzalez with music and lyrics by Diana Lawrence that began as an exploration of Black movement and trauma. The first iteration of the performance work was an embodied dance exploration with Alexandria Davis, a dancer from Gainesville, Florida. It was inspired by Zora Neale Hurston's essay "Characteristics of Negro Expression," first published in *The New Negro* anthology edited by the Harlem Renaissance author Alain Locke.[7] The essay was later reprinted in a volume called *Negro*, edited by Nancy Cunard. As a child, I discovered Cunard's collection of memorabilia about African American culture and history on my parents' bookshelf. I was entranced by the Hurston essay describing language and gestures of African American vernacular lifestyles, based on the author's experiences with all-Black communities in Florida. This writing was one of the earliest attempts to theorize what it means to embrace Black American vernacular expression as theory. It became the inspiration for Gonzalez and Davis to meet and work with Hurston's language to develop a movement vocabulary based on her descriptive imagery, one that would capture the feelings and flow of African American physical stances and gestures. The result was a series of movement phrases, including some that would later be incorporated into scenes within *Zora on My Mind*.

The next step was to assemble a team of artists that initially included the actor/deviser Antonio Disla, the Broadway performer Freddie Walker Browne, the composer Diana Lawrence, and the dancer Shaka Brown to begin to craft songs and music appropriate to a story that merged Zora Neale Hurston's writings with the life story of Eloise Nash-Nichols. Our devising team met in studios in New York City to discuss characters and create a musical vocabulary to complement the scenarios. We created a character named Key—a woman who does not know who she wants to be—as the central protagonist. The first song to emerge focused on the labor of Key as a Black woman who works multiple jobs while trying to find a sense of self-worth within a world that devalues her labor. The original lyrics read,

> I got this place
> I got this chair
> I got other folks' messes
> Scrubbing their floors
> Doing their hair
> Ain't I a queen
> That's what they say
> Ain't I a queen
> Ain't I a queen
> I got some property
> I got some clout
> But I'm still on my knees
> Begging please
> This can't be all that life's about
> Ain't I a queen
> They tell me someday
> Ain't I a queen
> Ain't I a queen
> I scrub with a smile
> So the white folks hire
> I twist and I braid

Like my sisters require
I rent out my rooms when the bottom line's dire but
What about me?
Who's that in the mirror?
Is that a queen that I see?
Or the edge of a pit drawing nearer and nearer and nearer
I'm down on my knees.
Always down on my knees.
Is this all life can mean?
All life can mean
All life can mean
Ain't I a queen?

The lyrics portray a downtrodden woman who seems incapable of finding a space for respite. The first impetus of the collaborators was to write about the pain and struggles of a woman seeking her place in Washington, DC. However, we later created a different framing for the story because the circumstances we first imagined were reiterating a trope about traumatizing circumstances of Black lives without celebrating the dignity and resiliency of Washington, DC, women and their networks of support. We wondered if we were not reinscribing stereotypes and archetypes from a biased imaginary.

The academic discipline of performance studies is deeply invested in how representations impact public perceptions of ethnic communities. Performance products in many cases determine how audience members label and imagine African American and other US minorities. Black actors, for example, are often asked to create characters that exist in the imagination of commercial writers or producers, and these "authors" of content conceive characters based on their own life experiences. This means that if a producer can only imagine African Americans to be "urban" or "southern," then they invent roles for the performer based on their limited imaginations. Often, characters are stereotyped— prescribed by the life experiences of the producing team and not the lived experiences of African Americans in all of their diversity. Therefore, African American and other ethnic performers struggle for opportunities to perform well-rounded characters because commercial producers tend to replicate existing tropes of ethnicity.

A good example is the audition experience that many actors undergo in order to find employment. A common practice is to enter a studio seeking work and then be asked to perform in a manner that reifies a producer's often-unarticulated typecast. Sometimes this can lead to a performer being asked to "act" like an imaginary Black person. Kevin Ray Johnson writes a blog in which he entreats, "Stop asking Black actors to 'sound Blacker' during auditions."[8] He asserts that Black is not an act and suggests that asking actors to perform Blackness will discourage young aspirants from continuing in the business. Entire comedy acts are available on YouTube channels about the experience of auditioning for roles as a Black actor.[9] The "Acting Black" videocast series hosted by Khalif J. Gillett and Yetunde Felix-Ukwu, for example, details intervention techniques for responding to stereotypical casting practices when attending auditions.[10] Their series represents a developing awareness of the need for cultural sensitivity in casting practices.

Two years into our developmental process, the *Zora on My Mind* team began to wonder if we might be unconsciously complicit in typecasting our central character, Key, as a disempowered woman without a sense of agency. We decided to directly address the problem by creating two new writer characters—one Black and one white—who would grapple with the challenge of "writing" a Black woman. While both fictional "writers" seek to create a character in the image of Zora Neale Hurston, each responds from their own preconceptions about who Key should be. Sophie, the middle-aged Black woman, wants Key to be strong, to struggle, and to represent the cotton fields of the deep South. Draft, in contrast, is a younger white woman who wants Key to succeed and be famous. By incorporating distinct narrative strategies for writing a Black woman directly into the story line, we were able to freely experiment with challenges of typing and defining Black women.

To advance the concept, we had both the fictional writers agree to introduce a man named Malik into the story, but for different reasons. The white character, Draft, wants to add a man into Key's life because it reifies the belief that a man-woman relationship and a heterosexual partnership is the ideal way of advancing in Euro-American society. This perspective ignores the role that the institution of slavery has had in destroying Black nuclear families. Racialized economic policies encouraged slave owners to separate enslaved family members for profit and control. Draft ignores this historical circumstance as she advocates for Key to enter into a romantic relationship with Malik and form a nuclear family.

Sophie, on the other hand, wants Key to have a partner because she believes that Key, as a generational inheritor of postslavery trauma, will be unable to support herself alone. Sophie adopts a rural southern perspective that believes a "good man" will help the protagonist to survive. If Key has a man, she presumes the man will support Key, and his presence will contribute to Key's status in a core Black community in a city where a "good working Black man" is hard to find. This resonates with the reality of lived experiences in Washington, DC, where employed Black women outnumber employed Black men substantially.[11] The journalist Ally Schweitzer writes, "Single, educated women who date men face a quandary in the D.C. region. There are lots of jobs for them here. But not enough men. For every 100 single, college-educated individuals in the Washington area, women outnumber men 53–47."[12] Sophie collaborates with Draft in creating a partner for Key even though each of them does so for a different reason.

Malik is cute and sexy, a good dancer and an encouraging partner. He first drops into Key's life as a boarding roommate and later offers his advice, encouraging her to expand her one-chair shop into a more lucrative online internet business. Conspiring with Draft, he urges Key to compete in a New York City beauty contest and expand her clientele. Sophie, on the other hand, wants Key to stay in the neighborhood and spend time with her community while remembering the traumas of the cotton field. Both writers are scribing a story about Key without her consent or cooperation. In the end, Key rejects all of the visions and expectations the writers have created for her. Instead, she creates a circle of health and healing where she can rest and begin to imagine her own potentiality.

The actual rehearsal process for the Georgetown University workshop production of *Zora on My Mind* was difficult. Director Kym Moore from Brown University was invited to lead the staging of the work for a public showing in June 2022. Several participants, who had once been devisers, were asked to enter the process as performers and respond to spatial and conceptual staging developed through the vision of the director. In some ways, their creative voices became more limited as they worked with the execution of the characters. Some felt traumatized by the experience of being written onto instead of writing the story of Black women's lives, yet Moore brought clarity and intent to each scene of the play and was instrumental in clarifying how the story might resolve. The campus presentations June 7 through 9, 2022, brought Washington, DC, community members into the theatrical space of the Devine Theater and invited audience response to histories and cultures of Black womanhood in Washington, DC. The African American studies scholar and dramaturg Jordan Ealey, who coleads the *Daughters of Lorraine* podcast, moderated the conversation.[13]

The postperformance conversation brought the community into a discursive consideration of Key's choices for achieving success. Should she have built on her success in New York City and moved more forcefully into entrepreneurship? Was Sophie right in wanting Key to stay connected to her community? How do rituals of self-care help us to sustain our path toward economic stability. Every audience member had a different response and a unique reflection. The performance offered a template for the audience to craft their own solution to the ever evolving conundrum of surviving as an African American woman in a racialized context. Every person in the room had in some ways struggled with how to establish a stable place in their home or work settings.

Placemaking

The notion of placemaking sits at the center of both the story of my grandmother and the creation of the chamber musical *Zora on My Mind*. The fictional character of Key navigates challenges familiar to contemporary Black women residents of Washington, DC, and beyond. In this section, I focus on several aspects of the Eloise Nash story that intersect with histories of placemaking in Washington, DC. *Zora on My Mind* situates the protagonist, Key, as a home owner who, like her inspiration, Eloise Nash, somewhat defied trends of Black domestics living in the homes of their employees.[14] The Depression of the 1930s deeply impacted Black communities that had traveled to northern cities in the United States to escape violence and lynching. Roosevelt's New Deal, implemented between 1933 and 1935, nearly tripled the number of federal workers in Washington, DC. As a result, the city became a boom town, with housing as one of the most challenging issues.[15] Even though housing developments and regulations sought to displace African Americans from neighborhoods like Georgetown, my grandmother was able to offer housing support to her relatives from South Carolina. Her utilization of the housing inventory she was able to acquire demonstrated both community solidarity among family members and resiliency. She kept her real estate in the community, using local Black resources to maintain and support sustainable economic streams.

Eloise Nash and the fictional character Key also participate in entrepreneur networks related to the beauty industry. Much has been written about Madame C. J. Walker, the entrepreneur and philanthropist who became one of the first African American women millionaires during the early 1900s.[16] Walker was one of a host of Black women who sustained their families through the beauty products and hair care industry.[17] Profitable beauty shops addressed the needs of local Black communities throughout the Americas, and the same is true of Washington, DC. The journalists Astrid Williams and Kaela Thomas write, "For many Black women the hair salon is an attainable means of community, support, and all-around self-care. The salon is a renowned place where we can discuss the chronicles of our day-to-day lives to local news highlights from the comfort of a salon chair."[18] Like many American women, Eloise Nash-Nichols used her beauty chair to supplement her income while also "beautifying" those who sought to acculturate into the urban and urbane institutions of the Black middle class. The character Key owns a beauty chair, but as a twenty-first-century character, she uses the internet. Malik teaches her how to advertise online and expand her clientele. Her "scribes" both want her to achieve financial success through an enterprise historically associated with African American advancement. Key does this and uses digital technologies to access local and global economies.

Neighborhood gentrification is another aspect of placemaking that is addressed in the musical. This housing and population shift, however, did not impact the life of my grandmother. During her lifetime, the neighborhood she lived in was segregated, and she never considered mixing and mingling with the "white folks." Today, Black, white and Latine families all live within the upper Northwest neighborhood. Yet gentrification is a part of the fictional world constructed around the character of Key because Draft transforms into a white character named Chelsea, who comes into Key's beauty shop asking her to "do" her hair. Chelsea is a bit clueless about the social justice challenges of moving into an area that was once predominantly Black, but she prides herself on supporting local Black businesses through her relationship with Key. She represents neoliberal politics in the twenty-first century.

Ultimately, issues of placemaking must resolve with Black women being willing to accept their own power to shape and control the circumstances of their own lives. Representation, or the enactment of stories relevant to Black women and their communities, is a part of this process. As I have written in the online blog *Medium*, "I want people to understand that Black women's stories matter and that theatre is an ideal place to write and share those stories. When Black women and girls perform, they embody a history where they are able to be themselves, let others see who they are, and work toward the empowerment, which happens when we center in self affirmation."[19] Black women recognizing their value and embracing their social and economic power allows us to make a place for ourselves and prosper in Washington, DC, and beyond.

NOTES

1 "Eloise N. Nichols in the U.S, Social Security Application and Claims Index, 1936–2007," Ancestry.com, accessed January 23, 2024, www.ancestry.com.
2 Personal archive of Amelia Govan, Esq., typewritten notes about the life of Eloise Nash Nichols.
3 Karen Cook Bell, "Slavery, Land Ownership, and Black Women's Community Networks," *Black Perspectives*, October 25, 2018, www.aaihs.org.
4 "Howard E. Nichols in the U.S., Public Records Index, 1950–1993," vol. 1, Ancestry.com, accessed January 23, 2024, www.ancestry.com.
5 American Postal Workers Union, "Black Women Advance Labor's Cause in an Unlikely Setting: 1881 Atlanta," December 31, 2009, https://apwu.org.
6 Shelly Bell, "Building the Ecosystem for Black Women Entrepreneurs in D.C.," D.C. Policy Center, September 5, 2019, www.dcpolicycenter.org.
7 Zora Neale Hurston, "Characteristics of Negro Expression (1934)," in *The New Negro: Readings on Race, Representation, and African American Culture, 1892–1938*, ed. Henry Louis Gates and Gene Andrew Jarrett (Princeton University Press, 2008).
8 Kevin Ray Johnson, "Stop Asking Black Performers to 'Sound Blacker' During Auditions," *On Stage Blog*, May 8, 2021, www.onstageblog.com.
9 Breakfast Club Power 105.1 FM, "DeRay Davis on 'How to Act Black,' Audition Stories, Comedy Beefs + More," November 6, 2017, www.youtube.com/watch?v=7BqGZPhMIuE.

10 *Acting Black*, hosted by Khalif J. Gillett and Yetunde Felix-Ukwu, YouTube, 2020, www.youtube.com/playlist?list=PLLsCkbcJXZWF47BNcW28hRiPDeU2Eamnk.

11 Laquitta M. Walker, Chanell N. Washington, Lydia R. Anderson, and George M. Hayward, "All the Single Ladies: Washington, D.C., Has the Highest Ratio of Unmarried Women to Unmarried Men," US Census Bureau, September 7, 2023, www.census.gov.

12 Ally Schweitzer, "Washington Has a Shortage of Single, Educated Men. Could Amazon Fix That?," WAMU 88.5 American University Radio, December 10, 2019, https://wamu.org.

13 Frederick Douglass Institute and Department of Black Studies, University of Rochester, "Jordan Ealey," accessed May 12, 2024, https://sas.rochester.edu; Jordan Earley, *Daughters of Lorraine Podcast*, HowlRound Theatre Commons, accessed May 12, 2024, https://howlround.com.

14 Elizabeth Clark-Lewis, *Living In, Living Out: African American Domestics in Washington, D.C., 1910–1940* (Smithsonian Books, 2010).

15 Chris Myers Asch and George Derek Musgrove, *Chocolate City: A History of Race and Democracy in the Nation's Capital* (University of North Carolina Press, 2017), 250–52.

16 A'Lelia Bundles, *On Her Own Ground: The Life and Times of Madame C. J. Walker* (Scribner, 2002).

17 Tiffany M. Gill, *Beauty Shop Politics: African American Women's Activism in the Beauty Industry* (University of Illinois Press, 2010).

18 Astrid Williams and Kaela Thomas, "The Black Beauty Industry–A Backbone of Our Community," *AFRO News: The Black Media Authority*, May 10, 2021, https://afro.com.

19 Anita Gonzalez, "Black Women Scholars on Identity, Research and Black Women's Studies: A Roundtable with Anita Gonzalez and Taifa Alexander," *Spark: Elevating Scholarship on Social Issues*, February 13, 2020, https://medium.com.

5

Rooted in Fertile Ground

Resilience, Resistance, and the Positive Development of Black Children

MARKETA BURNETT

I fashioned myself into a bouquet of miracles.
Pruned petals until prodigal.
Pieced together all of the broken and learned to make the
impossible, possible.
—Sama Beltran, "In Order to Bloom"

Black families share a collective history—entrenched in a rich and enduring tradition of resilience and resistance. Historical (mis)representations of
Black families and Black children too often engage in deficit-oriented perspectives that subsequently endorse harmful stereotypes and uphold racist
tropes as truth. By focusing on outcomes alone and not actively engaging
with process-oriented approaches, many scholars have missed the dynamic
ways that Black families continue to adapt and thrive despite these vul-
nerabilities. This chapter seeks to amplify the existing cultural strengths,
assets, and strategies Black families employ to assist their children in the
successful navigation of inequitable social and academic contexts. I assert
that Black families are creative cultivators of brilliance and are uniquely
equipped with the tools to prepare their children to traverse an oppressive
system while negotiating a healthy sense of self. Acknowledging that Black
families are not a monolith, this chapter honors the variation in Black family processes with particular attention given to the diverse ways in which
Black families empower their children to resist and overcome. The chapter concludes with future directions and tangible recommendations for
researchers, practitioners, and policy makers who seek to work *with* Black
families in the advancement of equity and lasting social change.

Framework

Research on Black families has disproportionately employed deficit frameworks and race-neutral justifications while ignoring the central role of systemic racism (Williams 2023). Racism is deeply rooted into the very foundation of the United States, and its existence compromises the healthy development of Black children (Iruka et al. 2022). Prior research frequently neglects to acknowledge the many structural manifestations of racism (e.g., inadequate access to quality health care, redlining, disproportionate school resources) that have deleterious impacts for Black families. Yet, we find that Black families use cultural strength-based coping assets that directly influence positive development, adjustment, and adaptation (Murry et al. 2018). Black families are sowing into fertile ground, utilizing what they have always known to pour into their children in culturally relevant and affirming ways. It is in this safe space where Black children are given the rare opportunity to laugh, to be curious, to grow without fear of being stifled or silenced.

Building on Mims et al.'s (2022) discussion of the "axiom of brilliance," I frame this chapter from the existing brilliance of Black children and Black families. I reject the dominant discourse of Black families that willfully chooses to ignore their strengths, conveniently forgets their long-standing history of resilience, and seeks to disrupt the progress born out of their resistance. In this chapter, I begin with an overview of the pervasiveness of racism and discrimination in educational settings with particular attention given to how racism and discrimination impact Black children at the individual and structural levels. Next, I briefly introduce the connected nature of resilience and resistance as concepts related to Black children's thriving. Then, I discuss several cultural assets and strategies that Black families utilize to promote the positive development of their Black children. Lastly, I provide future recommendations to consider for researchers, practitioners, and policy makers.

Unearthing the Pervasiveness of Racism and Discrimination in Educational Settings

Decades of empirical research have focused on achievement "gaps" and disparities in academic outcomes among Black students, with little attention given to the social conditions that facilitate them. However, an emergence of scholarship has sought to contextualize Black students' schooling experiences—highlighting the stark inequities, opportunity gaps, and oppressive practices that shape their broader educational trajectories (Annamma et al. 2019; Ladson-Billings 2006; Milner 2012; Morris 2016). These inequities emerge early for Black children, with research revealing the ways teachers in early childhood learning spaces perceive Black children's behaviors differently than that of children of other races (Gilliam et al. 2016). The adultification and dehumanization of Black children by adults results in Black children being seen as inherently less innocent, more adult-like, and less needing of nurturing and care (Epstein et al. 2017; Goff et al. 2014; Perillo et al. 2023). This bias contributes to the alarming rates of Black preschoolers being suspended and expelled across the country (Allen et al. 2021; Wesley and Ellis 2017). These disproportionate rates of exclusionary discipline continue throughout the K–12 period and have lasting impacts on Black children's thriving. For example, Edward Morris and Brea Perry (2016) found that Black students were more likely to be suspended than were their white and Asian peers in the same schools. Moreover, suspensions accounted for one-fifth of the Black-white differences in school performance, which further underscores the ways Black students' learning potential is hindered due to being disproportionately exposed to exclusionary discipline (Morris and Perry 2016). Despite legislation seeking to eliminate hair discrimination across the country (see the CROWN Act), Black students are still being suspended for wearing their natural hair in schools (James-Gallaway et al. 2024; Mbilishaka et al. 2020; Rogers et al. 2022). What does this signal to Black children about how the world sees them and their worth?

Black youth are keenly aware of racial discrimination as manifested in the differential treatment they receive in schools, which has significant impacts on their adjustment and well-being (Bell 2020; Byrd and Carter Andrews 2016; English et al. 2020; Griffin et al. 2020). In a recent longitudinal study, Shauna Cooper et al. (2022) found that experiencing school discrimination was associated with lower school satisfaction, lower academic persistence, and greater depressive symptoms among Black adolescents. Further, awareness of discipline inequities resulted in lower educational aspirations for Black girls (Cooper et al. 2022). Extending beyond school disciplinary inequities, research has illuminated the ways Black students perceive differences in treatment as a result of teachers' and counselors' lower educational expectations and negative stereotypical beliefs about Black students' academic abilities (Francis et al. 2019; Hope et al. 2015; McKown and Weinstein 2008; Pringle et al. 2012). This is particularly important as it is directly related to the underrepresentation of Black students in gifted education, as they are less likely to be recommended for advanced courses compared to their peers (Ford 2014; Ford et al. 2020). For Black students, who are more likely to attend lower-resourced schools with fewer advanced course offerings available, this deliberate inaction by teachers and counselors has lasting impacts on Black youth's academic and career preparation.

Peers can also be perpetrators of racial violence in schools. For instance, Black youth have reported experiencing racialized bullying such as being called racial slurs and being teased for their physical features (e.g., natural hair texture, size of their lips) by their classmates (Burnett et al. 2022; Henderson et al. 2020; Mims and William 2020). With the rise in social media usage and online communication among peers, this extended exposure to peers beyond the school day warrants added attention. In a fourteen-day daily diary study, Devin English et al. (2020) found that Black adolescents reported an average of over five racial discrimination experiences a day, with the internet being the most frequent context for racial discrimination experiences. Additionally, daily racial discrimination predicted short-term increases in depressive symptoms (English et al. 2020). The threat of racial discrimination is constant for Black youth, and its lasting impact on their mental health is of immediate concern. In a recent review, Enrique Neblett (2023) provides four areas of racial, ethnic, and cultural resilience factors related to African American youth's mental health. These resilience factors included ethnic-racial socialization, ethnic-racial identity, religiosity and spirituality, and family/parenting, further underscoring the varied ways Black families may help their children engage in adaptive coping mechanisms in the face of racial discrimination.

Deep Roots: The Interplay of Resilience and Resistance

Resilience has been described by previous scholarship as "ordinary magic," a naturally occurring adaptive response to the challenges and adversities experienced throughout life (Masten 2001). For Black families, this ordinary magic is intentional—informed by a shared legacy and embedded in cultural traditions and values (Murry et al. 2018). The resilience of Black families is not a replacement for institutional and systematic change but should serve as a reminder for why this change is necessary. The resilience of Black families was not crafted in isolation but hand in hand with resistance.

In a recent review, Velma McBride Murry et al. sought to disentangle the difference between resilience and resistance, saying, "While resilience is portrayed as the capacity to overcome odds and succeed despite adversity, resistance aims to undermine oppressive structures by either attempting to alter them or fighting against the logic of imposed socially constructed prescriptions" (2023, 6). Three distinct differences between resilience and resistance are (1) intent, (2) orientation, and (3) subsequent responses to oppressive systems (Murry et al. 2023). Despite these distinctions, it remains true that resilience and resistance in practice often intersect. For instance, a mother who is preparing her child with strategies to navigate the unfair treatment they experienced at school very well may be engaging in an act of resistance, but the encouragement and adaptive skills acquired in the process may aid in the child's capacity to succeed despite adversity in the future, which would be a by-product of resilience.

Blooming by Any Means Necessary: The Positive Development of Black Children

Ethnic-racial socialization (ERS) is one tool that Black families use to communicate their values, attitudes, and beliefs about the meaning and significance of race, racism, and culture to their children (Hughes et al. 2006; Lesane-Brown 2006). ERS aims not only to prepare Black children for the world but also to empower them with strategies to cope and successfully navigate the world (Anderson and Stevenson 2019; Jones et al. 2021). Not only is this communicated through words, but also it is exhibited through the behaviors and actions taken by family members. For example, Black children may learn more about Black history and the resilience of Black people when celebrating Juneteenth as a family, just as they can be introduced to the power of resistance by witnessing a grandparent organize a protest. Through the years, scholars have demonstrated the great variability in the content, frequency, and motivations that prompt ERS messaging among Black families (Hughes et al. 2006; Banerjee et al. 2018; Cooper et al. 2020). Some of the leading dimensions of ERS found in prior literature include *racial pride* (the teaching of cultural history, values, customs, and traditions), *preparation for bias* (preparing youth for the reality of racism while also providing adaptive coping strategies), and *egalitarian* (strategies that center the individual over groups due to the belief that all groups are equal; Burnett et al. 2022; Hughes et al. 2006; Umaña-Taylor and Hill 2020). For Black youth, ERS messages often promote positive academic and psychosocial outcomes and protect against the harms of racism and discrimination (Banerjee et al. 2018; Burnett et al. 2022; Wang and Huguley 2012; Umaña-Taylor and Hill 2020). For instance, positive messages about one's racial group related to pride, history, and tradition as well as preparation for bias messages have been found to attenuate the negative effect of teacher and peer discrimination on Black youth's educational aspirations, grade point average, self-concept, and self-efficacy (Banerjee et al. 2018; Wang and Huguley 2012). Also, research has found that the benefits of racial socialization messages extend to Black adolescents' coping with general stressors in addition to racialized stressors (Anderson et al. 2019).

Caregivers often find it necessary to tailor their messaging depending on their child's gender and the context (Bowman and Howard 1985; Cooper et al. 2020; Burnett et al. 2022; Huguley et al. 2021). For example, Shauna Cooper et al. (2020) found that when engaging with their sons, Black fathers prioritized conversations around risk avoidance, unsupportive school contexts, and personal safety. With their daughters, Black fathers focused on promoting positive self-esteem, encouraging healthy relationships, and highlighting the importance and utility of education (Cooper et al. 2020). As schools in particular are a place where Black children spend the majority of their time, Black caregivers frequently provide distinct messages and strategies to ensure their children succeed. Characterized as *racial bias academic socialization*, James Huguley et al. (2021) posit that Black caregivers engage in distinct strategies to help their children cope with both overt and implicit experiences of racial discrimination in school. These strategies included engaging in positive conversations about resilient racial histories, providing strategies for how to respond to educational discrimination, and framing high achievement as a way to overcome systemic oppression. Emerging literature has also explored the ways parental socialization messages and behaviors may promote Black youth's sociopolitical development (Anyiwo et al. 2019; Anyiwo et al. 2023). For example, Nkemka Anyiwo et al. (2023) found that when Black parents engaged in more conversations that prepared their children for racial discrimination and engaged in more cultural enrichment behaviors, Black youth had a higher awareness of racial inequality as well as greater confidence in addressing racism through racial justice actions.

Despite living in a society that devalues them, Black children still find ways to resist and thrive. A significant contributor to Black youth's resilience and resistance is related to their identity development. Though the exact configuration may differ, it is important to examine how Black children integrate the knowledge of societal perceptions into their own understanding of who they are and who they are capable of becoming. Ethnic-racial identity is multidimensional in nature and considers how salient one's race is to their sense of self (centrality), how an individual views their own racial group (private regard), and how they perceive others view their racial group (public regard; Sellers et al. 1997). Ethnic-racial identity is particularly important to the development of Black youth, as it has been linked to psychosocial and academic outcomes (Butler-Barnes et al. 2018; Decuir-Gunby 2009; Leath et al. 2019; Rivas-Drake et al. 2014; Quintana 2007; Sellers et al. 2006) and may even be protective in nature (Neblett et al. 2012; Tynes et al. 2012). For instance, several empirical studies have found that ethnic-racial identity acted as a buffer or mitigated the effects of school-based discrimination on various academic outcomes such as academic self-perceptions, engagement, and achievement (Chavous et al. 2008; Leath et al. 2019; Thomas et al. 2009). In a 2022 study, Marketa Burnett et al. found that despite experiencing racialized bullying and discrimination within their schools, Black adolescent girls were still proud to be a Black girl and maintained a positive racial identity. Girls in this study attributed their sustained confidence and academic persistence to the affirmations they received from their families, which encouraged them to see the beauty in their Blackness and celebrate their differences (Burnett et al. 2022). Thus,

Black caregivers are uniquely equipped to support their children's continued development and thriving in ways that are culturally relevant and affirming.

Planting the Seeds: Future Recommendations

It is imperative that researchers reevaluate how they approach working with Black families. Research with Black families should be strengths and assets based, provide critical contextualization of their experiences, and prioritize their voices. Of particular importance is including the perspectives of Black children, especially in the creation of solutions that are intended to serve them. Operating from an axiom of brilliance, we must recognize Black children also as knowledge producers. Black children are the experts of their own experiences, and there is much that we could learn if we took the time to ask and listen.

Acknowledging the expertise of Black caregivers in the positive development of Black children, schools should seek to partner with Black families and the larger community in the hopes of creating a more just and equitable learning environment. Schools should facilitate listening sessions to promote open dialogue among families and community stakeholders. Currently, schools are not always safe places for Black children to learn and develop. Many Black children are pushed out of the classroom altogether and into the criminal legal system as a result of racial bias, negatively held stereotypes of Black children, and inequitable exclusionary discipline policies. Prospective and current educators must address how these deficit ideologies show up in their pedagogy and educational praxis. Further, creative programming that centers Black children's lived experiences and joy and affirms them is needed in both formal and informal learning environments.

Addressing the current social conditions at the local and national level will greatly improve the educational experiences of Black children and their overall well-being. This will take an intentional commitment among policy makers to critically evaluate the current practices and policies that exist and invest the necessary time and capital to ensure Black children are given the resources and support to thrive. Changes must be made *with* communities. Their needs and their solutions should be prioritized to ensure meaningful and sustainable change. We all have a responsibility to ensure the positive development of Black children. When we invest in Black children, we invest in our future—a future that is fruitful and bright.

REFERENCES

Allen, Rosemarie, et al. 2021. "Creating Anti-Racist Early Childhood Spaces." *YC Young Children*, vol. 76, no. 2, pp. 49–54.

Anderson, Riana Elyse, and Howard C. Stevenson. 2019. "RECASTing Racial Stress and Trauma: Theorizing the Healing Potential of Racial Socialization in Families." *American Psychologist*, vol. 74, no. 1, pp. 63–75.

Anderson, Riana Elyse, et al. 2019. "What's Race Got to Do with It? Racial Socialization's Contribution to Black Adolescent Coping." *Journal of Research on Adolescence*, vol. 29, no. 4, pp. 822–31.

Annamma, Subini Ancy, et al. 2019. "Black Girls and School Discipline: The Complexities of Being Overrepresented and Understudied." *Urban Education*, vol. 54, no. 2, pp. 211–42.

Anyiwo, Nkemka, et al. 2019. "Sociocultural Influences on the Sociopolitical Development of African American Youth." *Child Development Perspectives*, vol. 12, no. 3, 2018, pp. 165–70.

Anyiwo, Nkemka, et al. 2023. "They Raised Me to Resist: Examining the Sociopolitical Pathways Between Parental Racial Socialization and Black Youth's Racial Justice Action." *Journal of Community and Applied Social Psychology*, vol. 33, no. 2, pp. 270–86.

Banerjee, Meeta, et al. 2018. "The Relationships of School-Based Discrimination and Ethnic-Racial Socialization to African American Adolescents' Achievement Outcomes." *Social Sciences*, vol. 7, no. 10, pp. 208–26.

Bell, Charles. 2020. "'Maybe If They Let Us Tell the Story I Wouldn't Have Gotten Suspended': Understanding Black Students' and Parents' Perceptions of School Discipline." *Children and Youth Services Review*, vol. 110, March, pp. 1–11. https://doi.org/10.1016/j.childyouth.2020.104757.

Bowman, Phillip J., and Cleopatra Howard. 1985. "Race-Related Socialization, Motivation, and Academic Achievement: A Study of Black Youths in Three-Generation Families." *Journal of the American Academy of Child Psychiatry* vol. 24, no. 2, pp. 134–41.

Burnett, Marketa, et al. 2022. "'When I Think of Black Girls, I Think of Opportunities': Black Girls' Identity Development and the Protective Role of Parental Socialization in Educational Settings." *Frontiers in Psychology*, vol. 13, July, pp. 1–16. http://doi.org/10.3389/fpsyg.2022.933476.

Butler-Barnes, Sheretta T., et al. 2019. "The Importance of Racial Socialization: School-Based Racial Discrimination and Racial Identity Among African American Adolescent Boys and Girls." *Journal of Research on Adolescence*, vol. 29, no. 2, pp. 432–48.

Byrd, Christy M., and Dorinda J. Carter Andrews. 2016. "Variations in Students' Perceived Reasons for, Sources of, and Forms of In-School Discrimination: A Latent Class Analysis." *Journal of School Psychology*, vol. 57, pp. 1–14.

Chavous, Tabbye M., Deborah Rivas-Drake, Ciara Smalls, Tiffany Griffin, and Courtney Cogburn. 2008. "Gender Matters, Too: The Influences of School Racial Discrimination and Racial Identity on Academic Engagement Outcomes Among African American Adolescents." *Developmental Psychology*, vol. 44, no. 3, pp. 637–54.

Cooper, Shauna M., et al. 2020. "'That Is Why We Raise Children': African American Fathers' Race-Related Concerns for Their Adolescents and Parenting Strategies." *Journal of Adolescence*, vol. 82, pp. 67–81.

Cooper, Shauna M., et al. 2022. "School Discrimination, Discipline Inequities, and Adjustment Among Black Adolescent Girls and Boys: An Intersectionality-Informed Approach." *Journal of Research on Adolescence*, vol. 32, no. 1, pp. 170–90.

DeCuir-Gunby, Jessica T. 2009. "A Review of the Racial Identity Development of African American Adolescents: The Role of Education." *Review of Educational Research*, vol. 79, no. 1, pp. 103–24.

English, Devin, et al. 2020. "Daily Multidimensional Racial Discrimination Among Black US American Adolescents." *Journal of Applied Developmental Psychology*, vol. 66, February, pp. 1–12. https://doi.org/10.1016/j.appdev.2019.101068.

Epstein, Rebecca, et al. 2017. *Girlhood Interrupted: The Erasure of Black Girls' Childhood*. Center on Poverty and Inequality, Georgetown Law.

Ford, Donna Y. 2014. "Segregation and the Underrepresentation of Blacks and Hispanics in Gifted Education: Social Inequality and Deficit Paradigms." *Roeper Review*, vol. 36, no. 3. pp. 143–54.

Ford, Donna Y., et al. 2020. "A Matter of Equity: Desegregating and Integrating Gifted and Talented Education for Under-Represented Students of Color." *Multicultural Perspectives*, vol. 22, no. 1, pp. 28–36.

Francis, Dania V., et al. 2019. "Do School Counselors Exhibit Bias in Recommending Students for Advanced Coursework?" *BE Journal of Economic Analysis and Policy*, vol. 19, no. 4, July, pp. 1–17. http://doi.org/10.1515/bejeap-2018-0189.

Gilliam, Walter S., et al. 2016. *Do Early Educators' Implicit Biases Regarding Sex and Race Relate to Behavior Expectations and Recommendations of Preschool Expulsions and Suspensions*. Yale University Child Study Center, Sept. 28.

Goff, Phillip Atiba, et al. 2014. "The Essence of Innocence: Consequences of Dehumanizing Black Children." *Journal of Personality and Social Psychology*, vol. 106, no. 4, pp. 526–45.

Griffin, Charity Brown, et al. 2020. "Racial Fairness, School Engagement, and Discipline Outcomes in African American High School Students: The Important Role of Gender." *School Psychology Review*, vol. 49, no. 3, pp. 222–38.

Henderson, Dawn X., et al. 2020. "A Phenomenological Study of Racial Harassment in School and Emotional Effects Among the Retrospective Accounts of Older Black Adolescents." *Urban Review*, vol. 52, pp. 458–81.

Hope, Elan C., et al. 2015. "'It'll Never Be the White Kids, It'll Always Be Us': Black High School Students' Evolving Critical Analysis of Racial Discrimination and Inequity in Schools." *Journal of Adolescent Research*, vol. 30, no. 1, pp. 83–112.

Hughes, Diane, et al. 2006. "Parents' Ethnic-Racial Socialization Practices: A Review of Research and Directions for Future Study." *Developmental Psychology*, vol. 42, no. 5, September, pp. 747–70.

Huguley, James P., et al. 2021. "African American Parents' Educational Involvement in Urban Schools: Contextualized Strategies for Student Success in Adolescence." *Educational Researcher*, vol. 50, no. 1, pp. 6–16.

Iruka, Iheoma U., et al. 2022. "Effects of Racism on Child Development: Advancing Antiracist Developmental Science." *Annual Review of Developmental Psychology*, vol. 4, pp. 109–32.

James-Gallaway, Chaddrick D., et al. 2024. "'It's in [Their] Roots:' A Critical Race Discourse Analysis of Media Accounts Depicting Black Hair Discrimination in K–12 School." *Urban Review*, vol. 56, no. 1, pp. 35–58.

Jones, Shawn C. T., et al. 2021. "Not the Same Old Song and Dance: Viewing Racial Socialization Through a Family Systems Lens to Resist Racial Trauma." *Adversity and Resilience Science*, vol. 2, pp. 225–33.

Ladson-Billings, Gloria. 2006. "From the Achievement Gap to the Education Debt: Understanding Achievement in US Schools." *Educational Researcher*, vol. 35, no. 7, pp. 3–12.

Leath, Seanna, et al. 2019. "Racial Identity, Racial Discrimination, and Classroom Engagement Outcomes Among Black Girls and Boys in Predominantly Black and Predominantly White School Districts." *American Educational Research Journal*, vol. 56, no. 4, pp. 1318–52.

Lesane-Brown, Chase L. 2006. "A Review of Race Socialization Within Black Families." *Developmental Review*, vol. 26, no. 4, pp. 400–426.

Masten, Ann S. 2001. "Ordinary Magic: Resilience Processes in Development." *American Psychologist*, vol. 56, no. 3, pp. 227–38.

Mbilishaka, Afiya M., et al. 2020. "Don't Get It Twisted: Untangling the Psychology of Hair Discrimination Within Black Communities." *American Journal of Orthopsychiatry*, vol. 90, no. 5, pp. 590–99.

McKown, Clark, and Rhona S. Weinstein. 2008. "Teacher Expectations, Classroom Context, and the Achievement Gap." *Journal of School Psychology*, vol. 46, no. 3, pp. 235–61.

Milner, H. Richard, IV. 2012. "Beyond a Test Score: Explaining Opportunity Gaps in Educational Practice." *Journal of Black Studies*, vol. 43, no. 6, pp. 693–718.

Mims, Lauren C., and Joanna L. Williams. 2020. "'They Told Me What I Was Before I Could Tell Them What I Was': Black Girls' Ethnic-Racial Identity Development Within Multiple Worlds." *Journal of Adolescent Research*, vol. 35, no. 6, pp. 754–79.

Mims, Lauren C., et al. 2022. "Black Brilliance and Creative Problem Solving in Fugitive Spaces: Advancing the Blackcreate Framework Through a Systematic Review." *Review of Research in Education*, vol. 46, no. 1, pp. 134–65.

Morris, Edward W., and Brea L. Perry. 2016. "The Punishment Gap: School Suspension and Racial Disparities in Achievement." *Social Problems*, vol. 63, no. 1, pp. 68–86.

Morris, Monique. 2016. *Pushout: The Criminalization of Black Girls in Schools*. New Press.

Murry, Velma McBride, et al. 2018. "Excavating New Constructs for Family Stress Theories in the Context of Everyday Life Experiences of Black American Families." *Journal of Family Theory and Review*, vol. 10, no. 2, pp. 384–405.

Neblett, Enrique W., Jr. 2023. "Racial, Ethnic, and Cultural Resilience Factors in African American Youth Mental Health." *Annual Review of Clinical Psychology*, vol. 19, pp. 361–79.

Neblett, Enrique W., Jr. Deborah Rivas-Drake, and Adriana J. Umaña-Taylor. 2012. "The Promise of Racial and Ethnic Protective Factors in Promoting Ethnic Minority Youth Development." *Child Development Perspectives*, vol. 6, no. 3, pp. 295–303.

Perillo, Jennifer T., et al. 2023. "Examining the Consequences of Dehumanization and Adultification in Justification of Police Use of Force Against Black Girls and Boys." *Law and Human Behavior*, vol. 47, no. 1, pp. 36–52.

Pringle, Rose M., et al. 2012. "Factors Influencing Elementary Teachers' Positioning of African American Girls as Science and Mathematics Learners." *School Science and Mathematics*, vol. 112, no. 4, pp. 217–29.

Quintana, Stephen M. 2007. "Racial and Ethnic Identity: Developmental Perspectives and Research." *Journal of Counseling Psychology*, vol. 54, no. 3, pp. 259–70.

Rivas-Drake, Eleanor K. Seaton, Carol Markstrom, Stephen Quintana, Moin Syed, Richard M. Lee, Seth J. Schwartz, et al. 2014. "Ethnic and Racial Identity in Adolescence: Implications for Psychosocial, Academic, and Health Outcomes." Child Development, vol. 85, no. 1, pp. 40–57.

Rogers, Leoandra Onnie, et al. 2022. "'They're Always Gonna Notice My Natural Hair': Identity, Intersectionality and Resistance Among Black Girls." *Qualitative Psychology*, vol. 9, no. 3, pp. 211–31.

Sellers, Robert M., Nikeea Copeland-Linder, Pamela P. Martin, and R. L'Heureux Lewis. 2006. "Racial Identity Matters: The Relationship Between Racial Discrimination and Psychological Functioning in African American Adolescents." *Journal of Research on Adolescence*, vol. 16, no. 2, pp. 187–216.

Sellers, Robert M., Stephanie A. J. Rowley, Tabbye M. Chavous, J. Nicole Shelton, and Mia A. Smith. 1997. "Multidimensional Inventory of Black Identity: A Preliminary Investigation of Reliability and Contract Validity." *Journal of Personality and Social Psychology*, vol. 73, no. 4, pp. 805–15.

Thomas, Oseela N., Cleopatra Howard Caldwell, Nkesha Faison, and James S. Jackson. 2009. "Promoting Academic Achievement: The Role of Racial Identity in Buffering Perceptions of Teacher Discrimination on Academic Achievement Among African American and Caribbean Black Adolescents." *Journal of Educational Psychology*, vol. 101, no. 2, pp. 420–31.

Tynes, Brendesha M., Adriana J. Umaña-Taylor, Chad A. Rose, Johnny Lin, and Carolyn J. Anderson. 2012. "Online Racial Discrimination and the Protective Function of Ethnic Identity and Self-Esteem for African American Adolescents." *Developmental Psychology*, vol. 48, no. 2, pp. 343–55.

Umaña-Taylor, Adriana J., and Nancy E. Hill. 2020. "Ethnic-Racial Socialization in the Family: A Decade's Advance on Precursors and Outcomes." *Journal of Marriage and Family*, vol. 82, no. 1, pp. 244–71.

Wang, Ming-Te, and James P. Huguley. 2012. "Parental Racial Socialization as a Moderator of the Effects of Racial Discrimination on Educational Success Among African American Adolescents." *Child Development*, vol. 83, no. 5, pp. 1716–31.

Wesley, LaWanda, and Addie Lucille Ellis. 2017. "Exclusionary Discipline in Preschool: Young Black Boys' Lives Matter." *Journal of African American Males in Education*, vol. 8, no. 2, pp. 22–29.

Williams, Deadric T. 2023. "Racism and the Mechanisms Maintaining Racial Stratification in Black Families." *Journal of Family Theory and Review*, vol. 15, no. 2, pp. 206–18.

6

Expectant and New Black Fathers

The Paradox of Hypervisibility and Invisibility

DEREK M. GRIFFITH, TRISTAN PORTER, EMILY C. JAEGER,
PERRI PEPPERMAN, AND ERIKA WICHMANN

In celebrating fatherhood, we must be able, finally, to put to
rest the stereotypes and myths that inhibit our understanding
of the diversity of roles played by the Black father in his family.
—John Lewis McAdoo (1986)

Kira Johnson was a thirty-nine-year-old expectant mother who went
into Cedars-Sinai Medical Center in Los Angeles on April 12, 2016, to
deliver her second child, Langston (Pahr 2023). Her pregnancy had been
normal. The Johnsons had one son already, Charles Johnson V. It was
Kira's husband, Charles Johnson IV, who accompanied her to the hospital for the scheduled cesarean section; shortly after Langston was born,
it became apparent that Kira's recovery was anything but normal (Pahr
2023). Charles noticed that her catheter turned pink with blood, and
after he brought it to the attention of the staff, nurses ordered a CT scan.
He asked an hour later why the scan had not been done and continued
to plead with the nursing staff, but he remained invisible to them. Kira
Johnson was left for more than ten hours with a hemorrhage bleeding
into her abdomen, and once staff finally intervened, the medical team
was unable to revive her (Pahr 2023). Kira's life was wrongfully lost as a
result of the providers' negligence.

Since this time, there has been a groundswell of attention, resources,
policy, and research dedicated to addressing Black maternal death (Bond
et al. 2021; Lister et al. 2019; Collier and Molina 2019; Joseph et al. 2021;
Walker and Boling 2023; Amutah-Onukagha et al. 2023; Lane 2021). In
remembrance of his wife, Charles Johnson founded the 4Kira4Moms

organization to promote maternal health legislation, offer financial and counseling services, and provide educational resources to families. To this day, the foundation advocates for equitable maternal care and co-alition building, and Charles Johnson remains a staunch advocate for maternal health. This chapter is dedicated to Charles Johnson and other Black fathers who, despite their best efforts, remain invisible.

Much like the protagonist featured in Ralph Ellison's *Invisible Man* more than seventy years ago (Ellison 1995), the humanity, strengths, values, and experiences of Black fathers remain invisible (Gilbert et al. 2016). Yet, Black fathers are hypervisible in negative cultural tropes and policy narratives regarding fatherhood (Connor and White 2011). Some people have even suggested that fathers are inessential to families and that perhaps families even fare better without fathers (Connor and White 2011).

Building from the legal scholar Kimberlé Crenshaw's (1995) concep-tualization of structural, political, and representational intersectionality, this chapter not only discusses narratives and policy approaches to pa-ternal involvement but also shows how expectant and new fathers report experiencing society, health care, and the institutionalization of narra-tives that often render them invisible and irrelevant to their families. However, before we delve into intersectionality, we briefly review the literature on fatherhood and Black fathers to contextualize Black pater-nal engagement within gendered, anti-Black structural racism (Griffith et al. 2021). We argue that this level of precision in describing structural racism is necessary to illuminate the narratives and institutional barriers that intersect to often hinder Black fathers' involvement during preg-nancy, childbirth, and children's lives.

Father: What Is the Role?

Men have defined their role in the family as being a provider for the past few thousand years (Reeves 2022). Men are expected to put others before themselves, providing for and protecting children and family members (Reeves 2022). Expectations for fathering have expanded in recent decades. Fathers are increasingly expected to be involved in their children's lives, beyond contributing as breadwinners (Goldberg 2015; Pragg and Knoester 2017). The provider role nevertheless tends to be one of the more important ways men connect to family and social life (Reeves 2022).

The traditional family structure, wherein men are providers and women are caretakers, was an effective social institution as it made both men and women necessary (Reeves 2022). This institution, however, often came with problematic cultural and power dynamics associated with patriarchy, tightly prescribed roles, and oppressive expectations harmful to women and men alike (Reeves 2022). For example, four out of five American adults with a high school education or lower believe a man's ability to financially support a family is very important; this is also true of three out of five American adults with a bachelor's degree (Reeves 2022). Ironically, the men least able to fulfill the role of traditional breadwinner are those most likely to be judged by their breadwinning potential (Reeves 2022). Consistent with the notion of precarious manhood (Vandello and Bosson 2013; Vandello et al. 2019), the inability to fulfill key family and social roles is often used to judge men's character and values, rather than their behavior.

The provider role traditionally was linked to marriage. As attitudes toward unmarried parenthood have become far more relaxed, men have struggled to redefine their identities in ways that provide the same level of meaning and purpose (Reeves 2022). Without the traditional provider role, Richard Reeves (2022) argues that men struggle to find meaning, purpose, and utility in family and social life. As compared to women, men tend to have a narrower range of roles that provide them sources of identity and meaning, making them particularly vulnerable to existential questions and mental health challenges (Reeves 2022).

Maternal and child health scholars have questioned the utility, relevance, and importance of fathers (Pleck 2010; Connor and White 2011). On the other hand, the very notion that fathers are important is rooted in the premise, and finding, that outcomes are better for mothers and children when fathers are involved (Griffith et al. 2023; Pleck 2010; Alio et al. 2013; Caldwell 2019). In addition to being important, the notion that fathers are "essential" suggests that fathers' contribution to child development are qualitatively different from mothers' (Pleck 2010). These factors are particularly important as we consider Black fathers.

Black Fathers and the Paradox of Invisibility

Since the publication of E. Franklin Frazier's landmark book *The Negro Family in the United States* more than eighty years ago, scholars have been debating the plight of Black families and the relevance and importance of Black fathers (Frazier 1939). Often, political pundits and researchers point to the "Moynihan Report" more than twenty-five years after its publication (Moynihan et al. 1965) and fail to realize that much of the research informing this report came from Frazier and his scholarly colleagues. One of the biggest critiques of the work of Frazier and Moynihan is that they tend to approach Black fathers from a deficit lens, pathologizing and psychologizing Black fathers as absent and uninvolved primarily by choice (Cooper et al. 2023; Semmes 2001). Moynihan, among others, specifically failed to capture the impact of structural racism and the unique forms it takes in the lives and context of Black men, particularly those Black men who are fathers (Connor 2011; Connor and White 2011; Gadsden et al. 2001; Gilbert et al. 2016; Griffith et al. 2021). The assumption that white fathers should be the standard for measuring the effectiveness of Black fathers and that Black fathers are a homogeneous group have dominated the literature on Black fathers (Cooper et al. 2023). While "deadbeat dads" has been primarily used to characterize contemporary Black fathers, the original men who fit this characterization were white slave masters during the era of chattel slavery, who took no responsibility, financial or otherwise, for the children they fathered with Black slaves (Connor 2011).

For more than forty years, Black psychologists and researchers have dedicated their careers to countering these narratives and demonstrating the need for research reflecting heterogeneity among Black fathers (Cooper et al. 2023). The research that provided the foundation for narratives pathologizing Black fathers tended to overgeneralize from small, nonrepresentative samples of Black fathers with extreme psychosocial problems and suggested that the deficits of Black fathers were the root causes of underachievement rather than the structural barriers that shaped them (Bowman and Sanders 1998; Summers 2013, 2004). The studies that emphasized Black fathers' deviance from white middle-class norms failed to recognize the adaptive coping that Black fathers employed to mobilize cultural strengths and overcome structural racism and other institutional barriers (Bowman and Sanders 1998; Cooper et al. 2023; Gilbert et al. 2016; Griffith et al. 2021).

One of the biggest flaws in research on Black fathers has been the lack of context (Cooper et al. 2023). The social, historical, cultural, political, and economic conditions that shape Black men's lives before and after they become fathers is critical to accurately understanding their contributions and impact on Black families, children, and society (Bowman and Sanders 1998; Connor and White 2011; Cooper et al. 2023; Gilbert et al. 2016; Griffith et al. 2021). One of the more recent factors that has come to light is the unique implication of the labor market on Black men (Reeves 2022; Allen 2016). While overall gender gaps are narrowing, racial gaps in the labor market are widening, and Black men are experiencing particularly slow growth in wages (Reeves 2022). In contrast to every other racial group, Black women are more likely than Black men to be the primary household breadwinner (Reeves 2022). This is consistent with the pattern that Black men lag behind Black women in educational attainment, upward mobility, employment, wages, and breadwinning status (Reeves 2022; Cooper et al. 2023). These educational and economic factors add additional context and a more refined lens to the question of why the men least able to fulfill the role of traditional breadwinner are the most likely to be judged by their breadwinning potential (Reeves 2022). While some people may consider this focus on the breadwinner role outdated and sexist, it is a reality of how men in general and Black men in particular are judged for their suitability as a potential mate (Reeves 2022). Among Black Americans, 84 percent say that it is "very important" for a man to be "able to provide for their family," but only two in three white Americans (67 percent) value providing so highly (Reeves 2022).

Despite the volume of research demonstrating that paternal involvement has positive implications for pregnancy, maternal health, and infant outcomes (Lu et al. 2010; Alio et al. 2013; Poh et al. 2014; Xue et al. 2018), few studies have described the barriers and facilitators of paternal involvement, particularly from the perspective of fathers. According to Vivian Gadsden et al. (2001) and others (Allen 2016; Caldwell et al. 2019; Cooper et al. 2023; Griffith et al. 2023), researchers and policy makers should consider the unique obstacles that Black fathers face by hearing about these challenges from their perspective. Moreover, few studies have explored fatherhood involvement in pregnancy and childbirth. To address this gap, we completed a series of focus groups with fathers to examine social, cultural, and environmental factors that influence behaviors among new fathers, while also providing community perspectives on men's experiences seeking care pre- and postdelivery. The two key questions explored through our data are the following:

1. How do expectant and new fathers understand the ways that they are perceived and treated in society?
2. What are the implications of the ways that expectant and new fathers understand their reception and treatment in efforts to support a mother's pregnancy, birth, and health?

Methods

Setting and Context

The Alliance for Innovation on Maternal Health–Community Care Initiative (AIM CCI) is a federally funded cooperative agreement that connects the Health Resources and Services Administration (HRSA), the National Healthy Start Association, and community organizations across six sites with high maternal mortality and morbidity: Atlanta, Georgia; Fresno, California; Newark, New Jersey; New Orleans, Louisiana; Tulsa, Oklahoma; and Grand Rapids, Michigan. The goal of AIM CCI is to improve maternal health outcomes by developing, piloting, and evaluating the use of novel Maternal Safety Bundles in nonhospital settings. We conducted focus groups with fathers who identified that the mother of their child received birthing services in one of the AIM CCI cities serving as pilot sites in the prior two years. The goal of these focus groups was to inform the development of Maternal Safety Bundles (i.e., compilations of trainings, programs, and resources) in nonhospital settings for expectant and new fathers. All study procedures were approved by the Georgetown-MedStar Institutional Review Board. Electronic informed consent and verbal confirmation of consent were obtained from all participants. Participants received $100 each for participating in the focus group.

Between November 2021 and April 2022, we conducted two focus groups with fathers at each of the six sites; however, because we were unable to confirm that participants at the sixth site met the inclusion criteria outlined in the next section, we did not include the data from the focus groups from the sixth site in this chapter. Thus, this chapter includes data from the ten focus groups conducted across five of the six AIM CCI sites.

Recruitment and Inclusion Criteria

To complete the focus groups, we worked with AIM CCI partner community organizations to facilitate the recruitment of fathers with a child born in the past two years. We distributed study fliers via email distribution lists, posted in site offices or clinics, and shared information with relevant groups of men through the local AIM CCI site network (fatherhood groups etc.). Fathers were eligible to participate if they were eighteen years of age or older, had a biological child in the past two years, indicated they were comfortable completing an online survey and virtual focus group in English, and indicated that their child's mother received birthing services from within one of the cities with participating pilot sites. Ideally the fathers would have used some of the services of the AIM CCI community partner organizations, but that was not a requirement for participation in the focus groups. Men who expressed interest in study participation were screened for eligibility online via an electronic survey or over the phone by members of the research team.

Data Collection

The virtual focus groups took place via the Zoom online conference-call platform and were audio and video recorded. Only the audio recordings of the focus groups were used in data analysis. The audio recordings were transcribed verbatim by an external professional transcription service and checked by study staff for accuracy. The focus groups lasted approximately one and a half hours and included review of the consent process, the focus group questions, and closing remarks. Prior to the focus group, we sent participants a demographic survey via the REDCap survey platform, and we asked them to complete it prior to attending the group. We used a phenomenological approach (Creswell 2012) to design the semistructured, in-depth focus group protocol. This approach is appropriate when the goal is to explore the meanings and perspectives of individuals who have experienced the phenomenon of interest and asks them to describe the topic of interest in the context of their lived experience (Creswell 2012; Watkins and Gioia 2015).

Data Analysis

We imported the transcripts into a software program for thematic analysis, which allowed us to identify themes and classifications that relate to the data and to discover, organize, and describe interpretations of the data (Braun and Clarke 2006; Watkins and Gioia 2015). Two qualitative data analysts iteratively created the codebook. Their coding reached an interrater reliability Kappa score of 0.725, which is considered strong agreement. The focus group data were analyzed by (1) organizing direct quotes that could accurately be understood outside the context of the focus group, (2) double checking the quotes and notes, (3) coding quotes per the codebook, (4) combining coded restatements across focus groups, and (5) reviewing the consolidated document to identify themes and subthemes.

Demographic survey data was captured within the online survey database REDCap and analyzed by the same research team members who analyzed the qualitative data. REDCap data was exported into Excel, and summary statistics were recorded by each focus group site and focus group participants as a whole. Additionally, the research team facilitated a member-checking discussion with maternal health service providers from the AIM CCI pilot sites to receive feedback on the findings and to enhance our confidence that our findings were trustworthy and credible. The questions asked during the member-checking session were organized around three themes: How representative are the findings of the fathers you work with based on what you know of their everyday lived experiences? What is missing from the preliminary findings? Based on these findings, what information, programs, and supports should we create for expectant and new fathers?

Results

Participant Characteristics

The average age of participating fathers was 33.9 years, with a range of 24 to 61 years old. The majority (86.25 percent) of men were African

American, and approximately one-sixth of focus group participants (16.25 percent) were Hispanic or Latino. Most men were employed full-time (71.25 percent), and more than half of the participants earned a bachelor's degree or above (55 percent), though there were men who participated in the focus groups who were currently unhoused (2.5 percent) or had an income less than $20,000 a year (10 percent). Four out of five of the fathers were married (80 percent), and over 40 percent (43.75 percent) of the men were first-time fathers.

Themes

Building from the legal scholar Kimberlé Crenshaw's (1995) conceptualization of intersectionality, we explore the policy response to improve Black American men's roles as fathers and the structural limitations to optimizing the roles of fathers in the lives of their children. Intersectionality is a strategy to map the intersection of race and gender in ways that disrupt the tendency to see race and gender as separable structures (Crenshaw 1995). Crenshaw (1995) organizes intersectionality into structural, political, and representational intersectionality.

Structural Intersectionality

Structural intersectionality highlights how racism is qualitatively different for Black fathers than for fathers of other racial or ethnic groups. A simple Google search of "perceptions of Black fathers" presents recommended related search topics such as "absent Black fathers," "Black fathers' involvement," "incarcerated Black fathers," and "Black fathers' invisible presence." This negative framing may explain why terms such as "deadbeat dads" and assumptions that fathers are disinterested in being involved in the birth of their children and the lives of pregnant persons have persisted. For Black fathers, experiences with the healthcare system can best be understood through the lens of structural intersectionality. Due to the constant stress related to living with the negative characterization of Black men as a Black man, that may also permeate into an individual's concept of how others perceive them as a Black father and their rights or relevance to be present during prenatal visits and childbirth.

The Black fathers who participated in the fatherhood focus groups recognized the tropes of the deadbeat dad, but they actively sought to counter those narratives. These men also felt that there need to be better systems in place structurally "to allow you to know that as the father you matter," as one father said in a focus group: "As the father, you're there when you want to be there. The idea of the deadbeat goes around so much—is, like, they all assume that's a possibility within all men, and it's just not true. I wanted to be there every single step of the way, and it felt like there was other factors pushing me toward that type of lifestyle. . . . I don't understand how anybody could ever be a deadbeat. I don't understand how anybody could ever not be a part of their child's life."

One father described his experience within the health-care system during the hospital stay for the birth of his son: "I'm saying that because that's just where I saw the red flag from that lactation counselor that does help a lot of mothers at university hospital, and the narratives—it comes from the basis of, and excuse my language, of 'Oh, I'm dealing with an ancient nigger.' Little did she know, I'm highly educated. I have a college degree. I'm a business owner. So I'm well versed when it comes to things about, when it comes to the laws, what are my rights, and I'm also very well versed with being able to verbally express what I feel."

The legal system is also a structural barrier to a father's success. Like other systems, the legal system is not configured to help Black fathers, let alone Black men, thrive. Updates to these spaces and systems that are more representative of different types of family structures are sorely needed. A father explained his struggle:

> They need to change something with, as far as the legal system, when it comes to if you're not married, because a lot of people don't like the idea of marriage. A lot of people actually rather do partnership. So . . . I think joint custody needs to be established from as soon as the father and the mother are signing applications for the birth certificate because that basically will ensure to both parties that you both made this child and you both have the same equal rights without it having to be where—now I [have] to put myself at risk of a person that I never thought I would have to be putting myself at risk or I may have to be put on child support because I'm taking the initiative to file to the court for my custody and visitations because my baby mother wants to

make her own interpretations of the law of how I'm able to have—have access to a child that we both created.

Despite seeming to be easily understandable, a considerable number of requirements to get aid are either inadequately specified or insufficiently conveyed or both. The act of signing the birth certificate was a cautionary tale for one individual, since it grants legal authority to impose child-support obligations onto a person, notwithstanding the current relationship status. The limited availability of benefits for single dads, along with a general lack of awareness of existing benefits, has significantly hindered the capacity of Black fathers to be recognized as actively involved in their children's lives. Moreover, an examination of the patriarchal characteristics inherent in the structure of the nuclear family in the United States, along with its associated advantages for married individuals compared to single individuals, will demonstrate the historical role played by this arrangement in perpetuating the perception of Black men as deviant and their marginalization as involved fathers.

Another father expressed his frustrations with his experience with the legal system and how it serves as a barrier to his desire to be an active father: "So, and it's not fair for me, where I do have aspirations. . . . And now I'm putting myself at risk of being a part of these things professionally, with something attached to me of possible child support. And I think that's so not fair to Black men that actually want to be active fathers. That's my biggest critique for the legal system. They need to change that."

Political Intersectionality

Political intersectionality demonstrates the invisibility and political ambivalence toward Black men's efforts to be actively engaged as fathers. For example, in the delivery room, fathers are considered "support persons" and have no right to be present to witness or participate in the birth of their child. Also, the implications of political intersectionality help showcase men's negative experiences with Section 8 and the Food and Nutrition Service of the United States Department of Agriculture's Special Supplemental Nutrition Program for Women, Infants, and Children (WIC). Political intersectionality (Crenshaw 1995) explains how our national politics marginalize Black men's involvement, access, and navigation of the systems they may encounter when having a child. Viewing fathers, and specifically Black fathers, as partners through-out the pregnancy, childbirth, and child-rearing process rather than bystanders, support persons, or the assumed "absent father" has the abil-ity to improve mortality outcomes among Black mothers. Programming that focuses on Black fathers is uncommon and rarely receives explicit funding or policies beyond what was presumed to be beneficial to the mother and child.

Current hospital system structures primarily focus on the well-being of mother and child, while often neglecting to inquire about the fa-ther's mental state. Fathers in the focus group highlighted that they felt, "when it comes to the care for Black women, there's nothing wrong with prioritizing the care for Black women, but it should not be at the sacri-fice of where there is either passive aggressiveness or there is a neglect to the father's mental state." Access to mental health resources for fa-thers is a resource that is sorely needed. Fathers also highlighted other systems that they felt were inaccessible to Black fathers. One father in particular noted,

> I hope we get a chance to talk quickly about the system put in place for us, because I just found that it's very discouraging. It really does nothing for Black fathers, and we're trying to get the help—we're trying to get the Section 8 and all of that. I didn't know I had to go on food stamps. I didn't know I had to go on child support in order to get Section 8. I didn't know I had to get on child support in order for her to get food stamps. It damn near seemed like an improper decision to sign the birth certificate, be-cause now they can legally put me on child support. And we're together. We're right next to each other 24/7. I don't think that's who the system is meant for, you know?

Fathers continually expressed concern for the sense of responsibility placed on their shoulders. There was no issue about the responsibility of raising and loving a child but rather the financial strain of supporting a family. One father noted, "I say Black men, we would have kids all, all day, all year, if we had the money. If I was a millionaire, I wouldn't be in this group. I wouldn't feel like I had problems with supporting my family. It's the biggest problem is financial. I know how to love a child. I feel like there's no problem with that, but how do I support them and be there for them while also being there for myself?"

Another father expressed concern for the ease with which his child could be taken from him as a father: "There needs to be some systems in place. I didn't have to learn how to hold my child for the first time until the delivery room. But I would like to be prepared before that. I, like, would have got some practice before then. So, if I had got it wrong, somebody wouldn't be there to take him from me, because the idea of somebody taking him from me is so much present in our lives."

Representational Intersectionality

Representational intersectionality highlights how Black fathers' voices tend to be absent in efforts to inform policies and programs that seek to promote three key aspects of father involvement: accessibility (i.e., presence and availability), engagement (e.g., food roles, emotional support for mothers, encouraging mothers' healthy eating and activity, taking care of other children), and responsibility (e.g., participation in tasks such as arranging child care and talking with their children's teachers). Representational intersectionality centers the cultural construction and representation of Black men in explaining both the ways in which images of Black men are created and reproduced and how contemporary narratives explaining Black fatherhood marginalize Black men (Young 2017). Perceptions of Black fathers and societal standards for what a father should stand for, look like, and act like can create additional stress on top of the already stressful situation of being a father. Financial burdens and other related gender-role strains can greatly impact a father's ability to healthily cope with the many transitions that come with fatherhood (Bowman 1992; Bowman and Forman 1997). However, Black fathers are typically not presented quality resources that may prove beneficial for the transition into fatherhood.

During the focus groups, some fathers expressed concerns regarding their interactions with the health-care system, acknowledging historical trauma and years of Black voices being left unheard. One father noted, "One of the things, what I was dealing with, with the birth of my daughter, was just concerned about complications during childbirth and my wife dealing with . . . Black women have dealt with complications after childbirth and as far as level of care as well. And my wife did experience some stuff after she had our daughter, and that was a little nerve-racking." Other fathers noted that they appreciated seeing Black doctors during their experience at the hospital, which they felt led to a better overall experience. One father noted, "I was kind of more thankful, too, on that one. Also, I got to see a Black male actually in a role as a doctor, so that was more of a good experience, too. I like to see that." Another father had a similar positive experience with the doctor, saying, "As far as the prenatal visits, yeah, it was a male, Black doctor, Dr. Weston. He was there. We had the same doctor throughout the whole pregnancy. He delivered the baby, as well. He was a top-tier doctor."

Men also touched on the difficulties they felt Black fathers experience while navigating the relationship with the birthing person and the negative perceptions of nonmarried Black individuals who are trying to raise their child. One father stated,

> And if you don't have [an] already solid relationship with the person you're having this baby with it, it can turn into "baby mother," "baby daddy" real quickly instead of "mom and dad," and people don't even understand the difference between that. I don't refer to her as my "baby mother" because it's going to breed some negativity. That's just how I feel. It's going to put us in that place where we don't want to be. It's just going to put us back in a category that already exists. And we're trying to be a category that's rare. . . . We're trying to show Black love.

Discussion

How does it feel to be a problem?
—W. E. B. Du Bois (1903)

W. E. B. Du Bois asked this question 120 years ago, as an effort to try to make sense of the negative implications of the ways Black Americans were thought about and treated at the dawn of the twentieth century. The public and professional narratives regarding Black fathers leave Black fathers and scholars asking a similar question. It is evident from the opening story about Kira and Charles Johnson that the costs of viewing Black fathers through a negative, unidimensional lens not only is inaccurate but yields consequences for Black fathers, mothers, and children alike. While it is important to capture the perspectives of mothers regarding the roles of fathers in coparenting and supporting the healthy gestational development of babies during the prenatal period, it also is critical to capture and understand the perspectives of fathers, particularly Black fathers, if we are indeed interested in understanding the ways that Black fathers make decisions about how to support expectant and new mothers and prepare for children to be born.

Kimberlé Crenshaw, who popularized the term, argues that intersectionality is a strategy to map the intersections of race and gender in ways that disrupt the tendency to see race and gender as separable structures when in fact they are intertwined (Crenshaw 1995; Bowleg 2017). For more than a decade, intersectionality has been applied to men's health (Griffith 2012; Griffith et al. 2011). Intersectionality has been a tool to examine why sex and gender do not have the same meaning and influence within and across all men's lives (Griffith 2012). The goal of an intersectional approach is to consider how individual agency and choice, contextual and environmental influences, and physiological and biological factors combine to influence health (Rieker and Bird 2005). Intersectionality has provided an important lens and analytic tool to help researchers "radically contextualize" the web of conditions that shape the lives and health of men and that shape patterns of health and well-being (National Academies of Sciences, Engineering, and Medicine 2017). Intersectionality has shed important light on the cultural narratives that frame how we define and explain the patterns and the institutional arrangements that create and maintain Black fathers' roles, relationships, and fulfillment of these key roles (Griffith et al. 2010; Griffith et al. 2016). Intersectionality also has helped to shed light on the lives of Black fathers who remain invisible when we use the generic term "father" (Griffith et al. 2011), which as scholars have noted, has led to using an inaccurate lens through which to examine the quality and effectiveness of Black fathers' role performance (Connor and White 2011; Cooper et al. 2023).

As we saw from the quotations from the fathers in the focus groups, these fathers understood the tropes and narratives that shaped their experience in and outside the health-care system. This is consistent with the literature that explores not only structural racism and its implications for shaping Black fathers' experiences across sectors but also how cultural racism has seeped into the health-care system to harm not only mothers and children but fathers too (Michaels et al. 2023; Griffith et al. 2010). Cultural racism and the tropes and narratives that are used to explain Black fathers' presence, absence, roles, and responsibilities in family life and health care are the glue that connects and provides synergies across the societal and institutional sectors that yield many of the same patterns and outcomes (e.g., education, employment, criminal justice, health care). Thus, we name anti-Black gendered structural racism (Griffith et al. 2021) as a useful framework that applies an intersectional lens to Black men's experiences as fathers. The work of Richard Reeves (2022), among others, has highlighted the unique educational and economic patterns that shape paternal involvement and the importance of recognizing that Black fathers' efforts to fulfill the role of father are intertwined with their ability to perform as providers and breadwinners. It is critical to put Black fatherhood in context to effectively design programs and policies to increase paternal involvement and improve maternal health outcomes.

REFERENCES

Alio, Amina P., et al. 2013. "A Community Perspective on the Role of Fathers During Pregnancy: A Qualitative Study." *BMC Pregnancy and Childbirth*, vol. 13, no. 1, pp. 1–11.

Allen, Quaylan. 2016. "'Tell Your Own Story': Manhood, Masculinity and Racial Socialization Among Black Fathers and Their Sons." *Ethnic and Racial Studies*, vol. 39, no. 10, pp. 1831–48. https://doi.org/10.1080/01419870.2015.1110608.

Amutah-Onukagha, Ndidiamaka, et al. 2023. "Black Maternal Health Scholars on Fire: Building a Network for Collaboration and Activism." *Health Services Research*, vol. 58, no. 1, pp. 202–6.

Bond, Rachel M., et al. 2021. "Working Agenda for Black Mothers: A Position Paper from the Association of Black Cardiologists on Solutions to Improving Black Maternal Health." *Circulation: Cardiovascular Quality and Outcomes*, vol. 14, no. 2, e007643.

Bowleg, Lisa. 2017. "Towards a Critical Health Equity Research Stance: Why Epistemology and Methodology Matter More than Qualitative Methods." *Health Education and Behavior*, vol. 44, no. 5, pp. 677–84.

Bowman, Phillip J. 1992. "Coping with Provider Role Strain: Adaptive Cultural Resources Among Black Husband-Fathers." *African American Psychology: Theory, Research, and Practice*, edited by A. Kathleen Hoard Burlew et al., Sage, pp. 135–54.

Bowman, Phillip J., and Tyrone A. Forman. 1997. "Instrumental and Expressive Family Roles Among African American Fathers." *Family Life in Black America*, edited by Robert Joseph Taylor et al., Sage, pp. 216–47.

Bowman, Phillip J., and Reliford Sanders. 1998. "Unmarried African American Fathers: A Comparative Life Span Analysis." *Journal of Comparative Family Studies*, vol. 29, no. 1, pp. 39–56.

Braun, Virginia, and Victoria Clarke. 2006. "Using Thematic Analysis in Psychology." *Qualitative Research in Psychology*, vol. 3, no. 2, pp. 77–101.

Caldwell, Cleopatra Howard, et al. 2019. "Fatherhood as a Social Context for Reducing Men's Health Disparities: Lessons Learned from the Fathers and Sons Program." *Men's Health Equity: A Handbook*, edited by Derek M. Griffith et al., Routledge, pp. 42–56.

Collier, Ai-ris Y., and Rose L. Molina. 2019. "Maternal Mortality in the United States: Updates on Trends, Causes, and Solutions." *Neoreviews*, vol. 20, no. 10, pp. e561–e574.

Connor, Michael E. 2011. "African Descended Fathers: Historical Considerations." *Black Fathers: An Invisible Presence in America*, edited by M. E. Connor and J. White, 2nd ed., Taylor and Francis, pp. 3–19.

Connor, Michael E., and Joseph White, editors. 2011. *Black Fathers: An Invisible Presence in America*. 2nd ed., Taylor and Francis.

Cooper, Shauna M., et al. 2023. "Honoring Foundational Black Psychologists' Contributions to Research on Black Fathers." *American Psychologist*, vol. 78, no. 4, p. 535.

Crenshaw, Kimberlé Williams. 1995. "Mapping the Margins: Intersectionality, Identity Politics, and Violence Against Women of Color." *Critical Race Theory: The Key Writings That Formed the Movement*, edited by Kimberlé Williams Crenshaw et al., New Press, pp. 359–83.

Creswell, John W. 2012. *Qualitative Inquiry and Research Design: Choosing Among Five Approaches*. Sage.

Du Bois, W. E. B. 1903. *The Souls of Black Folk*. McClurg.

Ellison, Ralph. 1995. *Invisible Man*. 2nd ed., Vintage.

Frazier, Edward Franklin. 1939. *The Negro Family in the United States*. University of Chicago Press.

Gadsden, Vivian, et al. 2001. *How Urban Fathers Represent the Transition to Fathering: A Discourse Analysis of Fathering Narratives*. ERIC.

Gilbert, Keon L., et al. 2016. "Visible and Invisible Trends in African American Men's Health: Pitfalls and Promises for Addressing Racial, Ethnic and Gender Health Inequities." *Annual Review of Public Health*, vol. 37, no. 1. https://doi.org/10.1146/annurev-publhealth-032315-021556.

Goldberg, Julia S. 2015. "Identity and Involvement Among Resident and Nonresident Fathers." *Journal of Family Issues*, vol. 36, no. 7, pp. 852–79.

Griffith, Derek M. 2012. "An Intersectional Approach to Men's Health." *Journal of Men's Health*, vol. 9, no. 2, pp. 106–12. https://doi.org/10.1016/j.jomh.2012.03.003.

Griffith, Derek M., et al. 2010. "Cultural Context and a Critical Approach to Eliminating Health Disparities." *Ethnicity and Disease*, vol. 20 no. 1, pp. 71–76.

Griffith, Derek M., et al. 2011. "Considering Intersections of Race and Gender in Interventions That Address U.S. Men's Health Disparities." *Public Health*, vol. 125, no. 7, pp. 417–23. https://doi.org/10.1016/j.puhe.2011.04.014.

Griffith, Derek M., et al. 2016. "John Henry and the Paradox of Manhood, Fatherhood and Health for African American Fathers." *Boys and Men in African American Families*, edited by Linda M. Burton et al., Springer, pp. 215–26.

Griffith, Derek M., et al. 2021. "Using Syndemics and Intersectionality to Explain the Disproportionate COVID-19 Mortality Among Black Men." *Public Health Reports*, vol. 136, no. 5, pp. 523–31. https://doi.org/10.1177/00333549211026799.

Griffith, Derek M., et al. 2023. "Fathers' Perspectives on Fatherhood and Paternal Involvement During Pregnancy and Childbirth." *Health Education and Behavior*, vol. 50, no. 6, pp. 802–9. https://doi.org/10.1177/10901981231199710.

Joseph, K. S., et al. 2021. "Maternal Mortality in the United States: Recent Trends, Current Status, and Future Considerations." *Obstetrics and Gynecology*, vol. 137, no. 5, p. 763.

Lane, Richard. 2021. "Ndidiamaka Amutah-Onukagha: Advancing Maternal Health Justice." *The Lancet*, vol. 397, no. 10274, p. 571.

Lister, Rolanda L., et al. 2019. "Black Maternal Mortality—The Elephant in the Room." *World Journal of Gynecology and Women's Health*, vol. 3, no. 1. https://doi.org/10.33552/WJGWH.2019.03.000555.

Lu, Michael C., et al. 2010. "Where Is the F in MCH? Father Involvement in African American Families." *Ethnicity and Disease*, vol. 20, pp. 49–61.

McAdoo, John Lewis. 1986. "A Black Perspective on the Father's Role in Child Development." *Men's Changing Roles in the Family*, edited by R. A Lewis and M. B. Sussman, Routledge, pp. 133–50.

Michaels, Eli K., et al. 2023. "The Water Surrounding the Iceberg: Cultural Racism and Health Inequities." *Milbank Quarterly*, vol. 101, no. 3, pp. 768–814. https://doi.org/10.1111/1468-0009.12662.

Moynihan, Daniel Patrick, et al. 1965. *The Negro Family: The Case for National Action.* MIT Press.

National Academies of Sciences, Engineering, and Medicine. 2017. *Communities in Action: Pathways to Health Equity.* National Academies Press.

Pahr, Kristi. 2023. "Charles Johnson's Loss Launched a Maternal Health Revolution." *Parents*, Sept. 19.

Pleck, Joseph H. 2010. "Fatherhood and Masculinity." *The Role of the Father in Child Development*, edited by M. E. Lamb, Wiley, pp. 27–57.

Poh, Hui Li, et al. 2014. "An Integrative Review of Fathers' Experiences During Pregnancy and Childbirth." *International Nursing Review*, vol. 61, no. 4, pp. 543–54.

Pragg, Brianne, and Chris Knoester. 2017. "Parental Leave Use Among Disadvantaged Fathers." *Journal of Family Issues*, vol. 38, no. 8, pp. 1157–85.

Reeves, Richard. 2022. *Of Boys and Men: Why the Modern Male is Struggling, Why It Matters, and What to Do About It.* Brookings Institution Press.

Rieker, Patricia P., and Chloe E. Bird. 2005. "Rethinking Gender Differences in Health: Why We Need to Integrate Social and Biological Perspectives." *Journals of Gerontology; Series A; Biological Sciences and Medical Sciences*, vol. 60B, pp. 40–47.

Semmes, Clovis E. 2001. "E. Franklin Frazier's Theory of the Black Family: Vindication and Sociological Insight." *Journal of Sociology and Social Welfare*, vol. 28, no. 2, pp. 3–21.

Summers, Martin. 2004. *Manliness and Its Discontents: The Black Middle Class and the Transformation of Masculinity, 1900–1930*. University of North Carolina Press.

Summers, Martin. 2013. "Manhood Rights in the Age of Jim Crow: Evaluating End-of-Men Claims in the Context of African American History." *Boston University Law Review*, vol. 93, pp. 745–67.

Vandello, Joseph A., and Jennifer K. Bosson. 2013. "Hard Won and Easily Lost: A Review and Synthesis of Theory and Research on Precarious Manhood." *Psychology of Men and Masculinity*, vol. 14, no. 2, pp. 101–13. https://doi.org/10.1037/a0029826.

Vandello, Joseph A., et al. 2019. "Precarious Manhood and Men's Health Disparities." *Men's Health Equity: A Handbook*, Routledge, pp. 27–41.

Walker, Denetra, and Kelli Boling. 2023. "Black Maternal Mortality in the Media: How Journalists Cover a Deadly Racial Disparity." *Journalism* vol. 24, no. 7, pp. 1536–53.

Watkins, Daphne C., and Deborah Gioia. 2015. *Mixed Methods Research*. Oxford University Press. Pocket Guides to Social Work Research Methods.

Xue, Weilin Lynn, et al. 2018. "Fathers' Involvement During Pregnancy and Childbirth: An Integrative Literature Review." *Midwifery*, vol. 62, pp. 135–45. https://doi.org/10.1016/j.midw.2018.04.013.

Young, Alford A., Jr. 2017. "The Character Assassination of Black Males: Some Consequences for Research in Public Health." *Perspectives on Health Equity and Social Determinants of Health. National Academy of Medicine*, National Academies Press, pp. 47–62.

7

Harnessing the Power of Caregivers from the Child's Community

SOLANGEL MALDONADO

The majority of pregnant women who are denied an abortion do not make an adoption plan.[1] They instead attempt to parent the child. In fact, only 9 percent of women who are denied an abortion choose to place the child for adoption.[2] One year after the *Dobbs* decision, almost 25 percent of pregnant women residing in states with abortion bans who would have had an abortion (had they been able to get one) carried their pregnancies to term.[3] But few of these children will end up in adoptive homes—at least not initially. Instead, a disproportionate number may end up in foster care, and approximately 25–50 percent of those will have their birth parents' rights terminated and be adopted.[4]

Pregnant persons who lack access to abortions are likely to be young, poor, and nonwhite and to have small children at home.[5] Thus, these women face significant hardships when parenting a child that was unplanned or unwanted. They are also at higher risk of state intervention for alleged child maltreatment—specifically neglect deriving from poverty or lack of adequate child care. These women (and their children) are disproportionately Black, multiracial (part Black), and Native American. Foster and adoptive parents, however, are disproportionately white.[6]

Numerous studies have demonstrated the importance of racial identity and racial socialization to a healthy self-esteem.[7] Yet, the federal Multiethnic Placement Act of 1994 (as amended by the Interethnic Adoption Provisions of the Small Business Job Protection Act of 1996; MEPA-IEAP) prohibits agencies that receive federal funding from considering the race or ethnicity of the child or the foster or adoptive family when placing a child in a foster or adoptive home.[8] Although the original statute permitted agencies to consider race or ethnicity as a factor when placing children in foster or adoptive homes, when Congress amended the act in 1996, it repealed the provisions that had allowed states to consider a child's "cultural, ethnic or racial background."[9] As the federal Children's Bureau's guidance on MEPA-IEAP currently provides, "Public agencies may not routinely consider race, national origin and ethnicity in making placement decisions," and "any placement policy that takes race or ethnicity into account is subject to strict scrutiny."[10]

While MEPA-IEAP requires colorblindness in most cases, it also requires states to diligently recruit "potential foster and adoptive families that reflect the ethnic and racial diversity of children in the State for whom foster and adoptive homes are needed."[11] States, however, have failed to develop adequate diligent recruitment plans. Indeed, a study of MEPA-IEAP conducted twenty-five years after its enactment concluded that the diligent recruitment plans of thirty-four states were unsatisfactory.[12]

This chapter examines the challenges to recruiting foster and adoptive families that reflect the racial and ethnic makeup of children in the child protection system. It proposes reforms to create a pool of racially and ethnically diverse families who can help children develop a healthy self-esteem and racial identity that will allow them to flourish and achieve their full potential. The first section briefly describes the disproportionate representation of Black, multiracial, and Native American children in the foster care system and the evidence demonstrating the importance of placement with families who will nurture their racial and ethnic identity. The second section examines the barriers to recruitment of Black and Native American families as foster and adoptive parents. The third section proposes ways to remove these barriers and grow the pool of caregivers who can nurture every aspect of a child's development when their birth parents are unable to adequately care for them.

A few caveats: First, I agree with scholars who have argued that the state removes too many children from their parents' care unnecessarily. Rather than removal and draconian conditions to reunification, the state should provide parents with support, including economic resources, that will enable them to care for their children at home. Yet, even with such supports, there may be times during which parents are unable to care for their children, at least temporarily, due to illness (including substance use), incarceration, or other extraordinary circumstances. In those cases, the state may need to find another adult, preferably a "relative or person with a significant relationship with the child or the child's family," to provide care for the child.[13] The proposals in this chapter aim to further the law's diligent recruitment mandate by increasing the pool of potential caregivers from the same racial and ethnic communities as the children needing care, thereby maximizing the likelihood that children will be placed with adults who are equipped to help them develop a healthy racial identity.

Second, MEPA-IEAP's colorblind provisions do not apply to "Indian children" as defined by the Indian Child Welfare Act (ICWA).[14] Instead, states must comply with ICWA's preferences for placement of "Indian children" with extended family members and tribal families.[15] However, not all Native American children are "Indian children" as defined by ICWA, and thus, placements of such children are subject to MEPA-IEAP's provisions. Given the overrepresentation of Native American children in the foster care system, states must diligently recruit families who are able to help Native American children develop a healthy identity and self-esteem when ICWA's placement preferences do not apply to them.

Self-Esteem and Racial Identity: The Importance of Caregivers from the Child's Community

African American children, multiracial children with a Black parent, and Native American children are overrepresented in the foster care system.[16] As compared to other children, they are less likely to be reunited with their families and more likely to be placed with foster and adoptive families of a different race or ethnicity.[17] While Latino children are not overrepresented in the foster care system, there are more than seventy-nine thousand Latino children in foster care, and of these, approximately twenty-five thousand are waiting to be adopted.[18] They are also significantly more likely than white children to be adopted by a family of a different race.[19]

Studies have shown that children who were removed from their birth families are at higher risk of psychological and emotional challenges than are other children. These risks increase for nonwhite children placed with families of a different race—they are more likely than children placed with a family of the same race to experience placement instability.[20] While the majority of children raised by a family of a different race do well psychologically and socially, some "struggle to fit in with peers, the community in general and, sometimes, their own families."[21] For example, African Americans who were adopted by white families as children have reported that they felt they did not fit in with either their adoptive white families or African Americans.[22] They felt awkward around African Americans because they did not grow up in an African American home or community but also felt "different" from their white family members. As one transracial adoptee explained, they "experience a kind of racial neutering in which they feel no sense of belonging to any racial group."[23] As illustrated in the groundbreaking documentary *Dawnland*, some Native American children placed with non-Native families felt they were no longer part of the Native community.[24] Children who do not feel a sense of belonging may experience greater behavioral challenges. In fact, studies have found that Black and Brown children who were adopted from foster care by families of a different race experience more behavioral problems than do children in same-race placements.[25]

Race is an important element of self-identity for many racial and ethnic minorities.[26] Children with a strong racial or ethnic identity tend to have higher self-esteem, which is associated with fewer emotional and behavioral challenges.[27] Black and Brown children placed with families of a different race, however, are more likely than their peers in same-race placements to experience ambivalence about their racial or ethnic background.[28] Such ambivalence is associated with greater psychological distress and behavioral problems.[29]

Can White Parents Raise Children of Color with a Positive Racial Identity?

I am not suggesting that only a foster or adoptive parent who shares a child's racial or ethnic background can raise a child with a positive racial identity. A Latino foster parent, for example, may or may not be able to raise an African American child with a positive racial identity, but we should not make any assumptions about the prospective foster or adoptive parent's abilities on the basis of their race or ethnicity. Rather, we must evaluate each potential foster and adoptive parent as an individual and assess their specific strengths and weaknesses. Moreover, every child has different needs, so when placing a child, we must determine what this particular child needs to develop a healthy identity and maintain a connection to their community of origin.

Foster and adoptive parents can learn the skills needed to nurture a child of a different race and help the child develop a strong and positive racial identity. But they must first understand how racial identity impacts a child's emotional development, identity, and self-esteem. Foster and adoptive parents must also be aware of the role of race, racism, and discrimination in our society and be willing to learn strategies to help the child cope.[30] They must also be part of, or be prepared to join, a community of individuals who share the child's racial or ethnic background. Unfortunately, not all prospective foster and adoptive parents have this knowledge, willingness to learn, or community support. Even after the murders of George Floyd, Ahmaud Arbery, and Trayvon Martin, some Americans continue to believe that talking about race and acknowledging how race affects our opportunities, interactions, and perceptions is unnecessary and potentially detrimental to our society.[31] Consequently, even the most loving and committed foster and adoptive parents sometimes fail to address the role of race in their children's lives.[32] Individuals who were adopted by parents of a different race as children have discussed the challenges they faced as children, adolescents, and young adults growing up in families in which they were the only person of color, with parents who were oblivious to their struggle to fit in and the racial microaggressions they experienced in their predominantly white neighborhoods.[33]

Given the prevalence of racism and discrimination in our society, Black and Brown children need to learn to cope with racial prejudice and how to navigate cross-racial interactions.[34] Children typically learn these skills from parents, relatives, and fictive kin who have firsthand experience navigating the challenges Black and Brown children are likely to face, such as teachers' assumptions that they are less capable than white students, disproportionate school discipline, and negative interactions with police or school resource officers.[35] Children are more likely to have the benefit of "The Talk" and feel comfortable discussing race with adults who share their racial markers.[36]

Although some Black and Brown children placed with white families will learn these skills from their white foster or adoptive parents, many will not, especially if the parents subscribe to colorblindness or are un-willing to talk about race. These children may also lack opportunities to learn these coping skills from their teachers, friends, or other members of the community, especially if they reside in predominantly white neighborhoods and attend predominantly white schools.

Private Agencies

Placing a Black or Brown child with a family that is not prepared for the challenges that child is likely to confront is not in that child's best interest. Private adoption agencies (which do not receive any government funding) have recognized the need to make families aware of the challenges that Black and Brown children might experience, and thus, they assess whether a prospective adoptive family understands the challenges transracial adoptees may face before approving that family to adopt transracially. They have also created programs to help applicants acquire the tools they will need to raise a child of a different race with a positive racial identity.[37] They increasingly require families considering transracial adoption to complete additional education courses that explore racial identity, implicit bias, helping a child cope with racism and microaggressions, and creating a racially inclusive home, environment, and community. They also provide ongoing support to transracial families such as counseling and parenting groups.

MEPA-IEAP prohibits agencies that receive federal funding from engaging in similar efforts. For example, the US Department of Health and Human Services Office of Civil Rights has interpreted MEPA-IEAP as barring state agencies from considering a prospective foster or adoptive parent's views about the role of racial or ethnic identity for a child's self-esteem, whether the applicant has any friends of the same race as the child to be placed in their home, or whether the applicant lives in a racially or ethnically diverse neighborhood. It has also interpreted MEPA-IEAP to prohibit public agencies from imposing any additional requirements on individuals willing to foster or adopt a child of a different race, such as education courses that focus on race and racial identity, unless they are also required for individuals who are only willing to accept a same-race placement.[38] As the head of one agency observed, "A child welfare agency cannot even consider how a non-white child may experience racism in a particular family—even if members of that family belong to a white supremacist organization—for fear of violating MEPA."[39]

In 2003, for example, the Office of Civil Rights (OCR) determined that an Ohio agency had violated MEPA-IEAP and Title VI of the Civil Rights Act of 1964—which prohibits agencies receiving federal funds from discriminating on the basis of race—when it required applicants seeking to adopt a child of a different race to explain how they would address the child's cultural identity and assessed the racial composition of their neighborhood. OCR explained that state agencies may not impose additional requirements on persons seeking to adopt a child of a different race and concluded that by giving preference to a single white female applicant over a white couple seeking to adopt an African American child because the single white female lived "in an integrated neighborhood and had bi-racial brothers," the state had impermissibly sought out information about white applicants' contacts with the Black community and the racial makeup of the local school system.[40]

In an effort to prepare families to adopt transracially without running afoul of MEPA-IEAP, some agencies that receive federal funding require all prospective adoptive families to complete courses on race and racial identity, implicit bias, helping a child cope with racism, and creating a racially inclusive community.[41] While these types of courses are beneficial for all families, they divert resources away from transracial families that need them most and need them immediately to facilitate the healthy emotional development of Black and Brown children.[42] Effective programs require extensive resources, including small groups and interactive exercises with trained facilitators. While private agencies can pass these costs onto families seeking to adopt, public agencies cannot do the same and thus may be unable to provide transracial families with the support they need.

Child advocates have long argued that MEPA-IEAP's colorblind approach is not in children's best interests and urged Congress to repeal the 1996 amendment and return to the 1994 MEPA, which allowed states to consider a child's "cultural, ethnic or racial background" as one factor when placing a child.[43] Indeed in 2007, the US Commission on Civil Rights heard testimony from experts advocating its repeal.[44] More recently, in 2021, Bethany Christian Services, one of the largest family social services organization in the country, issued a report documenting the harms of MEPA-IEAP's colorblind approach and calling for a return to the 1994 MEPA. Bethany further proposed that the law "proactively require social workers to assess a "family's ability to effectively parent transracially" and "provide additional training to families who may be well-intentioned but not yet equipped to parent transracially."[45] Despite these efforts, Congress has not repealed the 1996 amendment barring consideration of race. Moreover, given the attacks on race-conscious policies after the Supreme Court's 2023 decision in *Students for Fair Admissions, Inc. v. President and Fellows of Harvard College*, holding that race-conscious college admissions policies violate the Equal Protection Clause and Title VI, Congress is highly unlikely to revisit MEPA-IEAP.[46] Even if it did, any allowance for consideration of race would surely be challenged.

In light of MEPA-IEAP's restrictions on a public agency's ability to assess whether a prospective foster or adoptive parent is likely to be able to raise a child of a different race with a positive racial identity, child advocates must find other ways to increase the likelihood that all children who enter the foster care system are placed with families who are able and willing to nurture their racial identity. Enforcement of the diligent recruitment mandate may be that tool. By increasing the pool of prospective foster and adoptive families that reflect the racial and ethnic diversity of the children in need of care, lawmakers can increase the likelihood that children will be placed in homes and communities with people who understand the challenges Black and Brown children are likely to face and can help them develop a healthy racial identity.

Barriers to Recruitment of Foster and Adoptive Parents Who Share the Racial and Ethnic Background of Children in State Care

Children placed in kinship foster care do better—behaviorally, psychologically, emotionally, and academically—than children placed with strangers or individuals outside their community.[47] As Dorothy Roberts has explained, kinship foster care "preserves family, community, and cultural ties," and children in such placements are more likely to report "that they felt loved and happy."[48] Lawmakers recognize that placement with relatives, fictive kin, and members of their community is in children's best interests, and thus, federal law encourages states to give preference to relatives when placing a child.[49] In fact, the federal government has recognized that "improving efforts to place children with relatives/fictive kin at the onset of foster care placement" will contribute to "improvements in outcomes related to both permanency and child and family well-being."[50] The federal government has recognized that placement with relatives and kin helps to "preserve children's cultural identity and relationship to their community" and that "for youth in foster care, having a strong cultural identity can lead to greater self-esteem, higher education levels, improved coping abilities, and decreased levels of loneliness and depression."[51] Thus, the federal government recommends that states "make placement decisions that carefully consider a child's connections to their community."[52] State laws similarly give preference to relatives and fictive kin when placing a child in foster care.[53] Yet only about a third of children in foster care are living with a relative or fictive kin; most children in foster care live with strangers.[54]

In our racially segregated society, members of the child's community (such as friends, classmates, church members, and neighbors) are likely to be of the same race and ethnicity as the child. The mandate to diligently recruit families that reflect the racial and ethnic background of the children in need of placement suggests that Congress recognized that all children should have the *opportunity* to be placed with a family that shares their racial or ethnic background, which is not possible if such families are not in the pool of potential foster parents. Congress also sought to ensure that individuals of all racial and ethnic backgrounds would have opportunities to be foster and adoptive parents. Yet, the pool of prospective foster and adoptive parents who share the racial or ethnic background of the children in need of care is small. This section examines the barriers to recruitment of Black and Brown foster and adoptive parents.

African American, Native American, and Latino families are more likely than white and Asian American families to be poor.[55] In fact, although poverty is not a ground for removal of a child from their parents' care, poverty is one of the reasons Black and Native American children enter foster care at higher rates than do children of other racial and ethnic backgrounds.[56] Poverty in Black and Native communities is not limited to families with children in the foster care system but is also experienced by grandparents and other extended family members, as well as neighbors and family friends.[57] Black and Native individuals are also more likely to experience poor physical and mental health, especially when caring for their relatives' and kin's children without adequate state support, and are less likely to have a partner who can share the day-to-day responsibility of caring for a child.[58] They are also less likely to have access to information on becoming a foster parent and the resources available to support them.[59]

The law itself discourages Black and Native individuals from becoming foster and adoptive parents. The requirements to become a licensed foster parent are onerous. They include financial and medical reviews; literacy, transportation, and language requirements; age limits; assessment of the suitability of the home (including size of the home and number of bedrooms); criminal and child protective services background checks for everyone in the household; interviews with each member of the household; and intensive and time-consuming foster parent training classes.[60] These requirements disproportionately affect Black, Native, and Latino individuals, who are more likely to be indigent and to reside in modest homes and are more likely to have experienced (or live with individuals who have experienced) past involvement with child protective services or the criminal justice system.

The communities that reflect the racial and ethnic background of children in need of foster homes have a "historical distrust of the child welfare agency."[61] This distrust continues today. One study found that African Americans and Latinos were more likely than whites to believe that the state does not do enough to keep families together and "to say the foster care system harms more than helps the children in its care."[62] Moreover, individuals who have dealt with child protective services or been involved with the criminal justice system may seek to avoid any further involvement with state agencies. Foster parents, however, are under constant surveillance. They must allow agency caseworkers to visit their home periodically to make sure they are complying with the agency's requirements and must repeatedly share private medical and financial information.

Black, Native, and Latino individuals must also deal with caseworkers who do not understand or value the role they play in helping to raise their relatives' and friends' children. Many foster parents fear that the state will scrutinize their daily child-rearing decisions and deny them the deference all parents need when caring for a child.[63] This lack of respect and deference is magnified when the foster parent is Black, Latino, or Native American and especially if they are a relative or kin. For example, Elizabeth Bartholet, one of the strongest supporters of MEPA-IEAP, opposes the preference for kinship caregivers who are typically members of the community where the children needing care came from because that environment led to circumstances requiring removal.[64] Members of these communities sense the harsh judgment and disapproval from caseworkers who share Bartholet's views. They wish to avoid further scrutiny by agencies and caseworkers who do not respect them, especially when caseworkers' personal biases may lead to their rejection as foster parents.[65] Indeed, 25 percent of African Americans and 20 percent of Latinos report that racial or ethnic discrimination is an obstacle to considering becoming a foster or adoptive parent, and the federal government has investigated allegations that racial or ethnic discrimination resulted in denial of relative or kinship placements.[66] Black and Brown individuals who distrust state actors view the foster care system as too intrusive and are dissuaded from becoming foster parents.[67]

The federal government reimburses states for foster care payments made to licensed providers.[68] Although states determine their licensing standards and can waive non-safety-related licensure requirements for kinship caregivers, until recently, the requirements for a kinship caregiver to become a licensed foster parent have typically been the same as for an unrelated individual who had no prior relationship with the child. Kinship caregivers who did not satisfy the state's licensing standards for foster parents were denied foster care maintenance payments.[69] While unlicensed caregivers could obtain financial assistance from Temporary Assistance for Needy Families (TANF), TANF assistance amounts are typically less than half of the amount of foster care maintenance payments.[70] Thus, kin who wished to provide a home for a child but could not meet the foster care licensing requirements were often unable to do so unless they had other sources of support.[71] Moreover, even licensed foster parents who receive foster care maintenance payments sometimes struggle financially, as the payments are intended to help offset the child's expenses but do "not cover the costs of adding another child (or children) to the household."[72] Although "foster parenting is a full-time job," foster parents must often work outside the home in order to support themselves and their families.[73] Indeed, state agencies expect foster parents to work full-time, a situation that may lead them to leave the children in their care alone unsupervised.[74] Financial constraints are a significant barrier, especially for African Americans, who are more likely than other groups to list "the amount of money required" as an obstacle to becoming a foster parent.[75]

Diligent Recruitment of Foster and Adoptive Families That Reflect the Ethnic and Racial Diversity of Children in State Care

The majority of states have failed to diligently recruit foster and adoptive parents that "reflect the ethnic and racial diversity of children in the State for whom foster and adoptive homes are needed."[76] As noted, the federal government's own 2020 study concluded that thirty-four states lacked adequate diligent recruitment plans.[77] This section describes recent actions by the federal government that may facilitate recruitment of foster and adoptive parents from the communities where the children in need of care come from and proposes other reforms that may reduce the barriers to fostering and adopting by members of these communities.

The federal government has taken several actions to increase the pool of foster and adoptive parents who reflect the racial and ethnic diversity of the children in state care. In November 2023, the Administration for Children and Families amended the federal regulations to make it easier for relatives and kin to become licensed foster parents. The new regulations authorize states to adopt different licensing standards for relative and kinship foster family homes versus nonrelative foster family homes.[78] Under the new regulations, states may adopt foster home licensing standards for "individuals related to a child by blood, marriage, or adoption" or "who have an emotionally significant relationship with the child, including fictive kin," that differ from the standards applied to an unrelated individual who is not kin or fictive kin.[79] A kinship caregiver who meets the state's foster home licensing requirements for kinship foster parents is eligible for the same foster care payments as unrelated foster parents who must satisfy different licensing requirements. Moreover, the state is entitled to federal reimbursement for these payments.[80]

The new regulations will make it easier for many Black, Native, and Latino individuals to become foster parents. As noted, strict licensing requirements prevent and discourage disproportionate numbers of individuals from these communities from becoming licensed foster parents. Under the new regulations, states may choose to, for example, "extend age limits for relative or kinship foster care providers; allow relative children to share sleeping spaces; disregard certain income, transportation, literacy, language, and education requirements; and remove disqualifications for non-child-related past crimes such as issuing bad checks."[81] As the Administration for Children and Families recognized, the new regulations will "especially provide a support to low-income prospective relative caregivers, many of whom are families of color."[82]

Congress is also considering action that may increase the pool of Black and Brown foster and adoptive parents. The bipartisan Recruiting Families Using Data Act was initially introduced in 2023.[83] The act seeks to "improve foster and adoptive parent recruitment and retention" and would amend the diligent recruitment mandate to require states to develop a family partnership plan "in consultation with birth, kinship, foster and adoptive families, community-based service providers, technical assistance providers, and youth with lived experience with foster care and adoption."[84] The act requires states to address how they plan "to identify, notify, engage, and support relatives (and others connected to the child) as potential placement resources for children."[85] As noted, in our racially segregated society, relatives and kin are likely to share the racial and ethnic background of the children entering care. Requiring states to indicate how they will identify and recruit relatives and kin may result in a larger pool of foster and adoptive parents who share the racial and ethnic background of the children in care.

The act also requires each state to address how it "plans to develop and implement child-specific recruitment plans for every child . . . who needs a foster or adoptive family."[86] A child-specific recruitment plan would presumably require consideration of a specific family's ability to nurture the specific child's emotional development. Thus, this requirement should allow states to consider how a specific foster or prospective adoptive family would help the child develop a positive racial identity.

Finally, the act would require states to provide an annual report analyzing the "specific challenges or barriers to recruiting, licensing, and utilizing families who reflect the racial and ethnic background of children in foster care in the State, and the State's efforts to overcome those challenges and barriers."[87]

As of March 2025, the act (which was reintroduced in January 2025 after the Senate failed to take action on the 2023 bill) had passed the House and was pending in the Senate.[88] While I am hopeful that the act's requirements will incentivize states to develop adequate diligent recruitment plans and lead to greater accountability, stronger enforcement mechanisms are needed to ensure compliance. MEPA-IEAP imposes financial penalties on states that consider race or ethnicity when placing a child in a foster or adoptive home. As discussed, Ohio and South Carolina faced those penalties, and the federal government's guidance explains that both MEPA-IEAP and Title VI of the Civil Rights Act of 1964 "impose significant legal penalties for race-based discrimination in adoption and foster care," including "suspension or termination of, or the refusal to grant, Federal financial assistance."[89] In contrast, no state has faced financial penalties for failure to comply with the diligent recruitment mandate. The absence of legal penalties for violation of the diligent recruitment requirement signals that it is not a priority. Thus, it is not surprising that a majority of states are not in compliance. The same legal penalties that apply to violations of MEPA-IEAP's colorblindness requirement should apply when a state does not comply with the diligent recruitment mandate.

States have resources available to guide them as they develop and implement diligent recruitment plans.[90] The federal Children's Bureau's guidance directs child welfare agencies to include "specific strategies to reach all parts of the community" and to train "staff to work with diverse cultural, racial, and economic communities."[91] It clarifies that states can engage in "targeted recruitment" of minority families who can provide foster and adoptive homes, including hiring a private recruitment agency that understands "the needs of a specific community."[92] The guidance advises agencies to partner with organizations, including "religious institutions and neighborhood centers," in the communities in which children in need of care come from, noting that dissemination of information is more effective when agencies partner with these groups.[93] Child advocacy organizations have similarly urged states to engage in these types of partnerships and outreach.[94] States that have heeded this advice and worked with faith-based organizations and involved current foster parents and youth (currently or formerly) in foster care in their recruitment efforts were better able to reach and engage with the communities where the children in need of care come from.[95] Most states, however, have not engaged in adequate outreach. As one commentator has noted, "I have never seen foster agencies advertising in areas that are predominantly Black."[96]

Outreach alone is not sufficient. Child welfare agencies and their staff must earn the trust of Black, Latino, and Native American individuals. Thus, an effective diligent recruitment plan must address how the state will ensure that caregivers are treated with the respect and deference they deserve and need to care for children day to day. Several states already require the agency and other stakeholders to treat foster parents "with consideration, dignity, respect, and trust as a primary caregiver for foster children, including respect for the family values and routines of the foster parent."[97] Federal law should require the same. Child welfare agencies must also train staff about the important role that Black, Native, and Latino relatives and kin play in the upbringing of children and demonstrate respect for parents' reliance on relatives and kin. Building trust requires hiring and training caseworkers who are committed to finding homes for children in the communities they come from, even if the homes in those communities lack some comforts. It also requires states to consider reducing the oversight that is typically unwarranted when children are cared for by relatives and kin and that is perceived as overly intrusive. Finally, agencies must address caseworkers' implicit (and explicit) biases that lead to rejection of Black and Brown applicants and discourage members of these communities from applying.

Conclusion

African Americans are more likely than other racial and ethnic groups to have experience with the foster care system, to know someone who is a foster parent, or to know someone who is or was in foster care.[98] They are also more likely than other groups to have considered becoming a foster parent and adopting from foster care.[99] Yet, the barriers to fostering and adopting have prevented many African Americans from formally bringing children in need of care into their homes. They have also forced many individuals to care for their relatives' and kin's children informally, without adequate state support. The government can and should do a lot more to support individuals who step in to care for children when parents are unable to do so. It should increase the amount of foster maintenance payments, which would allow more individuals, and especially racial and ethnic minorities, to become foster parents. It should also "identify, notify, engage, and support [all] relatives (and others connected to the child) as potential placement resources for children," as the Recruiting Families Using Data Act, if enacted, requires.[100] Diligent recruitment of families that reflect the racial and ethnic background of the children in need of care will not remedy the injustices of our family regulation system or provide the support they need, but it may increase the likelihood that children will find loving homes with individuals who will nurture every aspect of their identity.

NOTES

1 Gretchen Sisson, *Relinquished* (St. Martin's, 2024), 63–64. I recognize that transgender men and binary individuals may become pregnant and seek abortion care. However, the majority of pregnant persons are cis-women. Thus, I use the terms "pregnant women" and "pregnant persons" interchangeably.

2 Sisson, *Relinquished*, 61.

3 Claire Cain Miller and Margot Sanger-Katz, "How Many Abortions Did the Post-Roe Bans Prevent?," *New York Times*, November 22, 2023.

4 Julianne Hill, "Family Limbo: Movement to Repeal a Clinton-Era Law Sparks Debate About Foster Care and Adoption," *ABA Journal* 110 (2024): 60.

5 Kiara Alfonseca, "Why Abortion Restrictions Disproportionately Impact People of Color," *ABC News*, June 24, 2022.

6 National Data Archive on Child Abuse and Neglect, "Kinship Caregivers in the Child Welfare System," National Survey of Child and Adolescent Well-Being Research Brief, NSCAW No. 15 (2014): 3, www.acf.hhs.gov; Nicholas Zill, "The Changing Face of Adoption in the United States," Institute for Family Studies, August 8, 2017.

7 Ndidi Okeke-Adeyanju, Lorraine C. Taylor, Ashley B. Craig, Rachel E. Smith, Aqiyla Thomas, Alaina E. Boyle, and Melissa E. DeRosier, "Celebrating the Strengths of Black Youth: Increasing Self-Esteem and Implications for Prevention," *Journal of Primary Prevention* 35 (2014): 357–69.

8 42 U.S.C. § 1996b(1) (1996).

9   Howard Metzenbaum Multiethnic Placement Act of 1994, 42 U.S.C. § 5115a (1994), repealed by Act of Aug. 20, 1996, Pub. L. 104-188, § 1808(d), 110 Stat. 1904.

10 Children's Bureau, Administration for Children and Families, "4.3 MEPA/IEAP, Guidance for Compliance," in *Child Welfare Policy Manual* (US Department of Health and Human Services, March 5, 2025), www.acf.hhs.gov.

11 42 U.S.C. § 622(b)(7); Children's Bureau, Administration for Children and Families, "4.1 MEPA/IEAP, Diligent Recruitment," in *Child Welfare Policy Manual* (US Department of Health and Human Services, April 11, 2014), www.acf.hhs.gov.

12 Office of the Assistant Secretary for Planning and Evaluation, *The Multiethnic Placement Act and Transracial Adoption 25 Years Later* (US Department of Health and Human Services, 2020), https://aspe.hhs.gov.

13 American Law Institute, "§ 2.22 Permanent Placement Options and Permanency Hearings," in *Restatement of the Law, Children and the Law* (2025).

14 25 U.S.C. § 1904(4) (defining an "Indian child" as "any unmarried person who is under age eighteen and is either (a) a member of an Indian tribe or (b) is eligible for membership in an Indian tribe and is the biological child of a member of an Indian tribe"); 42 U.S.C. § 1996b(3).

15 25 U.S.C. § 1915.

16 Children's Bureau, Administration for Children and Families, *AFCARS Report No. 30* (US Department of Health and Human Services, 2024), www.acf.hhs.gov.

17 Hill, "Family Limbo," 60; Office of the Assistant Secretary for Planning and Evaluation, *Transracial Adoption from Foster Care in the U.S.* (US Department of Health and Human Services, December 2020), 3–4, www.aspe.hhs.gov; Elisha Marr, "U.S. Transracial Adoption Trends in the 21st Century," *Adoption Quarterly* 20, no. 3 (2017): 236–42, 247.

18 Children's Bureau, *AFCARS Report No. 30*.

19 Office of the Assistant Secretary for Planning and Evaluation, *Transracial Adoption*.

20 Catherine A. LaBrenz, Jangmin Kim, Marian S. Harris, Jandel Crutchfield, Mijin Choi, Erica D. Robinson, et al., "Racial Matching in Foster Care Placements and Subsequent Placement Stability: A National Study," *Child and Adolescent Social Work Journal* 39 (2022): 583–94.

21 Rita J. Simon, Howard Altstein, and Marygold Shire Melli, *The Case for Transracial Adoption* (American University Press, 1994); Evan B. Donaldson, *Finding Families for African American Children: The Role of Race and Law in Adoption from Foster Care* (Adoption Institute, May 5, 2008), 23, www.ncap-us.org.

22 Donaldson, *Finding Families*; Gene Demby and Shereen Marisol Meraji, "Code Switch: Transracial Adoptees on Their Racial Identity and Sense of Self," *All Things Considered*, NPR, podcast, October 13, 2018, www.npr.org.

23 Lena Williams, "Beyond 'Losing Isaiah': Truth in Shades of Gray," *New York Times*, March 23, 1995, C1, www.nytimes.com.

24 Adam Mazo and Ben Pender-Cudlip, dirs., *Dawnland* (PBS Independent Films, 2018).

25 Donaldson, *Finding Families*, 24, 41.

26 Donaldson, *Finding Families*, 19.
27 Donaldson, *Finding Families*, 24; APA Working Group for Addressing Racial and Ethnic Disparities in Youth Mental Health, , *Addressing the Mental Health Needs of Racial and Ethnic Minority Youth—A Guide for Practitioners* (American Psychological Association, 2017), 6, www.apa.org.
28 Donaldson, *Finding Families*, 24–25.
29 Donaldson, *Finding Families*, 25; LaBrenz et al., "Racial Matching," 3.
30 Donaldson, *Finding Families*, 7; Maria Vidal de Haymes and Shirley Simon, "Transracial Adoption: Families Identify Issues and Needed Support Services," *Child Welfare* 82, no. 2 (2003): 261–62.
31 J. Nicky Sullivan, Jennifer L. Eberhardt, and Steven O. Roberts, "Conversations About Race in Black and White U.S. Families: Before and After George Floyd's Death," *Psychological and Cognitive Sciences* 118, no. 38 (2021): e2106366118.
32 Carla Goar, Jenny L. Davis, and Bianca Manago, "Discursive Entwinement: How White Transracially Adoptive Parents Navigate Race," *Sociology of Race and Ethnicity* 3, no. 3 (2017): 339.
33 Nicole Chung, *All You Can Ever Know* (Thorndike, 2019); Angela Tucker, *You Should Be Grateful* (Beacon, 2023); Rebecca Carroll, *Surviving the White Gaze: A Memoir* (Simon and Schuster, 2021); Adoptive and Foster Family Coalition, *Struggle for Identity: Issues in Transracial Adoption*, video (PhotoSynthesis Productions, July 8, 2016), https://affcny.org.
34 *Petition of R.M.G.*, 454 A.2d 776, 802 (D.C. 1982).
35 Christopher Redding, "A Teacher like Me: A Review of the Effect of Student–Teacher Racial/Ethnic Matching on Teacher Perceptions of Students and Student Academic and Behavioral Outcomes," *Review of Educational Research* 89, no. 4 (August 2019): 499–35; American Bar Association, "School-to-Prison Pipeline Statistics," July 11, 2023, www.americanbar.org/; Kristin Henning, *The Rage of Innocence: How America Criminalizes Black Youth* (Pantheon Books, 2021).
36 Ernie Suggs, "When White Parents Have 'The Talk' with Their Black Children," *Atlanta Journal-Constitution*, September 26, 2020.
37 Solangel Maldonado, "Discouraging Racial Preferences in Adoptions," *University of California Davis Law Review* 39 (2006): 1462; Cheri Williams and Julia Fukuda, *What the Pandemic Taught Us: Innovative Practice Report* (Bethany Christian Services, 2021), 21, https://bethany.org.
38 Children's Bureau, "4.3 MEPA/IEAP, Guidance for Compliance."
39 Cheri Williams and Nathan Bult, "We Celebrate Transracial Adoption. But Child Welfare Can't Ignore Race," *Newsweek*, May 6, 2021.
40 Letter of Findings from US Department of Health and Human Services to Suzanne A. Burke and Tom Hayes, Director, Department of Health and Human Services, Re: Docket No. 05997026 (October 20, 2003), www.hhs.gov.
41 Williams and Bult, "We Celebrate Transracial Adoption."
42 White families adopting white children need this information, albeit with a different focus, to help them raise nonracist children. Margaret A. Hagerman, *White*

Kids: Growing Up with Privilege in a Racially Divided America (New York University Press, 2020); Ibram X. Kendi, *How to Raise an Anti-Racist* (One World, 2022).

43 Howard Metzenbaum Multiethnic Placement Act of 1994, 42 U.S.C. § 5115a (1994), repealed by Act of August 20, 1996, Pub. L. No. 104-188, § 1808(d), 110 Stat. 1904.

44 US Commission on Civil Rights, *Multiethnic Placement Act: Minorities and Foster Care and Adoption: A Briefing Before the United States Commission on Civil Rights, Washington, D.C.* (US Commission of Civil Rights, 2010), 4–5, www.usccr.gov (reporting on the September 21, 2007, briefing).

45 Williams and Fukuda, *What the Pandemic Taught Us*, 18.

46 Nikole Hannah-Jones, "The 'Colorblindness' Trap: How a Civil Rights Ideal Got Hijacked," *New York Times*, March 13, 2024; Julian Mark, "Next Front in the Attack on Affirmative Action: State Diversity Programs," *Washington Post*, March 9, 2024; *Students for Fair Admissions, Inc. v. President and Fellows of Harvard College*, 600 U.S. 181 (2023).

47 The federal government defines "kinship foster care" as "any living arrangement in which a relative or someone else emotionally close to the child takes primary responsibility for rearing a child." National Data Archive on Child Abuse and Neglect, "Kinship Caregivers in the Child Welfare System," 1; Child Welfare Information Gateway, Administration for Children and Families, *Kinship Care and the Child Welfare System* (US Department of Health and Human Services, 2022), 3, www.childwelfare.gov.

48 Dorothy Roberts, "Kinship Care and the Price of State Support for Children," *Chicago-Kent Law Review* 76 (2001): 1619.

49 42 U.S. § 671(a)(19) (2023).

50 Children's Bureau, Administration for Children and Families, *Achieving Permanency for the Well-Being of Children and Youth*, ACYF-CB-IM-21-01 (US Department of Health and Human Services, 2021), 4, www.acf.hhs.gov.

51 Children and Families Administration, "Separate Licensing Standards for Relative or Kinship Foster Family Homes," *Federal Register* 88, no. 30 (2023): 9414, www.federalregister.gov.

52 Children's Bureau, *Achieving Permanency*, 11.

53 Alaska Stat. Ann. § 47.14.100(e)(1), (3) (2018); Arkansas Code Ann. § 9-27-355(b)(1)(E)(i) (2019); California Welfare and Institutions Code, 361.3(a) (2018); Montana Code Ann. § 41-3-101(3) (2009).

54 Casey Family Programs, "Why Should Child Protection Agencies Adopt a Kin-First Approach?," August 12, 2020, www.casey.org.

55 Emily A. Shrider, Melissa Kollar, Frances Chen, and Jessica Semega, *Income and Poverty in the United States: 2020–Current Population Reports*, Report #P60-273 (US Census Bureau, September 2021), www.census.gov.

56 *In re S.S.*, 269 Cal. Rptr. 3d 484, 487 (Cal. 2020); *In the Interest of C.T. Children*, 648 S.E. 2d 708, 711 (Ga. 2007); *Tipton v. Marion County Department of Public Welfare*, 629 N.E. 2d 1262, 1268 (Ind. 1994); Dorothy Roberts, *Torn Apart: How the Child Welfare System Destroys Black Families—and How Abolition Can Build a*

Safer World (Basic Books, 2022), 36, 288; Joan Shaughnessy, "An Essay on Poverty and Child Neglect: New Interventions," *Washington and Lee Journal of Civil Rights and Social Justice* 21 (2014): 11–12.

57 Roberts, "Kinship Care," 1634.

58 Dayna Bowen Matthew, *Just Health: Treating Structural Racism to Heal America* (New York University Press, 2022), 33–37; National Data Archive on Child Abuse and Neglect, "Kinship Caregivers in the Child Welfare System," 3; Juliana Menasce Horowitz, Mikki Graf, and Gretchen Livingston, *Marriage and Cohabitation in the U.S.* (Pew Research Center, November 6, 2019), www.pewresearch.org.

59 Foster and Adoptive Care Coalition "The Coalition RESPONDs to the Need for African American Foster Parents," April 8, 2022, www.foster-adopt.org; National Child Welfare Resource Center for Tribes, accessed July 1, 2024, www.nrc4tribes.org.

60 Children and Families Administration, "Separate Licensing Standards," 9412; Alaska Stat. Ann. § 47.14.100(j) (2018); Ariz. Rev. Stat. Ann. § 8-514.03)B (2022); Ind. Code Ann. § 31-34-6-2 (2014).

61 CHAMPS, *A CHAMPS Guide on Foster Parent Recruitment and Retention: Strategies for Developing a Comprehensive Program* (CHAMPS, April 2019), 15.

62 Gallup, *Americans' Views of U.S. Foster Care: Elevating Black Americans' Perspectives and Experiences* (Gallup, 2024), 15–16, www.gallup.com.

63 Rachel Nielsen, "Foster Parents Say 'Retaliation' by Caseworkers Means Few Families to Help Kids in Need," *Crosscut*, January 15, 2020.

64 Elizabeth Bartholet, "Taking Adoption Seriously: Radical Revolution or Modest Revisionism?," *Capital University Law Review* 28 (1999): 77.

65 Kathleen Creamer, Rachael M. Miller, and Jenny Pokempner, "Investing in Youth and Families: The Importance of Family Bonds and Kinship Care," Juvenile Law Center, September 10, 2020, https://jlc.org.

66 Gallup, *Americans' Views*, 28; Civil Rights Division, US Department of Justice, "Title VI Child Welfare Guidance," updated December 19, 2019, www.justice.gov.

67 N. J. Hackensack, *The Kinship Treatment Foster Care Initiative Toolkit* (Foster Family-Based Treatment Association, 2015), 14, www.ffta.org.

68 45 Code of Federal Regulations § 1355.20.

69 Children and Families Administration, "Separate Licensing Standards," 9412.

70 Casey Family Programs, "Why Should Child Protection Agencies," 2; Nicholas Bogel-Burroughs, Ellen Barry, and Will Wright, "Ma'Khia Bryant's Journey Through Foster Care Ended with an Officer's Bullet," *New York Times*, May 8, 2021.

71 Casey Family Programs, "Why Should Child Protection Agencies," 2.

72 45 Code of Federal Regulations § 1355.20; Gladney Center for Adoption, "Do Foster Parents Get Paid and Why?," November 23, 2019, https://adoption.org.

73 Bogel-Burroughs et al., "Ma'Khia Bryant's Journey."

74 Bogel-Burroughs et al., "Ma'Khia Bryant's Journey."

75 Gallup, *Americans' Views*, 7.

76 42 U.S.C. § 622(b)(7).

77 Office of the Assistant Secretary for Planning and Evaluation, *Multiethnic Placement Act.*
78 45 Code of Federal Regulations § 1355.20(2).
79 Children and Families Administration, "Separate Licensing Standards," 9411.
80 Children and Families Administration, "Separate Licensing Standards," 9420.
81 Children and Families Administration, "Separate Licensing Standards," 9413.
82 Children and Families Administration, "Separate Licensing Standards," 9415.
83 H.R. 3058—Recruiting Families Using Data Act of 2023, House Ways and Means Committee, 118th Congress, 2nd session, House Report 118-347 (2023), www.congress.gov.
84 H.R. 3058, 1–2.
85 H.R. 3058, 2–3.
86 H.R. 3058, 3.
87 H.R. 3058, 4.
88 H.R. 579—Recruiting Families Using Data of 2025, 119th Cong., 1st sess. (2025).
89 Richard M. Campbell and Wade F. Horn, "OCR and HHS Administration on Children Disseminate Self-Assessment Tool to Facilitate Non-discrimination on the Basis of Race in Foster Care and Adoption," US Department of Health and Human Services, Office for Civil Rights, January 17, 2023, www.hhs.gov.
90 Casey Family Programs, "What Are Some Strategies for Finding and Keeping Traditional and Therapeutic Resource Families?," February 9, 2021, www.casey.org; CHAMPS, *CHAMPS Guide*, 7–8, 16–17; Jill Yordy, "Foster Parent Retention," National Conference of State Legislatures, April 2022, https://leg.mt.gov.
91 Children's Bureau, "4.1 MEPA/IEAP, Diligent Recruitment."
92 Children's Bureau, "4.1 MEPA/IEAP, Diligent Recruitment."
93 Children's Bureau, "4.1 MEPA/IEAP, Diligent Recruitment."
94 CHAMPS, *CHAMPS Guide*, 4, 12.
95 CHAMPS, *CHAMPS Guide*, 15; David Hansell, "A Roadmap for Recruiting Foster Parents: What We Learned with Home Away from Home," Who Cares, accessed April 21, 2025, www.fostercarecapacity.com.
96 Juwan Jessup, "Too Many Black Foster Kids, Not Enough Black Foster Parents," *The Imprint*, December 20, 2022, https://imprintnews.org.
97 Arkansas Code § 9-28-903; Rhode Island General Laws § 42-72.10-1.
98 Gallup, *Americans' Views*, 28.
99 Gallup, *Americans' Views*, 19–20.
100 H.R. 579.

8

Health Justice for Children of Color

YAEL ZAKAI CANNON

Families of color in the United States are disproportionately less healthy. People of color experience not only higher rates of a wide range of chronic health conditions but shorter life spans.[1] Children, despite their youth, are not immune from these disparities, which can be seen across an array of data, including data demonstrating wide inequities in infant mortality and childhood deaths from asthma.[2]

A growing body of research recognizes that these disparities are not primarily driven by a person's biology or the care they get at the doctor's office.[3] Instead, as much as 80 percent of health is driven by the conditions in which people live, eat, work, learn, and age.[4] These social, structural, and political determinants of health drive racial health inequities that harm—and kill—people of color.[5]

As a scholarly framework and a movement, health justice aims to leverage law, policy, and institutions to dismantle such conditions and the systems of subordination that drive health disparities, while building the power of individuals and communities to create and sustain conditions that support health equity.[6]

Health justice recognizes both that racism itself leads to poor health and that laws and policies steeped in structural racism have long driven health inequity for Black children and families in particular, as well as for other families of color in the United States.[7] For example, redlining and restrictive covenants have relegated children from Black families to neighborhoods with substandard housing conditions and environmental hazards, harming their health.[8] Just as law and policy have caused such disparities, health justice requires the leveraging of law and policy to instead actively promote health equity.

This chapter centers children of color in the fight for health justice. Children of color face harms resulting from structural racism and White supremacy throughout many aspects of "ordinary" life, as well as compounding harms from the subordination of people with intersectional identities based on gender, disability, class, and other identities.[9] Racial health inequities persist even across socioeconomic status.[10] These harms manifest themselves not only as injustice but as *health injustice* because they threaten the health and well-being of children of color. When children of color are evicted from their homes, live in unhealthy housing, face food insecurity, or go without health insurance, they can face immediate and lifelong health and mental health impacts. Research demonstrates the intergenerational nature of health: When a parent faces job discrimination, income insecurity, or domestic violence, a child's health and well-being can suffer as well.[11]

As a foundational step in the fight for health justice, this chapter argues that children of color are being deprived of the vital conditions for health and well-being—conditions needed to thrive. It names and frames how the absence of interconnected vital conditions contributes to health inequities for children and families of color. It identifies tangled threats of health injustice facing children of color as a key feature of structural inequality in our nation and centers those children and families, as researchers, advocates, and policy makers seek to create a vision for a healthier and more just nation in the twenty-first century. Building on a core value of health justice—that those who experience health inequity should drive the agenda for reform—the chapter calls for approaches that build the power and leadership of youth and families of color to serve as change agents for health justice.

The Vital Conditions for Health

While children and families of color have long experienced health inequity, the COVID-19 pandemic highlighted and compounded these disparities. People of color experienced disproportionately higher rates of infection, disease, and mortality, driven by structural inequity in a range of conditions.[12] For example, people of color are more likely to be employed in jobs that were deemed essential, limiting their ability to socially distance when the disease was raging. People of color are also more likely to be evicted and experience housing insecurity and

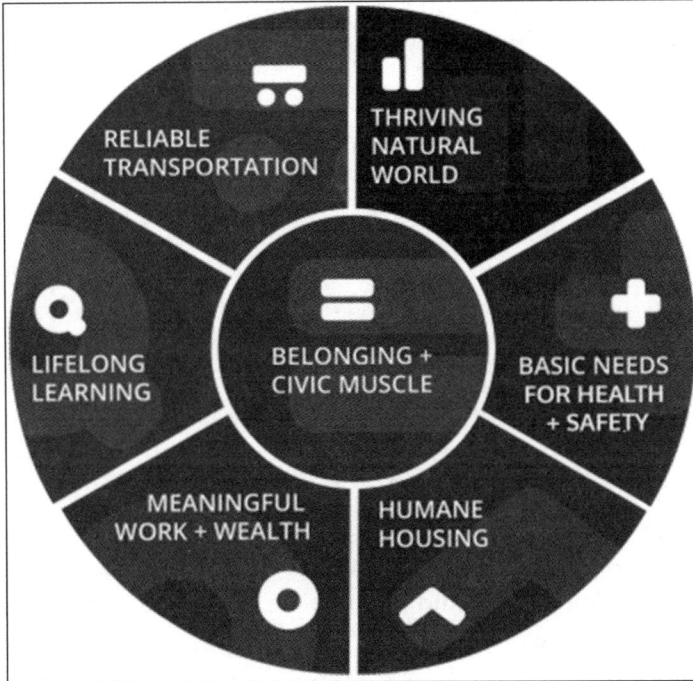

Figure 8.1. Components of belonging and civic muscle needed for health justice for children of color. Office of Disease Prevention and Health Promotion, "Framework," US Department of Health and Human Services, accessed January 10, 2024, https://health.gov.

overcrowding, conditions that made them more vulnerable to COVID-19 transmission and other health harms.[13]

As the country continues to recover from the pandemic and grapple with the health inequities that the pandemic laid bare, the US Department of Health and Human Services' Office of Disease Prevention and Health Promotion launched the *Federal Plan for Equitable Long-Term Recovery and Resilience for Social, Behavioral, and Community Health* to create a shared vision of "building community and individual resilience [that] recognizes the potential for federal partners to make significant changes to turn responses to tragedy into opportunities for renewal."[14] Twenty-eight federal departments, agencies, and institutions came together and published an interagency plan aimed at aligning federal actions to improve the seven "Vital Conditions for Health and Well-Being" over the next ten years and beyond.[15]

The *Federal Plan* selected the vital conditions framework, created by a cross-sector group of experts and community members, for its guiding principles for future investment and collaboration. The seven conditions that must be present for individuals and communities to thrive are (1) belonging and civic muscle, (2) thriving natural world, (3) basic needs for health and safety, (4) humane housing, (5) meaningful work and wealth, (6) lifelong learning, and (7) reliable transportation.[16]

This framework conceptualizes the conditions that allow people not just to experience the absence of disease or illness but to achieve holistic health and well-being and to thrive. By focusing on institutions and the structural mechanisms necessary for people to live healthy lives, it provides opportunities to analyze and address systemic inequities in health.[17] While "vital signs like heart rate, temperature, and weight tell us what is going in our body," the Vital Conditions for Health and Well-Being help us understand and evaluate the properties of places and institutions that shape the opportunities and exposures that allow people to thrive.[18] Current conditions are so entrenched because they are inherited from our predecessors and transmitted to future generations, perpetuating deep inequities and structural racism that continue to harm children of color generation after generation.[19]

Structural Inequities Keeping Children of Color from Thriving

This section examines the seven vital conditions and why they are essential to child health and well-being, as well as the stark interdisciplinary evidence that children of color are disproportionately and systematically deprived of these conditions, necessitating action to facilitate health justice.

Civic Muscle and Belonging

All people require "civic muscle and belonging," or fulfilling relationships and social supports, to lead healthy, thriving lives.[20] With social support from family and friends, including support in navigating challenges, together with a feeling of community belonging, people lead more resilient and fulfilling lives.[21] The US Surgeon General has argued that "civic muscle and belonging" are vital in and of themselves and as a component of the other six vital conditions because when people feel more connected, the other conditions become easier to attain.[22]

Both familial and community connections are especially vital to the health of children, who need a "sense of belonging" to feel safe and, beyond that, to thrive.[23] A lack of feeling of belonging is particularly harmful to children because it impacts their ability to form healthy relationships with caregivers and others, leading to inhibited adjustment and social development.[24] For example, children who are socially isolated have lower subsequent educational attainment, greater psychological distress, and higher risk of poor physical health in adulthood.[25]

Children removed from their families and communities by the family policing system (also known as the child welfare or family regulation system) and juvenile justice system are often isolated and deprived of the supports and connections they need to thrive, harming their sense of belonging.[26] Additionally, those children may face significant disruptions to schooling, experience disorientation as they adjust to new settings, and struggle with identity formation.[27]

Children seeking to maintain their culture and familial customs may be unable to do so in foster care, for example, leading to additional feelings of loss.[28] The American Academy of Pediatrics has identified that children in foster care have a higher prevalence of many health conditions when compared to any other group of children and are less likely to receive medical, dental, and optical care, vaccinations, and treatment for developmental needs.[29] Black children are 1.6 times more likely and Indigenous children are 2.8 times more likely than White children to enter foster care and experience the resulting health harms.[30]

Similarly, youth detention negatively impacts health, with youth involved in the juvenile justice system requiring ongoing clinical care for mental health disorders at a rate twice that of the general adolescent population and facing increased likelihood of depression, suicide, and self-harm, lower future earnings, and learning disabilities.[31] While Black youth do not engage in delinquent behavior at higher rates than White youth do, they are more likely to be arrested, detained, tried as adults, and confined in secure facilities and for longer periods—and to experience the associated health harms.[32]

A Thriving Natural World

A thriving natural world, including clean air, water, and land, as well as well-functioning ecosystems, homes, and communities free from hazards and pathogens, is vital for health.[33] Globally, one in four deaths of young children under five are attributable to environmental factors, such as air pollution, unsafe water, inadequate sanitation, and chemical exposure in both their homes and neighborhoods. Additionally, children are more easily exposed to and harmed by environmental contaminants because they breathe more air, drink more water, and eat more food per pound of body weight than adults do, their bodies are often less able to break down and get rid of harmful contaminants, and they have more time to develop health conditions caused by environmental exposure than do adults who are exposed later in life.[34]

Environmental conditions impacting children are particularly concerning in the United States, despite its many resources. Among thirty-nine peer countries, UNICEF found that the United States ranked twentieth for conditions affecting the world *of* the child (air pollution, water pollution, and lead poisoning) and twenty-eighth for conditions affecting the world *around* the child (overcrowding, urban green space, and road safety).[35]

Substandard housing quality in particular—including lead exposure, water leaks, poor ventilation, and infestation—contributes to poor child health, especially in early childhood, in light of the developmental process of immune development.[36] Mold, dampness, asbestos, pests, and overcrowding have been linked with increased risk of chronic illness, inadequate nutrition, greater emotional problems, and lower reading and math test scores, while insufficient ventilation, mold, and rodent and pest infestations in particular contribute to and exacerbate respiratory conditions like asthma.[37]

Residential lead hazards, such as peeling lead paint and lead in water, present a significant risk of cognitive and developmental delays.[38] Even low levels of lead exposure in children have been associated with cognitive delays, learning disabilities, hyperactivity, behavior problems, and later physical health problems, including hypertension, renal disease, reproductive problems, and developmental problems in offspring.[39]

Children of color disproportionately experience these types of housing hazards and are more often exposed to commercial hazardous waste facilities, which are frequently concentrated in communities of color and exact significant health harms.[40] One national survey found that 7.5 percent of non-Hispanic Black people lived in moderately substandard housing, compared with 2.8 percent of non-Hispanic White people, and substandard housing conditions in particular are more likely to impact extremely low-income renters, who are disproportionately Black, Indigenous, and Latino/a/x.[41] Additionally, studies have found that young Black children have higher rates of lead exposure than do young White children, and Black heads of households are more likely to have a child diagnosed with asthma than are White heads of households.[42]

Moreover, commercial hazardous waste facilities are disproportionately placed near communities of color, with Black families, in particular, experiencing higher health risks from exposure to air-particle pollution, including higher incidence of premature death in Black children and predispositions to heart attacks, stroke, impaired brain development, lung disease, and cancer.[43]

Basic Needs for Health and Safety

Basic needs for health and safety that are vital for optimal well-being include access to fresh and nutritious food, a life free from violence and toxic stress, and access to physical and mental health care, all of which affect health in childhood and have long-term impacts into adulthood.[44] Food insecurity is a powerful threat to health; it is associated with lower child health status, low birth weight, birth defects, more frequent colds and stomachaches, asthma, developmental risk, and mental health problems.[45] Children of color disproportionately experience food insecurity and these resulting health harms. In 2020, nearly one in three Black children and nearly one in four Latino/a/x children were in food-insecure households, meaning they struggled to afford and access healthy meals and were thus more likely to experience the related negative health effects.[46]

Exposure to unsafe and traumatic situations as a child also implicates health with ramifications into adulthood. Adverse childhood experiences (ACEs)—traumatic events such as abuse, neglect, witnessing domestic violence, or the death of a caregiver—have been shown by a robust body of research to undermine a child's sense of safety and stability, disrupt healthy brain development and social development, and have effects on lifelong health, including increased risk of diabetes, heart disease, cancer, and stroke.[47] As with food insecurity, ACEs and their associated health harms reflect racial disparities. Studies show that compared to White children, Black children are 45 percent more likely to experience one ACE, 29 percent more likely to experience two ACEs, and 21 percent more likely to experience three or more ACEs, making them more likely to experience the associated harms to their physical and mental health and development.[48]

Access to health care is critical to meeting children's basic health and safety needs. Uninsured children face barriers to accessing health care, with long-term consequences for health and development.[49] Conversely, children with health insurance are more likely to have a "medical home" where they routinely seek care and therefore access to vaccinations, preventive care, monitoring of developmental milestones, necessary prescriptions, and dental care.[50] While children of color constitute 50.5 percent of all children in the United States, they make up two-thirds of all uninsured children.[51]

Humane Housing

To thrive, individuals need "humane housing," or high-quality, affordable, and stable housing without health hazards. Housing access "can determine who thrives . . . and who struggles to survive" and has an impact on generations to come.[52]

To achieve good health and well-being, children require affordable, stable, and secure housing with adequate space.[53] Housing instability has been associated with negative child health outcomes such as developmental delays, depression, and even death.[54] Research has found that simply being behind on rent is linked to increased child hospitalizations and worse child health.[55] When children experience evictions, they are also more likely to experience poorer parent-reported child health, lower test scores, greater frequency of lead exposure, and higher rates of hospitalizations and developmental risk.[56]

Homelessness is also highly correlated with poor health in children. Studies show that infants born during a period of homelessness had lower birthweight and longer neonatal intensive care stays, while children of mothers who experienced homelessness during pregnancy or after birth had an increased risk of hospitalization and developmental delays.[57] Children who are unhoused have higher rates of immunization delay, severe hunger, and nutrition, developmental, and behavioral problems.[58]

Conversely, not only has home ownership "long been at the center of the American Dream," but it is also associated with positive child well-being, such as greater psychological health and better school performance, with studies also showing that improved self-esteem and reduced financial stress among parents may translate to improved developmental outcomes for children.[59]

However, children of color are disproportionately deprived of access to these positive health benefits, instead experiencing higher rates of housing insecurity, homelessness, and related health harms. Black renters make up only 18.6 percent of the renter population but 51.1 percent of those facing eviction filings and 43.4 percent of those evicted, and the risk of eviction is even higher for those with children, particularly Black women.[60] And in 2019, *more than half* of families who were unhoused were Black, and Black youth were 83 percent more likely than youth of other races to experience homelessness.[61] Additionally, racial disparities in income and wealth have similarly created racial inequities in home ownership.[62] In a similar vein, people of color disproportionately lack liquid financial assets, which are significant predictors of home ownership.[63]

The racial inequities evident in rates of housing instability and home ownership and their corresponding health effects have persisted due to racial discrimination and historical and ongoing racist housing policies such as "redlining" and exclusionary zoning practices, along with generational racial inequities in income and wealth.[64]

Meaningful Work and Wealth

Meaningful work and wealth includes personal, family, and community wealth; well-paying, fulfilling jobs and careers; and financial security.[65] This Vital Condition recognizes that poverty and financial insecurity impact health through toxic stress and poor health outcomes.[66]

For children, growing up in poverty affects physical and mental health and cognitive development and is associated with toxic stress, chronic illness, and nutritional deficits.[67] Children make up the largest age cohort of people experiencing poverty in the United States.[68]

A family's income and wealth influence a child's access to resources supporting health and well-being.[69] Families with higher incomes are more consistently able to access high-quality preventive health services, high-quality educational opportunities from early childhood through higher education, nutritious foods, and neighborhoods with less pollution and violence, all of which impact children's development.[70] Beyond impacting what a family is able to afford, a lack of family income and wealth can also influence a child's health through parental stress, mental wellness, and emotional resources, which can disrupt child development and negatively impact child health.[71] In contrast, stable employment enables families to ensure their children can access the resources needed to thrive.

Driven by historical and ongoing racial discrimination and structural racism, there are significant racial disparities in wealth, income, and unemployment.[72] Given the intergenerational nature of financial disadvantage, these gaps continue to grow.[73] White families continue to benefit from significantly higher median income and net worth in the United States.[74] For example, in 2019, the median income of White families with children ($95,700) was double that of Black ($43,900), Latino/a/x ($52,300), and Indigenous ($48,000) families with children, and the median net worth of White families ($188,200) was almost eight times more than Black families ($24,100) and five times more than Latino/a/x families ($36,100).[75] White family caregivers are also significantly more likely to have access to employment, with benefits to their children's health, than are caregivers in Black families and other families of color.[76]

Lifelong Learning

From early-childhood learning opportunities to meaningful careers, high-quality education and supportive learning environments that positively shape social development are necessary to young people's health and future success.[77] Education is not just an engine for social mobility but also an engine for lifelong health and well-being; whether a person graduates from high school is one of the greatest predictors of lifelong health and life expectancy.[78] Each stage of learning is both a building block for the next and critical to health in its own right. Conversely, gaps in access to education and educational attainment can persist across generations.[79]

Early childhood education (ECE) is especially impactful given the malleability of young children's developing brains.[80] ECE interventions improve social and cognitive development and educational outcomes and act as a protective factor against the future onset of disease and disability.[81] ECE can affect children's health directly through access to health screenings and improved nutrition and indirectly through increased school readiness, parental employment, and income—leading to improved health outcomes that carry into adulthood, such as improved cardiovascular and metabolic health.[82]

Families of color, particularly Latino/a/x and Indigenous families, are most likely to live in "child care deserts," or areas with little or no access to quality, licensed child care.[83] Studies also show that Black children are more likely to be enrolled in programs with lower ratings in child-to-adult ratio, emotional support, classroom organization, and instructional support.[84] By the beginning of kindergarten, Black children have fallen behind their White non-Hispanic peers, on average, by nearly nine months in math and seven months in reading.[85]

Academic attainment, positive school climate, and high-quality education in the K–12 years are also closely connected to health.[86] By age twenty-five, individuals with a high school degree are expected to live over ten years longer than those without.[87] Compared to graduates, students who do not graduate from high school are more likely to report suffering from at least one chronic health condition, such as asthma, diabetes, or heart disease.[88] Graduating from high school also lowers the risk of premature death.[89]

Racial disparities abound in high school graduation rates, with data from the 2018–19 schoolyear showing that, compared to 89 percent of White students, only 82 percent of Latino/a/x, 80 percent of Black, and 74 percent of American Indian/Alaska Native students attending public high schools graduate within four years of entering the ninth grade.[90] Children of color are also less likely to have access to high-quality K–12 education preparing them for successful graduation and careers and are more likely to attend underfunded K–12 schools with fewer high-quality teachers and curriculum resources, less student support, and larger class sizes.[91]

Academic attainment is also hindered by discriminatory school policing and exclusionary discipline, which push students into the school-
to-prison pipeline and harm students' health.[92] Black students and other
students of color are punished and policed at much-higher rates than
are their White peers throughout their education. In the 2021–22 school
year, despite representing only 8 percent of total K–12 student enrollment, Black boys made up 15 percent of students who received at least
one in-school suspension, 18 percent of students who received at least
one out-of-school suspension, and 18 percent of students who were expelled, and both Black and Indigenous students were disproportionately
referred to law enforcement or subjected to school-related arrests.[93] Research has also shown that Latino/a/x students are more likely to face
exclusionary discipline than White students are.[94]

Higher education is also connected to health outcomes.[95] College
completion correlates with lower prevalence of health conditions, like
heart disease and diabetes, and premature death.[96] Earning a bachelor's degree at any point in life has been correlated with better physical health.[97] Studies have also found that White and Asian American
students are far more likely to be enrolled in advanced college prepara-
tory tracks within their schools, while Black and Latino/a/x students are
disproportionately placed in noncollege tracks and have lower college
enrollment and graduation rates compared to White individuals, preventing them from reaping the associated health benefits.[98]

Reliable Transportation

Reliable transportation is not only a vital condition for health but a
bridge to the other six factors.[99] Reliable transportation allows children
to get to school, medical services, and green outdoor space and helps
parents get to work and grocery stores.[100] Lack of transportation can
serve as an economic barrier to health care, school, jobs, and healthy
food.[101] Conversely, reliable transportation can facilitate social mobility
and its resulting positive health outcomes and increase physical activity
with options like "walking, biking, and transit."[102]

Lack of transportation has been found to contribute to poorer health
outcomes, worsening of chronic illnesses, and higher health-care costs.[103]
People experiencing transportation barriers have less frequent doctors'

visits for routine care and for serious illnesses, more missed or rescheduled appointments, and more missed or delayed medication use.[104]

Moreover, lack of reliable transportation can have particularly cascading impacts on the health of children. Children with longer school commute times—disproportionately from low-income families and families of color, who often depend on public transit to get to school—get less sleep and exercise than do children with shorter school commute times.[105] Transportation barriers also impede children's access to health-care appointments.[106]

The prevailing transportation policy and funding schemes privilege drivers and car owners, in turn disadvantaging those who cannot drive or do not have access to a private vehicle.[107] This car-centric transportation landscape disproportionately harms Black households, particularly given that Black workers are up to six times less likely to own a car and four times more likely to rely on public transportation than are White workers, with significant impacts on parental and child well-being.[108] Lack of car ownership not only hinders parents' access to jobs but also hinders children's access to school and healthy food, especially as the placement of highways has displaced many families of color and created physical barriers between their neighborhoods and critical necessities.[109]

Responding to Tangled Threats to Health Injustice

Addressing the current racial disparities exposed by the seven Vital Conditions of Health and Well-Being and ensuring equity for children and families of color are critical to health justice. These vital conditions cannot be understood, analyzed, or addressed in isolation from each other.[110] Yet, "most of the research . . . available to decision makers . . . does not adequately account for the way that seemingly separate threats are, in fact, connected."[111]

Tangled Threats

For children of color, the vital conditions represent tangled threats of health injustice. In other words, while "each vital condition is distinct and indispensable, . . . they work together as a system to produce our legacies of health and well-being over time."[112]

Consider the story of six-year-old Erica, who lives in the majority-Black Ward 8 of Washington, DC, and the domino effects of the tangled threats to health and well-being that she has experienced.[113] A lead test in her pediatrician's office revealed that Erica had significantly elevated levels of lead in her blood, which could cause developmental delays and long-term brain damage impacting daily functioning and behaviors.[114] Erica's home had peeling paint, which was the source of her lead exposure, along with mold and other health hazards. Her mother could not afford better-quality housing, especially as she was having difficulty finding work and was falling behind on rent. The family had been erroneously terminated from the Supplemental Nutrition Assistance Program (SNAP) and Medicaid, resulting in food insecurity and difficulty accessing treatment for Erica's lead poisoning. Erica's family did not own a car, which was an added barrier to Erica's access to treatment.

Not receiving the special education services necessary to address the developmental delays resulting from her lead poisoning, Erica was struggling in school. As she got older, she faced suspensions, inhibiting her sense of belonging and pushing her into the school-to-prison pipeline. Lacking educational and social support, Erica increasingly avoided school and experienced isolation.

Erica and her family endured interconnected deprivations of their access to humane housing, a thriving natural world, meaningful work and wealth, basic needs for health and safety, reliable transportation, lifelong learning, and civic muscle and belonging. This intricate web of tangled threats systematically deprived Erica of the vital conditions she required not only to avoid disease and disability but to thrive.

As with Erica, for many children of color, deprivation exists not only *within* each of the vital conditions but also *across* multiple or even all seven conditions in interconnected ways, leading to enmeshed challenges and compounding, intersectional health harms. Such tangled threats represent entrenched structural problems that lead to interwoven and complex barriers to health. In other words, legal structures are root causes of the disproportionately harmful impacts of the social drivers of health on racially minoritized communities. The framing around tangled threats shifts the focus away from a destructive discourse blaming families for poor choices and misaligned priorities and instead recenters it on interconnected structures that drive racialized and intergenerational inequity that harms the health and well-being of children.[115]

Multisolving

Because of the interdependent structural nature of the vital conditions, they are most effectively addressed through cross-sector solutions that can have cascading positive impacts, or "multisolving." The concept of "multisolving" refers to the idea that "working across sectors to address multiple challenges with one policy or investment . . . accomplishes more [on] the same budget and aligns constituencies for greater impact," thus encouraging a variety of players "to step out of their silos of expertise."[116] Leveraging law, policy, and institutions to support multisolving approaches within any of the seven vital conditions will have positive domino effects.

If Erica's mother had access to well-paying employment and reliable transportation to get her to work, she would be more likely to generate income and accumulate wealth that would allow her to afford stable and safe housing, which, in turn, would reduce the likelihood of lead exposure and other health harms that result from substandard housing, as well as the anxiety, depression, and other mental health disorders that can arise from the stress of housing insecurity.[117]

In fact, the promotion of affordable, safe housing is also linked to access to lifelong learning and contact with a thriving natural world. When people can afford humane housing, their children are more likely to have upward economic mobility that allows them to move into neighborhoods with quality schools, health care, and grocery stores, as well as clean air and green space, the latter of which reaps myriad cascading health benefits.[118] Because families experiencing housing instability are more likely to be investigated by child protective services, increased affordable housing options can also reduce family policing system involvement and the resulting social exclusion.[119] Thus, leveraging legislative, executive, and judicial approaches to promote and safeguard affordable, safe housing represents multisolving that can create pathways for children of color to thrive by promoting myriad vital conditions for their health and well-being.

Such cross-sector, multisolving approaches are needed to improve outcomes in all seven categories. Multisolving will not only improve physical and mental health outcomes on the individual and community levels but also help to repair the multigenerational impacts of systemic harm that has disproportionately affected children, families, and communities of color.[120] The framing around vital conditions and the potential for "thriving," rather than health alone, has the additional effect of acknowledging that better health outcomes are not the ends in and of themselves but rather essential preconditions to fulfilling and prosperous lives.

Researchers have begun to study the opportunity that the seven vital conditions provide for multisolving. One study looked at tangled threats to health and well-being in large, urban counties and found that interventions targeted to reduce poverty and strengthen social support were most successful across the board. The study found that "regardless of county-to-county differences, interventions that expand meaningful work and wealth as well as belonging and civic muscle (thereby reducing poverty and strengthening social support) yield consistently better results than other interventions" and that "when looking over a longer 20-year time frame, youth education ranked among the highest contributors to multiple goals."[121]

Most approaches to health crises historically involved interventions, rather than preventive strategies.[122] As such, shifting to intentionally preventive multisolving approaches will be a challenge requiring significant political will. The *Federal Plan for Community Health* acknowledges that effectively and efficiently addressing future crises requires fundamentally changing the way resources have been invested and that "such a transformation requires interagency, multi-sectoral efforts that overtly address underlying and long-standing inequities in communities and in systems intended to support communities."[123] To that end, the *Federal Plan* includes "multisolver" recommendations specifically aimed at strengthening at least five vital conditions.[124]

The problems seem daunting, but this realignment of federal, state, and local investments in vital conditions for health can be cost-effective in the long-term. For example, supports for an individual experiencing chronic homelessness cost the public more than $35,000 per year, but investment in prevention services can reduce such costs by almost 50 percent.[125] Investments targeted at children have especially high returns. The Nobel laureate James Heckman and colleagues found that "every dollar invested in a high-quality, birth-to-5 years old program for children from families experiencing the most economic disadvantage resulted in $7.30 in benefits as children grew up healthier, were more likely to graduate high school and college, and earned more income as adults."[126]

Advancing racial equity has economic benefits for everyone, given findings that "closing racial gaps in wages, housing credit, lending opportunities, and access to higher education would amount to an additional $5 trillion in gross domestic product in the American economy over the next 5 years."[127] Such instrumental benefits strengthen the case for collaborative multisolving efforts to close existing gaps within the vital conditions.

To advance health justice for children of color, policy makers must acknowledge the interconnected nature of systems rooted in structural racism and White supremacy and the resulting tangled threats to health and well-being for children of color. A menu of discrete interventions is inadequate and falls short of the necessary multisolving: "When beset by multiple threats, decision makers face a crucial strategic choice: They either may confront each problem individually as it commands attention . . . or they may view the whole constellation of threats collectively as a matter of system design and then craft a strategy to transform that system in ways that better safeguard the population. . . . Leaders must work together as *stewards of a common system* and then build a portfolio of effective interventions . . . that can be enacted in their local context to achieve both short-term and long-term improvement."[128] To attain health justice, policy makers should act as "stewards of a common system," a system developed and led by families of color who are impacted by the health inequities.

Building Community Power to Multisolve

Health justice requires promoting the power of affected communities to lead both the development and implementation of multisolving reforms. For example, youth and parents of color are working toward increased access to culturally responsive school-based mental health services and police-free schools that can help support lifelong learning and open up opportunities for meaningful work and wealth.[129] Parents of color have also long been organizing for reform—and abolition—of the family policing system, which often disrupts a child's sense of belonging, with cascading effects on the other vital conditions.[130] Effectuating such changes requires acknowledging both youth and parents as "experts on what they need" and viewing them as "leaders of policy change" who should have the power to identify the tangled threats that are most harmful to them and have opportunities for multisolving in their own lives and communities.[131] To advance health justice, "shifting power to affected communities is a critical component to beginning to remedy the harms of long-standing disinvestment, discrimination, and disenfranchisement in frontline communities."[132]

Legislative-, executive-, and judicial-branch priorities need to be driven by goals identified by local communities for successful multisolving.[133] Maximizing the impact of the health justice framework for historically marginalized populations requires supporting these communities as they guide its goals and implementation, which should center their own ideas, lived experiences, visions, and goals.[134] Community-based participatory research and community-led policy making can provide structures for bringing community leadership into health interventions and policy reforms across systems. By involving parents who have been harmed by the family policing system to envision an alternative system of supports, for example, Rise and TakeRoot Justice, in developing an agenda for reforms, wielded community participatory research methods to support people who have experienced systemic harm.[135]

Research and policy-making efforts must be coupled with support for the power of movements for health justice that are working toward abolition and dismantling of subordinating systems.[136] Health justice necessitates such power building to ensure that the interconnected vital conditions for health and well-being are robust for children of color and their communities.

NOTES

1 Nambi Ndugga, Latoya Hill, and Samantha Artiga, "Key Data on Health and Health Care by Race and Ethnicity," Kaiser Family Foundation, June 11, 2024, www.kff.org.

2 Centers for Disease Control and Prevention, "Most Recent National Asthma Data," accessed April 16, 2025, www.cdc.gov.

3 Bobby Milstein, Becky Payne, Christopher Kelleher, Jack Homer, Tyler Norris, Monte Roulier, and Somava Saha, "Organizing Around Vital Conditions Moves

the Social Determinants Agenda into Wider Action," *Health Affairs Forefront*, February 2, 2023, https://doi.org/10.1377/forefront.20230131.673841.

4 Sanne Magnan, "Social Determinants of Health 101 for Health Care: Five Plus Five," National Academy of Medicine, October 9, 2017, https://nam.edu; Richard Wilkinson and Michael Marmot, introduction to *Social Determinants of Health: The Solid Facts*, ed. Richard Wilkinson and Michael Marmot (World Health Organization, 2003), 7; Daniel Dawes, *The Political Determinants of Health* (Johns Hopkins University Press, 2020).

5 Anuli Njoku, Marian Evans, Lillian Nimo-Sefah, and Jonell Bailey, "Listen to the Whispers Before They Become Screams: Addressing Black Maternal Morbidity and Mortality in the United States," *Healthcare* 11, no. 3 (2023): 483, https://doi.org/10.3390/healthcare11030438.

6 Lindsay F. Wiley, Ruqaiijah Yearby, Brietta R. Clark, and Seema Mohapatra, "Introduction: What Is Health Justice?," *Journal of Law, Medicine and Ethics* 50, no. 4 (2022): 636–37, https://doi.org/10.1017/jme.2023.2.

7 Ruqaiijah Yearby, "Structural Racism and Health Disparities: Reconfiguring the Social Determinants of Health Framework to Include the Root Cause," *Journal of Law, Medicine and Ethics* 48, no. 3 (2020): 518–26, https://doi.org/10.1177/1073110520958876.

8 Sheila Foster, Yael Cannon, and M. Gregg Bloche, "Health Justice Is Racial Justice: A Legal Action Agenda for Health Disparities," *Health Affairs Forefront*, July 2020, https://doi.org/10.1377/forefront.20200701.242395.

9 Chandra Ford and Collins O. Airhihenbuwa, "Critical Race Theory, Race Equity, and Public Health: Toward Antiracism Praxis," *American Journal of Public Health* 100, Suppl. 1 (April 2010): S30–35, https://doi.org/10.2105/AJPH.2009.171058. The author of this chapter has chosen to capitalize "White." Various periodicals and journals do not capitalize "white" out of concern that they may legitimize the beliefs of White supremacists. David Bauder, "AP Says It Will Capitalize Black but Not White," AP, July 20, 2020, https://apnews.com/ ("'We agree that white people's skin color plays into systemic inequalities and injustices, and we want our journalism to robustly explore these problems,' John Daniszewski, the AP's vice president for standards, said in a memo to staff Monday. 'But capitalizing the term white, as is done by white supremacists, risks subtly conveying legitimacy to such beliefs.'"). While those concerns may be legitimate, this chapter capitalizes "White" because not doing so, despite capitalizing "Black," risks implying that Whiteness is the standard or norm. Ann Thuy Nguyen and Maya Pendleton, "Recognizing Race in Language: Why We Capitalize 'Black' and 'White,'" Center for the Study of Social Policy, March 23, 2020 ("We believe that it is important to call attention to White as a race as a way to understand and give voice to how Whiteness functions in our social and political institutions and our communities."); Matiangai Sirleaf, "Rendering Whiteness Visible," *American Journal of International Law* 117 (2023): 2024, 2026 (arguing that capitalizing White does not ignore racism's complex roots

but rather encourages deep reflection on such history and that "the move to capitalize White challenges global conventions informed by anti-Blackness and White supremacy that seek to race certain groups of people and leave Whiteness untouched.").

10 Nambi Ndugga and Samantha Artiga, "Disparities in Health and Health Care: 5 Key Questions and Answers," KFF, May 11, 2021, www.kff.org.

11 Neil Halfon and Miles Hochstein, "Life Course Health Development: An Integrated Framework for Developing Health, Policy, and Research," *Milbank Quarterly* 80, no. 3 (2002): 433–79, https://doi.org/10.1111/1468-0009.00019.

12 Foster et al., "Health Justice."

13 Foster et al., "Health Justice."

14 Office of Disease Prevention and Health Promotion, *Federal Plan for Equitable Long-Term Recovery and Resilience for Social, Behavioral, and Community Health* (US Department of Health and Human Services, January 20, 2022), 21, https://health.gov.

15 Office of Disease Prevention and Health Promotion, *Federal Plan*, 8, 20.

16 Office of Disease Prevention and Health Promotion, *Federal Plan*, 10; Milstein et al., "Organizing Around Vital Conditions."

17 National Center for Chronic Disease Prevention and Health Promotion, Office on Smoking and Health, *Community Health and Economic Prosperity: Engaging Businesses as Stewards and Stakeholders—A Report of the Surgeon General* (US Department of Health and Human Services, January 2021), 85–108, www.hhs.gov.

18 Well Being Trust, *Vital Conditions Primers* (July 16, 2018), 2.

19 Well Being Trust, *Vital Condition Primers*.

20 Thriving Together, North Central Washington, "Belonging and Civic Muscle," accessed December 21, 2023, www.thrivingtogether.org; Win Network, "Vital Conditions," accessed February 13, 2022, https://winnetwork.org/vital-conditions.

21 Thriving Together, "Belonging and Civic Muscle."

22 National Center for Chronic Disease Prevention and Health Promotion, *Community Health*, 13–15.

23 Community Commons, "Belonging and Civic Muscle as a Vital Condition," accessed April 16, 2025, https://communitycommons.org; Child Welfare Information Gateway, *Belonging Matters—Helping Youth Explore Permanency* (September 2019), 2, www.childwelfare.gov.

24 Harriet Over, "The Origins of Belonging: Social Motivation in Infants and Young Children," *Philosophical Transactions of the Royal Society of London. Series B, Biological Sciences* 371, no. 1686 (January 19, 2016): 4, https://doi.org/10.1098/rstb.2015.0072.

25 Rebecca E. Lacey, Meena Kumari, and Mel Bartley, "Social Isolation in Childhood and Adult Inflammation: Evidence from the National Child Development Study," *Psychoneuroendocrinology* 50 (August 2014): 91, https://doi.org/10.1016/j.psyneuen.2014.08.007; Avshalom Caspi, HonaLee Harrington, and Terrie E. Moffitt, "Socially Isolated Children 20 Years Later: Risk of Cardiovascular Disease,"

Archives of Pediatrics and Adolescent Medicine 160, no. 8 (2006): 805, https://doi.org/10.1001/archpedi.160.8.805.

26 Child Welfare Information Gateway, *Belonging Matters*, 2; Community Commons, "Belonging and Civic Muscle."

27 Hannah Lantos, Tiffany Allen, Fadumo M. Abdi, Felipe Franco, Kristin Anderson Moore, and Jasmine Snell, "Integrating Positive Youth Development and Racial Equity, Inclusion, and Belonging Approaches Across the Child Welfare and Justice Systems," *Child Trends*, January 25, 2022, www.childtrends.org.

28 Shanta Trivedi, "The Harm of Child Removal," *N.Y.U. Review of Law and Social Change* 43 (2019): 540.

29 Trivedi, "Harm of Child Removal," 546–48.

30 Jerry Milner and David Kelly, "The Need for Justice in Child Welfare," *Child Welfare Journal: Poverty, Race, and Child Welfare* 99, nos. 3–4 (2021).

31 Barry Holman and Jason Ziedenberg, *The Dangers of Detention: The Impact of Incarcerating Youth in Detention and Other Secure Facilities* (Justice Policy Institute, November 28, 2006), 2–3, 8, https://justicepolicy.org.

32 Holman and Ziedenberg, *Dangers of Detention*, 3; Patricia Soung, "Social and Biological Constructions of Youth: Implications for Juvenile Justice and Racial Equity," *Northwestern Journal of Law and Social Policy* 6 (2010): 436; Kele M. Stewart, "Re-envisioning Child Well-Being: Dismantling the Inequitable Intersections Among Child Welfare, Juvenile Justice, and Education," *Columbia Journal of Race and Law* 12, no. 1 (July 2022): 644.

33 Bobby Milstein, Monte Roulier, Christopher Kelleher, Elizabeth Hartig, and Stacy Wegley, eds., *Thriving Together: A Springboard for Equitable Recovery and Resilience in Communities Across America* (CDC Foundation and Well Being Trust, July 4, 2020), 13, https://thriving.us.

34 CDC, "Environmental Health Tracking: Children's Environmental Health," accessed April 23, 2025, www.cdc.gov; "No Child Health Without Planetary Health," *The Lancet Child and Adolescent Health* 6 (June 30, 2022): 509, https://doi.org/10.1016/S2352-4642(22)00199-7.

35 Eszter Timar, Anna Gromada, Gwyther Rees, and Alessandro Carraro, *Places and Spaces: Environments and Children's Well-Being* (UNICEF Office of Research-Innocenti, 2022), 12–14, www.unicef-irc.org.

36 Lauren A. Taylor, "Housing and Health: An Overview of the Literature," *Health Affairs Health Policy Brief*, June 7, 2018, https://doi.org/10.1377/hpb20180313.396577; Allyson E. Gold, "No Home for Justice: How Eviction Perpetuates Health Inequity Among Low-Income and Minority Tenants," *Georgetown Journal on Poverty Law and Policy* 24 (2016): 70.

37 James Krieger and Donna L. Higgins, "Housing and Health: Time Again for Public Health Action," *American Journal of Public Health* 92, no. 5 (2002): 758–59; Rebekah Levine Coley, Tama Leventhal, Alicia Doyle Lynch, and Melissa Kull, *Poor Quality Housing Is Tied to Children's Emotional and Behavioral Problems* (MacArthur Foundation, September 2013), 2, www.macfound.org.

38 Emily A. Benfer, "Health Justice: A Framework (and Call to Action) for the Elimi-nation of Health Inequity and Social Justice," *American University Law Review* 65 (2015): 294–95.

39 Nick Farr and Cushing N. Dolbeare, "Childhood Lead Poisoning: Solving a Health and Housing Problem," *Cityscape: A Journal of Policy and Development Research* 2, no. 3 (September 1996): 167; CDC Agency for Toxic Substances and Disease Registry, "Lead Toxicity," accessed April 16, 2025, www.atsdr.cdc.gov.

40 Philip J. Landrigan, Virginia A. Rauh, and Maida P. Galvez, "Environmental Justice and the Health of Children," *Mount Sinai Journal of Medicine* 77 (2010): 178–82, https://doi.org/10.1002/msj.20173.

41 David E. Jacobs, "Environmental Health Disparities in Housing," *American Journal of Public Health* 101 (2011): S116; Office of Disease Prevention and Health Promo-tion, "Quality of Housing," Healthy People 2030, accessed December 18, 2023, https://health.gov; Andrew Aurano, Dan Emmanuel, Emma Foley, Matt Clarke, Ikra Rafi, and Diane Yentel, *The Gap: A Shortage of Affordable Homes* (National Low In-come Housing Coalition, March 2023), 1. The author has chosen to use "Latino/a/x" for the purpose of gender inclusivity, rather than simply "Latinx," which has been criticized by some in the community it intends to describe. Evan Odegard Pereira, "For Most Latinos, Latinx Does Not Mark the Spot," *New York Times*, June 15, 2021; Ana Maria del Rio-Gonzalez, "To Latinx or Not to Latinx: A Question of Gender Inclusivity Versus Gender Neutrality," *American Journal of Public Health* 111, no. 6 (2021): 1018–21, https://doi.org/10.2105/AJPH.2021.306238. However, the chapter uses "Hispanic" when this term is used in the underlying data.

42 Simisola O. Teye, Jeff D. Yanosky, Yendelela Cuffee, Xingran Weng, Raffy Luquis, Elana Farace, and Li Wang, "Exploring Persistent Racial/Ethnic Disparities in Lead Exposure Among America Children Aged 1–5 Years: Results from NHANES 1999–2016," *International Archives of Occupational and Environmental Health* 94 (2021): 723–24, https://doi.org/10.1007/s00420-020-01616-4; Helen K. Hughes, Elizabeth C. Matsui, Megan M. Tschudy, Craig E. Pollack, and Corinne A. Keet, "Pediatric Asthma Health Disparities: Race, Hardship, Housing, and Asthma in a National Survey," *Academic Pediatrics* 17 (2017): 131, https://doi.org/10.1016/j.acap.2016.11.011.

43 Jacqui Patterson and Nsedu Obot Witherspoon, *The Racism That Upends the Cradle: Black Children Caught in the Syndemic Crosshairs* (Chisholm Legacy Project and Children's Environmental Health Network, June 28, 2022), 10–11, 14, https://thechisholmlegacyproject.org.

44 Milstein et al., *Thriving Together*; Food Research and Action Center, *The Role of the Supplemental Nutrition Assistance Program in Improving Health and Well-Being* (December 2017), 3–9; Debra E. Houry and James A. Mercy, *Adverse Childhood Experiences (ACEs) Prevention Resource for Action: A Compilation of the Best Available Evidence* (Center for Disease Control and Prevention, 2019), 2–5, https://cdc.gov; David Murphey, "Health Insurance Coverage Improves Child Well-Being," *Child Trends*, May 12, 2017, www.childtrends.org.

45 Food Research and Action Center, *Role*, 3.
46 Alisha Coleman-Jensen, Matthew P. Rabbitt, Christian A. Gregory, and Anita Singh, *Statistical Supplement to Household Food Security in the United States in 2020*, APO-91 (US Department of Agriculture Economic Research Service, September 2021), 6, www.ers.usda.gov.
47 Houry and Mercy, *Adverse Childhood Experiences*, 7.
48 Patterson and Witherspoon, *Racism That Upends the Cradle*, 15.
49 Elizabeth Williams and Rachel Garfield, "How Could the Build Back Better Act Affect Uninsured Children?," Kaiser Family Foundation, November 11, 2021, www.kff.org.
50 Committee on Health Insurance Status and Its Consequences, *America's Uninsured Crisis: Consequences for Health and Health Care* (National Academies Press, 2009), 58, 116.
51 Williams and Garfield, "How Could the Build Back Better Act."
52 Community Commons, "Humane Housing as a Vital Condition," accessed December 21, 2023, https://communitycommons.org.
53 Milstein et al., *Thriving Together*, 32.
54 Taylor, "Housing and Health"; Ericka Petersen, "Building a House for Gideon: The Right to Counsel in Evictions," *Stanford Journal of Civil Rights & Civil Liberties* 16 (2020): 69.
55 Petersen, "Building a House."
56 Bruce Ramphal, Ryan Keen, Sakurako S. Okuzuno, Dennis Ojogho, and Natalie Slopen, "Evictions and Infant and Child Health Outcomes A Systematic Review," *JAMA Network Open* 6, no. 4 (April 2023): 8, https://doi.org/10.1001/jamanetworkopen.2023.7612.
57 Robin E. Clark, Linda Weinreb, Julie M. Flahive, and Robert W. Seifert, "Infants Exposed to Homelessness: Health, Health Care Use, and Health Spending from Birth to Age Six," *Health Affairs* 38, no. 5 (May 2019): 721, https://doi.org/10.1377/hlthaff.2019.00090; Megan Sandel, Richard Sheward, and Lisa Sturtevant, "Compounding Stress: The Timing and Duration Effects of Homelessness on Children's Health," *Insights from Housing Policy Research* 2 (June 12, 2015), https://childrenshealthwatch.org.
58 Roy Grant, Delaney Gracy, Grifin Goldsmith, Alan Shapiro, and Irwin E. Redlener, "Twenty-Five Years of Child and Family Homelessness: Where Are We Now?," *American Journal of Public Health* 103 (December 2013), https://doi.org/10.2105/AJPH.2013.301618.
59 Brian Rahmer, Mary Ayala, and Patrick Jordan, "Humane Housing: Place-Based Resiliency and Equitable Recovery" (Human Housing Deep Dive, June 2020), https://thriving.us; William M. Robe and Mark Lindblad, "Reexamining the Social Benefits of Homeownership After the Housing Crisis" (Joint Center for Housing Studies, Harvard University, August 2013), 27, www.jchs.harvard.edu.
60 Nick Graetz, Carl Gershenson, Peter Hepburn, Sonya R. Porter, Danielle H. Sandler, and Matthew Desmond, "A Comprehensive Demographic Profile of

the US Evicted Population," *PNAS* 120, no. 41 (October 2, 2023): 1, 3, https://doi.org/10.1073/pnas.2305860120.

61 Meghan Henry, Rian Watt, Anna Mahathey, Jillian Ouellette, and Aubrey Sitler, *The 2019 Annual Homeless Assessment Report (AHAR) to Congress* (Office of Community Planning and Development, US Department of Housing and Urban Development, January 2020), 9, www.huduser.gov; Chapin Hall and Voices of Youth Count, *Missed Opportunities: Youth Homelessness in America* (Chapin Hall, October 2017), 12, https://voicesofyouthcount.org.

62 Dedrick Asante-Muhammed, Chuck Collins, Josh Hoxie, and Emanuel Nieves, *The Ever-Growing Gap: Without Change, African-American and Latino Families Won't Match White Wealth for Centuries* (Institute for Policy Studies, August 2016), 7–8, https://ips-dc.org.

63 Christopher E. Herbert and Winnie Tsen, *The Potential of Downpayment Assistance for Increasing Homeownership among Minority and Low-Income Households* (US Department of Housing and Urban Development, January 2005), vi.

64 Jeramy Townsley and Unai Miguel Andres, "The Lasting Impacts of Segregation and Redlining," SAVI, June 24, 2021, www.savi.org; Asante-Muhammed et al., *Ever-Growing Gap*, 7–8.

65 Milstein et al., *Thriving Together*, 36.

66 Milstein et al., *Thriving Together*, 36.

67 Annie E. Casey Foundation, "Child Poverty in America More Than Doubled in 2022," updated September 29, 2023, www.aecf.org; Office of Disease Prevention and Health Promotion, "Poverty," Healthy People 2030, accessed December 20, 2023, https://health.gov.

68 Office of Disease Prevention and Health Promotion, "Poverty."

69 Joan Alker and Alexandrea Corcoran, *Children's Uninsured Rate Rises by Largest Annual Jump in More than a Decade* (Georgetown University Health Policy Institute Center for Children and Families, October 2020), 10, https://ccf.georgetown.edu; Vanessa Wight, Neeraj Kaushal, Jane Waldfogel, and Irv Garfinkel, "Understanding the Link between Poverty and Food Insecurity Among Children: Does the Definition of Poverty Matter?," *Journal of Child Poverty* 20, no. 1 (January 2014): 8–10, https://doi.org/10.1080/10796126.2014.891973; Milstein et al., *Thriving Together*, 36.

70 Elizabeth R. Wolf, Camille J. Hochheimer, Roy T. Sabo, Jennifer DeVoe, Richard Wasserman, and Erik Geissal, "Gaps in Well-Child Care Attendance Among Primary Care Clinics Serving Low-Income Families," *Pediatrics* 142 (2018): 1, 2, https://doi.org/10.1542/peds.2017-4019; W. Steven Barnett and Donald J. Yarosz, "Who Goes to Preschool and Why Does It Matter?," (Preschool Policy Brief, National Institute for Early Education Research, November 1, 2007), 7, https://nieer.org; Josh Kinsler and Ronni Pavan, "Family Income and Higher Education Choices: The Importance of Accounting for College Quality," *Journal of Human Capital* 5, no. 4 (2011): 469–76; Wight et al., "Understanding the Link," 8–10; Landrigan et al., "Environmental Justice," 182; Ashli J. Sheidow, Deborah Gorman-Smith, Patrick H. Tolan, and David B. Henry, "Family and Community Charac-

teristics: Risk Factors for Violence Exposure in Inner-City Youth," *Journal of Community Psychology* 29, no. 3 (2001): 346–48; Greg J. Duncan, Katherine Magnuson, and Elizabeth Votruba-Drzal, "Moving Beyond Correlations in Assessing the Consequences of Poverty," *Annual Review of Psychology* 68 (2017): 419–21.

71 Kelsey Allard Crowder, "The Effects of the Family Stress Model on Child Mental Health" (Iowa State University, Theses and Dissertations, 2013), 1, 5–7, 8–9, 10–12, https://dr.lib.iastate.edu.

72 US Bureau of Labor Statistics, "Labor Force Characteristics by Race and Ethnicity 2022," (BLS Reports, November 2023), www.bls.gov.

73 Dorothy Brown, *The Whiteness of Wealth: How the Tax System Impoverishes Black Americans—and How We Can Fix It* (Crown, 2021).

74 Neil Bhutta, Andrew C. Chang, Lisa J. Dettling, and Joanne W. Hsu, "Disparities in Wealth by Race and Ethnicity in the 2019 Survey of Consumer Finances," Board of Governors of the Federal Reserve System, September 28, 2020, www.federalreserve.gov.

75 Annie E. Casey Foundation, "Median Family Income Among Households with Children by Race and Ethnicity in the United States," Kids Count Data Center, updated December 2020, https://datacenter.aecf.org; Bhutta et al., "Disparities in Wealth."

76 Christian E. Weller and Lily Roberts, *Eliminating the Black-White Wealth Gap is a Generational Challenge* (Center for American Progress, March 19, 2021), 1, 2–5, https://americanprogress.org.

77 Milstein et al., *Thriving Together*, 40–47.

78 Community Commons, "Lifelong Learning as a Vital Condition," accessed December 21, 2023, www.communitycommons.org; Thalia González, Alexis Etow, and Cesar De La Vega, "An Antiracist Health Equity Agenda for Education," *Journal of Law, Medicine and Ethics* 50 (2022): 33.

79 Community Commons, "Lifelong Learning."

80 Thriving Together, "Lifelong Learning: Cradle to Career," accessed December 21, 2023, https://thriving.us.

81 Robert A. Hahn, W. Steven Barnett, John A. Knopf, Benedict I. Truman, Robert L. Johnson, and Jonathan E. Fielding, "Early Childhood Education to Promote Health Equity: A Community Guide Systematic Review," *Journal of Public Health Management and Practice* 22, no. 5 (2016): E4–E6, https://doi.org/10.1097/PHH.000000000000378; Neal Halfon and Miles Hochstein, "Life Course Health Development: An Integrated Framework for Developing Health, Policy, and Research," *Milbank Quarterly* 80, no. 3 (2002): 451, https://doi.org/10.1111/1468-0009.00019.

82 Taryn Morrissey, "The Effects of Early Care and Education on Children's Health," *Health Affairs*, April 25, 2019, 4–5, https://doi.org/10.1377/hpb20190325.519221.

83 Rasheed Malik, Katie Hamm, and Leila Schochet, *America's Child Care Deserts in 2018* (Center for American Progress, December 6, 2018), 3, 11, https://americanprogress.org.

84 Daphna Bassok and Eva Galdo, "Inequality in Preschool Quality? Community-Level Disparities in Access to High-Quality Learning Environments," *Early*

Education and Development, 27, no. 1 (2016): 136–37, https://doi.org/10.1080/10409 289.2015.1057463.

85 Allison Friedman-Krauss and W. Steven Barnett, *Access to High-Quality Early Education and Racial Equity* (National Institute for Early Education Research, June 16, 2020), 1, https://nieer.org.

86 Community Commons, "Lifelong Learning."

87 González et al., "Antiracist Health Equity Agenda," 33.

88 Office of Disease Prevention and Health Promotion, "High School Graduation," Healthy People 2030, accessed December 22, 2023, https://health.gov.

89 Office of Disease Prevention and Health Promotion, "High School Graduation."

90 Office of Disease Prevention and Health Promotion, "High School Graduation."

91 Children's Defense Fund, *The State of America's Children 2021* (2021), 26, https:// childrensdefense.org.

92 González et al., "Antiracist Health Equity Agenda," 33; Andrew Bacher-Hicks, David J. Deming, and Stephen B. Billings, "Proving the School-to-Prison Pipeline: Strict Middle Schools Raise the Risk of Adult Arrest," *Education Next* 21, no. 4 (2021): 52, 54–57.

93 Office for Civil Rights, *Student Discipline and School Climate in U.S. Public Schools* (US Department of Education, November 2023), 7, 10, www2.ed.gov; Juan Del Toro and Ming-Te Wang, "The Roles of Suspensions for Minor Infractions and School Climate in Predicting Academic Performance Among Adolescents," *American Psychologist* 77, no. 2 (September 2021): 179, https://doi.org/10.1037/ amp0000854.

94 Nicholas A. Gage, Antonis Katsiyannis, Kelly M. Carrero, Rhonda Miller, and Danielle Pico, "Exploring Disproportionate Discipline for Latinx Students With and Without Disabilities: A National Analysis," *Behavioral Disorders* 47, no. 1 (2021): 9, https://doi.org/10.1177/0198742920961356.

95 Community Commons, "Lifelong Learning"; Office of Disease Prevention and Health Promotion, "Enrollment in Higher Education," Healthy People 2030, accessed December 22, 2023, https://health.gov.

96 Office of Disease Prevention and Health Promotion, "Enrollment in Higher Education."

97 Office of Disease Prevention and Health Promotion, "Enrollment in Higher Education."

98 Todd McCardle, "A Critical Historical Examination of Tracking as a Method for Maintaining Racial Segregation," *Educational Considerations* 45, no. 2 (March 2020): 12, https://doi.org/10.4148/0146–9282.2186; Jeannie Oakes, *Keeping Track: How Schools Structure Inequality*, 2nd ed. (Yale University Press, 2005), 230; Patterson and Witherspoon, *Racism That Upends the Cradle*, 8; Office of Disease Prevention and Health Promotion, "Enrollment in Higher Education."

99 Community Commons, "Reliable Transportation as a Vital Condition," accessed December 21, 2023, www.communitycommons.org.

100 Community Commons, "Reliable Transportation."

101 Milstein et al., *Thriving Together*, 48–51.

102 Milstein et al., *Thriving Together*, 48.

103 Richard Wallace, Paul Hughes-Cromwick, Hillary Mull, and Snehamay Khasnabis, "Access to Health Care and Nonemergency Medical Transportation: Two Missing Links," *Transportation Research Record* 1924, no. 1 (2005): 80, 82, https://doi.org/10.1177/0361198105192400110.

104 Wallace et al., "Access to Health Care"; Samina T. Syed, Ben S. Gerber, and Lisa K. Sharp, "Traveling Towards Disease: Transportation Barriers to Health," *Journal of Community Health* 38, no. 5 (December 2013): 980, https://doi.org/10.1007/s10900-013-9681-1.

105 Brendan Chen, "How Students' Transportation Options—or Lack Thereof—Affect Educational and Health Outcomes," Housing Matters, Urban Institute, April 26, 2023, https://housingmatters.urban.org.

106 Roy Grant, Delaney Gracy, Grifin Goldsmith, Morissa Sobelson, and Dennis Johnson, "Transportation Barriers to Child Health Care Access Remain After Health Reform," *JAMA Pediatrics* 168, no. 4 (April 2014): 385–386, https://doi.org/10.1001/jamapediatrics.2013.4653.

107 Community Commons, "Reliable Transportation."

108 Michael Swistara, "A Fare Share: A Proposed Solution to Address the Racial Disparity in Access to Public Transportation Funding in America," *Michigan Journal of Race and Law* 26 (2021): 523, https://doi.org/10.36643/mjrl.26.2.fare.

109 Regan F. Patterson, *New Routes to Equity: The Future of Transportation in the Black Community* (Congressional Black Caucus Foundation, September 2020), 8, www.cbcfinc.org; Anthony Foxx et al., *Beyond Traffic 2045* (2017), 95, www.transportation.gov.

110 Milstein et al., "Organizing Around Vital Conditions."

111 Bobby Millstein and Jack Homer, "Which Priorities for Health and Well-Being Stand Out After Accounting for Tangled Threats and Costs? Simulating Potential Intervention Portfolios in Large Urban Counties," *Milbank Quarterly* 98, no. 2 (June 2020): 385, 391, https://doi.org/10.1111/1468-0009.12448.

112 Well Being Trust, *Vital Conditions Primers*, 2.

113 This story is based on a family with whom the author's medical-legal partnership collaborated. The child's name and some details have been changed to protect the family's identity.

114 Benfer, "Health Justice," 293–95.

115 Nicholas Kristof, "We Are a Nation of Child Abusers," *New York Times*, February 3, 2021.

116 Community Commons, "Multisolving 101: Co-Creating Vital Conditions for Thriving Together," accessed December 20, 2023, www.communitycommons.org.

117 Office of Disease Prevention and Health Promotion, "Quality of Housing"; Maya Brownstein, "Childhood Housing Insecurity Linked to Short- and Long-Term Anxiety and Depression," Harvard T. H. School of Public Health, July 12, 2023, www.hsph.harvard.edu.

118 Kriti Ramakrishnan, Elizabeth Champion, Megan Gallagher, and Keith Fudge, *Why Housing Matters for Upward Mobility* (Urban Institute, January 2021), 1, https://urban.org; Areeba Haider, *Basic Facts About Children in Poverty* (Center for American Progress, January 12, 2021), www.americanprogress.org; Suchitra Sugar, "The Necessity of Urban Green Space for Children's Optimal Development," UNICEF, July 26, 2021, www.unicef.org.

119 Hina Haveed, *"If I Wasn't Poor, I Wouldn't Be Unfit": The Family Separation Crisis in the US Child Welfare System* (Human Rights Watch, November 17, 2022), 92, www.hrw.org; JoAnn S. Lee and Jessie Patton, "The Social Exclusion of Dually-Involved Youth: Toward a Sense of Belonging," *Journal of Sociology & Social Welfare* 44, no. 1 (March 2017): 58–59, https://doi.org/10.15453/0191-5096.3856.

120 Milstein et al., "Organizing Around Vital Conditions."

121 Milstein and Homer, "Which Priorities for Health," 394.

122 Office of Disease Prevention and Health Promotion, *Federal Plan*, 19.

123 Office of Disease Prevention and Health Promotion, *Federal Plan*, 41.

124 Office of Disease Prevention and Health Promotion, *Federal Plan*, 41.

125 Office of Disease Prevention and Health Promotion, *Federal Plan*, 135; National Alliance to End Homelessness, "Ending Chronic Homelessness Saves Taxpayers Money," February 17, 2017, 1, https://endhomelessness.org.

126 Office of Disease Prevention and Health Promotion, *Federal Plan*, 187; Jorge Luis García, James J. Heckman, Duncan Ermini Leaf, and María José Prados, "The Life-Cycle Benefits of an Influential Early Childhood Program" (National Bureau of Economic Research Working Paper, December 2016), 1, www.nber.org.

127 Joseph R. Biden Jr., "Executive Order on Advancing Racial Equity and Support for Underserved Communities Through the Federal Government," White House, January 20, 2021, www.whitehouse.gov.

128 Milstein and Homer, "Which Priorities for Health," 374.

129 Yael Cannon and Nicole Tuchinda, "Critical Perspectives to Advance Educational Equity and Health Justice," *Journal of Law, Medicine and Ethics* 50, no. 4 (2023): 784, https://doi.org/10.1017/jme.2023.19.

130 Dorothy E. Roberts, *Torn Apart: How the Child Welfare System Destroys Black Families—and How Abolition Can Build a Safer World* (Hachette, 2022).

131 Cannon and Tuchinda, "Critical Perspectives," 784.

132 Thalia González, Alexis Etow, and Cesar De La Vega, "A Health Justice Response to School Discipline and Policing," *American University Law Review* 71, no. 5 (2022): 1964, https://doi.org/10.2139/ssrn.3919216.

133 Office of Disease Prevention and Health Promotion, *Federal Plan*, 46.

134 Cannon and Tuchinda, "Critical Perspectives," 783.

135 Rise PAR Team, *An Unavoidable System: The Harms of Family Policing and Parents' Vision for Investing in Community Care* (Rise, Fall 2021), 9, www.risemagazine.org.

136 Amna A. Akbar, "Non-Reformist Reforms and Struggles over Life, Death, and Democracy," *Yale Law Journal* 132, no. 8 (2023): 2562–71.

9

Essential Workers and Their Families

AZIZA AHMED AND JASON JACKSON

This chapter considers the way the family and household was exceptionalized in the early response to COVID-19.[1] The exceptionalization of the family mirrored a longer history of the privatization of the family and household in state public health response. The impact of this exceptionalization shaped the lives and families of essential workers who faced repeated exposure while at work to the virus that causes COVID. These essential workers were largely racial minorities and often lived with their families, in kinship networks, or in housing arrangements that mimic households to facilitate their employment. The racial dimensions of the erasure of the home in the public health response are clear in the early data on COVID, which showed that Black, Native, and Latinx individuals were contracting COVID and dying of the virus at higher numbers. We argue that the obfuscation of the home in the public health response contributed to health disparities flowing from the pandemic.

Essential Workers and Their Families

In the early part of the pandemic, state governments issued stay-at-home orders. One group was exempted from the orders: essential workers. These workers were deemed necessary for government function, food infrastructure, safety, and medical care. Many of these essential workers were gig workers (delivering groceries and food or working in restaurants), while others were care workers (keeping nursing homes functioning, caring for the elderly, and staffing hospitals). Many others were working behind the scenes in places like meat-packing plants. In each of these settings, essential workers were facing repeated and frequent exposure to the virus that causes COVID and often falling sick.

The data collected during COVID revealed a highly racialized and gendered essential workforce. The essential health-care and community-based services workforce was 76 percent women. Fifty percent of agricultural workers are people of color. In the essential labor force, 5.2 million people were undocumented. And two-thirds of essential workers were frontline workers.[2]

Nearly a quarter of all essential workers live in low-income families with incomes below 200 percent of the poverty line, according to a 2020 report of the Center for Economic and Policy Research. One in ten frontline workers lack health insurance. One-third of frontline workers have a child under eighteen in their home. One-third of frontline workers are over fifty, while 16 percent live with someone who is older.[3]

Essential workers face a difficult and stressful work environment: A report from the University of Massachusetts Labor Center documented that essential workers felt unsafe at work, linked to the absence of basic safety equipment, and lacked paid time off to deal with sickness or family emergencies. Essential workers were unable to practice social distancing. The lack of savings or low savings forced people into the workplace, as well as a need to pay for food and housing. Yet 43 percent of essential workers in Massachusetts were low-wage workers, making less than twenty dollars per hour. These low-wage workers were often unable to meet basic needs and faced food insecurity. These work conditions existed despite relatively strong labor protections. Moreover, the Labor Center's reporting found that issues arising for essential workers were "consistently worse for African American and Latino workers."[4]

At high risk for COVID exposure, given the lack of masks and the general state of expert-generated nonknowing in the pandemic, essential workers would go home at the end of their workday and expose their families to the virus. This was particularly true for families and households for people living in cramped conditions. A recent study in *JAMA: The Journal of the American Medical Association* utilized data from the universal testing of pregnant women in New York City to find that the building-level variables measured by household membership, household crowding (greater than one person per room), and low socioeconomic status were associated with a higher prevalence of COVID.[5]

Difficult and precarious economic conditions, in the midst of a pandemic, impacted families and their children. Mental health issues surged among the children of essential workers. The children of workers, especially young children under thirteen, "females, and non-conforming youth had a higher risk of specific crisis events during the COVID-19 pandemic."[6] There was a deep economic and psychological toll for Latina mothers who were essential workers and their families. Stress came from the threat of layoffs, low incomes in general and incomes lower than white counterparts, and an inability to protect themselves from exposure. Latino workers were more likely to work in occupations that made social distancing impossible, increasing their likelihood of contracting COVID.[7]

The pieces of data that exist indicate a troubling story: Essential workers, many of whom are people of color, struggled economically and financially, facing housing insecurity and mental health crises in their families.

The Failing Public Health Response

Reading the Centers for Disease Control's (CDC's) early response to the COVID crisis, it was clear that the agency did not have the families of economically insecure essential workers in mind. Its advice, which suggested separating from people who tested positive with COVID and using separate bathrooms, assumed that families had access to multiple rooms and multiple bathrooms, in rooms where you could socially distance. As noted earlier, this was not the reality of the highly racialized and economically precarious essential workforce. Instead, the CDC's advice focused on individuals who would be able to easily opt to mitigate exposure to COVID and live an isolated life once infected. Families and interhousehold transmission did not register as a point of intervention for the CDC.

Obfuscation of the private, or the home and household, during the pandemic response is in part the product of the public/private divide, which furthers the exceptionalization of the family. The legal scholars Janet Halley and Kerry Rittich have offered the frame of "family law exceptionalism" to describe the phenomenon of how families are elided in law: "Family and family law are often treated as occupying a unique and autonomous domain—as exceptional—and for a wide variety of reasons: they are unique because (unlike the market) they house intimate, private, emotional, and vulnerable relationships; they are unique because they preserve (against modernity and/or the global or foreign) the traditional, the national, the indigenous; they are unique because (as against the secular) they derive from sacred command."[8]

The family becomes essentialized in part through the separation of public and private. For Fran Olsen, who theorized the public/private divide, the core of this distinction is the imagined dichotomy between the sphere of the market and the sphere of the family. The private sphere is associated with affective life in the home, with family and culture, care, and child rearing, all of which are deeply intertwined with notions of gender.[9] The public sphere is associated with employment and the market.[10] For the legal scholars Duncan Kennedy and Fran Olsen, the public/private divide was so deeply ingrained in the way the world functions that we should consider it a "structure of consciousness": "a shared vision of the social universe that underlies a society's culture and also shapes the society's view of what social relationships are 'natural' and, therefore, what social reforms are possible."[11] This public/private divide plays an important role in structuring a gendered world in which women exist in the private sphere and men in the public sphere.[12]

Halley and Rittich offer a broad view of framing the private inclusive of the household: "human association bounded through social negotiation and aimed at securing human reproduction, including reproduction from day to day of its members as well as the production of new human beings."[13] This broader framing is necessary in considering the condition of essential workers, at least some of whom lived in migrant "households" or shared housing with coworkers.

Drawing on this robust critical legal and feminist literature, we argue that family law exceptionalism, manifested through the public/private divide as operationalized in public health law, produced a public health response that excluded interfamily and interhousehold transmission. This was despite early evidence that many people testing positive for COVID were contracting the virus in their homes, often in crowded housing conditions.

The history of excluding the family from public health interventions can be traced, in part, to economists leaning into these ideas in the context of HIV and AIDS. This influential set of ideas, echoed in the work of leading scholars including Richard Posner and Thomas Phillipson, seemed to suggest that there was a mitigating effect of disease spread based on a person's willingness to act differently in familial or long-term relationships. In the case of HIV/AIDS, a person might be more willing to be cautious with their wife or girlfriend and less so with a stranger. Their ideas harked back to Gary Becker, who described how the economic man was rational, selfish, and disciplined, while the same man in the context of the family was nurturing, caring, affective, and altruistic.[14]

The failure of the pandemic response to take the home into account was reminiscent of arguments that feminist scholars have long made with regard to domestic violence: that the police stop at the door on the assumption that the private space is governed by a different set of norms and practices that is outside the purview of state intervention. This logic appeared inherent in the COVID response. Focused on the individual and the middle-class family—with money and resources to stay home and protect themselves—public health agencies appeared unaware of the fact that interhousehold transmission was commonplace and that the families of people who were essential workers, given repeated exposure to the virus, would be most likely to suffer the harms of COVID. Instead, the operating assumption in the public health response seemed to be that if people took time to wear masks and social distance in public, they would arrive to a risk-free zone in their home. The individual in a public space is treated as the primary point of intervention. The political and economic conditions that require essential workers to work and expose themselves, and their families, to COVID are ignored or elided.

What Would a Household Intervention Look Like?

To be sure, there were attempts to keep people in their homes, evidenced most vividly by the CDC eviction moratorium, which allowed some people to stay in their rental properties despite economic precarity. The CDC's eviction moratorium represented the commonsense idea that if people were moving around and facing housing insecurity, filling shelters, transmission of the virus would go up. But housing security did not protect people from intrahome transmission of the virus. Again, the private lives of families were ignored even in the context of housing itself being a concern.

There are many examples of what could have been done to prevent intrahousehold transmission. A few of these examples stand out. As the idea emerged that the virus was aerosolized, rather than solely transmitted from respiratory particles, it became clear that buildings would need to be properly ventilated and cleaned in order for the air to be cleared of the virus.[15] Air filters were recommended by the CDC as a way to clean air of the virus.[16] The availability of air filters would have reduced intra-home transmission. While people who could afford air filters were able to access them for their homes and sales of air filters went up dramatically in response to public health guidance, this was not the case for individuals who struggled financially, who could not afford them.[17] There was no distribution of air filters to essential workers or to households. A basic approach would have been to equip families with air filters to ensure some mitigation of transmission even in instances of close living spaces.

Another clear issue arising in tight living quarters was the inability to isolate when carrying the virus. In homes with close living quarters, or few bedrooms and shared bathrooms, it was impossible to be away from other people. There was a commonsense response needed: a place to allow individuals to isolate away from their home. This would have also been effective way to curb intrahome transmission. Some jurisdictions made this possible but often failed to do so in an effective way, including Los Angeles and New York City. New York City allowed people to isolate at hotels for up to ten days for free.[18] However, rooms were in short supply, and often there were no rooms available. Los Angeles catered its rooms to its unhoused community but faced shortages in rooms.[19] At least one study has shown that these programs were effective in containing the spread of COVID-19.[20]

Conclusion: Ongoing Racial Impacts, Ongoing Elision of the Household

Even as COVID data suffer from lack of systematic tracking, the data that exist continue to reveal racial disparities in health outcomes and health prevention efforts. In May 2023, the Kaiser Family Foundation noted that on the third-year anniversary of the pandemic, it is Black, Hispanic, and American Indian and Alaskan Native individuals who have borne the heaviest health impact of the pandemic. Age-adjusted data show higher rates of infection and hospitalization for Black, Asian, and Hispanic people compared with whites. Black and Hispanic people are half as likely as whites to have received the updated bivalent booster. Latino people are more likely than whites to suffer long COVID.[21]

As in the start of the pandemic, these numbers are probably the product of structural inequalities that pushed people into precarious work with little to no COVID protections, exacerbated by the lack of systematic tracking of COVID and the lifting of nearly all COVID-related public health measures.

We know little about how the families of workers will fare as public health attention to COVID declines even as the virus continues to mutate and spread, particularly among vulnerable populations. The current rates of infection, death, and long COVID suggest that in many instances families of color will be widely represented among those bearing the brunt of a pandemic ignored. This is not happenstance—it is, as this chapter argues, the family being exceptionalized in the official public health response to the pandemic.

NOTES

1 This chapter is a version of the Bodenheimer Lecture delivered by Aziza Ahmed at UC Davis School of Law. The lecture and this chapter summarize Jason Jackson and Aziza Ahmed's "The Public/Private Distinction in Public Health: The Case of COVID-19," *Fordham Law Review* 90, no. 6 (2022): 2541–59; and Aziza Ahmed and Jason Jackson's "Race, Risk, and Personal Responsibility in the Response to COVID-19," *Columbia Law Review* 121, no. 3 (2021): 47–70.

2 Shruti Magesh, Daniel John, Wei Tse Li, Yuxiang Li, Aidan Mattingly-App, Sharad Jain, et al., "Disparities in COVID-19 Outcomes by Race, Ethnicity, and Socioeconomic Status," *JAMA Network* 4, no. 11 (November 11, 2021), www.ncbi.nlm.nih.gov.

3 Hye Jin Rho, Hayley Brown, and Shawn Fremstad, "A Basic Demographic Profile of Workers in Frontline Industries," Center for Economic and Policy Research, April 7, 2020, https://cepr.net.

4 Clare Hammonds, Jasmine Kerrissey, and Donald Tomaskovic-Devey, *Stressed, Unsafe, and Insecure: Essential Workers Need a New, New Deal* (University of Massachusetts Amherst College of Social and Behavioral Sciences, 2020), 4, www.umass.edu.

5 Ukachi N. Emeruwa, Samsiya Ona, Jeffrey L. Shaman, Amy Turitz, Jason D. Wright, Cynthia Gyamfi-Bannerman, and Alexander Melamed, "Associations Between Built Environment, Neighborhood Socioeconomic Status, and SARS-

CoV-2 Infection Among Pregnant Women in New York City," *JAMA* 324, no. 4 (2020): 390–92, https://doi.org/10.1001/JAMA.2020.11370.

6   Margaret M. Sugg, Jennifer D. Runkle, Lauren Andersen, Jaclyn Weiser, and Kurt D. Michael, "Crisis Response Among Essential Workers and Their Children During the COVID-19 Pandemic," *Preventive Medicine* 153, no. 106852 (December 2021), www.sciencedirect.com.

7   Leah C. Hibel, Chase J. Boyer, Andrea C. Buhler-Wassmann, and Blake J. Shaw, "The Psychological and Economic Toll of the COVID-19 Pandemic on Latina Mothers in Primarily Low-Income Essential Worker Families," *Traumatology* 27, no. 1 (2021), psycnet.apa.org.

8   Janet Halley and Kerry Rittich, "Critical Directions in Comparative Family Law: Genealogies and Contemporary Studies of Family Law Exceptionalism," *American Journal of Comparative Law* 58, no. 4 (2010): 754.

9   Martha Albertson Fineman, "Contract and Care," *Chicago-Kent Law Review* 76 (April 2001): 1416 (discussing separate spheres); Martha Albertson Fineman, "What Place for Family Privacy?," *George Washington Law Review* 67 (1999): 1207, 1218; Naomi R. Cahn, "Models of Family Privacy," *George Washington Law Review* 67 (1999): 1225 (discussing separate spheres and the public/private distinction); Gary S. Becker, "Altruism in the Family and Selfishness in the Market Place," *Economica* 48 (1981): 1.

10 Fineman, "What Place for Family?," 1207.

11 Fran Olsen, "The Family and the Market: A Study of Ideology and Legal Reform," *Harvard Law Review* 96 (1983): 1498. See also Duncan Kennedy, *The Rise and Fall of Classical Legal Thought* (AFAR, 1998). The public/private distinction is similarly so deeply ingrained in the history of legal thought that Kennedy and Olsen understand it to be embedded in legal consciousness. See also Jackson and Ahmed, "Public/Private Distinction in Public Health."

12 Fineman, "Contract and Care," 1403; Cahn, "Models of Family Privacy," 1225.

13 Halley and Rittich, "Critical Directions in Comparative Family Law," 759.

14 Becker, "Altruism in the Family," 1. Becker begins by assuming that only one actor in the family is altruistic, while all others are "selfish beneficiaries" of his altruistic preferences. Becker's model of the altruistic household assumes a male head of the household and then operationalizes this assumption to account for coordinated behavior in the family that maximizes a single household utility curve (rather than a set of individual and heterogeneous utility curves, as would be expected in the public sphere of the market).

15 New York City, "Isolation Hotel Program for Those with COVID-19," March 2022, www1.nyc.gov.

16 William G. Lindsley, Raymond C. Derk, Jayme P. Coyle, Stephen B. Martin Jr., Kenneth R. Mead, Francoise M. Blachere, et al., "Efficacy of Portable Air Cleaners and Masking for Reducing Indoor Exposure to Simulated Exhaled SARS-CoV-2 Aerosols—United States, 2021," *Morbidity and Mortality Weekly Report* 70, no. 27 (July 9, 2021): 972–76. This was a controversial idea at the start of the pandemic,

as the Trump administration attempted to downplay the aerosolized virus as a route of transmission in order to push a "reopen the economy" agenda. Laurel Wamsley, "CDC Publishes—Then Withdraws—Guidance on Aerosol Spread of Coronavirus," *NPR*, September 21, 2020, www.npr.org.

17 Daniela Sirtori-Cortina, "Covid-19 and Wildfires Spell Big Business for the Air Purifier Industry," *Bloomberg Green*, August 5, 2021, www.bloomberg.com; US Department of Education, "Improving Ventilation in Schools, Colleges, and Universities to Prevent COVID-19," accessed April 16, 2025, www.ed.gov. Students have also protested for better investment in air quality and masks. Laura Meckler and Hannah Natanson, "Students, Seeing Lax Coronavirus Protocols, Walk Out and Call in Sick to Protest In-Person Classes," *Washington Post*, January 14, 2022, www.washingtonpost.com. There were some attempts by people to construct home air-filtration systems out of box fans and filters.

18 NYC Health + Hospitals, "Take Care," March 23, 2022, www.nychealthandhospitals.org.

19 County of Los Angeles, "COVID-19: Medical Sheltering," March 23, 2022, https://covid19.lacounty.gov.

20 Jonathan D. Fuchs, Henry Clay Carter, Jennifer Evans, Dave Graham-Squire, Elizabeth Imbert, Jessica Bloome, et al., "Assessment of a Hotel-Based COVID-19 Isolation and Quarantine Strategy for Persons Experiencing Homelessness," *JAMA Network* 4, no. 3 (March 2, 2021): e210490.

21 CDC, "Long Covid Basics," February 3, 2025, www.cdc.gov.

10

Black Families and the Gaping Absence of the US Family Support System

MAXINE EICHNER

Devon Carbado describes critical race theory (CRT) as "repudiat[ing] the view that status quo arrangements are the natural result of individual agency and merit." According to Carbado, "We all inherit advantages and disadvantages, including the historically accumulated social effects of race. This racial accumulation . . . structures our life chances. CRT exposes these inter-generational transfers of racial compensation."[1] In keeping with this important function of CRT, this chapter centers the large role that the US system of routine family supports (actually, the almost complete absence of such a system of supports) plays in perpetuating the structural inequality of Black Americans.

Scholars' focus on structural racism during the past twenty years has delineated the effects of many areas of US law in perpetuating the inequality of African Americans. Of these, the criminal justice system's link to continued racial subordination has perhaps received the most attention.[2] But scholars have also carefully traced how a number of other areas of US law have contributed to ongoing inequalities based on race. They have documented, among others, the role played by voter registration laws and other voting requirements in diminishing African Americans' power at the ballot box;[3] the ways the Social Security Act's exclusions have left African American families less financially stable than white families;[4] the historical effects that the redlining of home mortgages have had on Black families' home ownership and wealth;[5] the ways that laws allowing school segregation have contributed to the racial achievement gap;[6] how US higher-education funding policies make it far more difficult for African Americans to graduate college and therefore contribute to the racial income gap;[7] the path through which laws governing evictions lead to disproportionate numbers of African

American families being evicted from their homes;[8] and how the legal framework governing the child welfare system rips a disproportionate number of Black children away from their families, causing trauma to both children and their parents.[9]

Laws relating to US family supports have received less attention in this literature. The partial exception is that the nation's paltry system of safety-net, or "welfare," benefits has been shown to be deeply influenced by racism—both in terms of how the framework surrounding the Temporary Assistance for Needy Families of 1996 (TANF) was constructed at passage and in terms of how TANF benefits have been administered by states.[10] However, the relationship between our US system (or absence thereof) of routine family supports and structural racism has been relatively unexplored. As this chapter demonstrates, however, this system plays a fundamental role in transmitting racial inequality between generations in the United States.

The first section begins by comparing the virtual absence of US family supports with the far more extensive family supports that other wealthy democracies provide, including routine cash subsidies for children, paid parental leave, subsidized day care and prekindergarten, and laws reconciling work and family. The second section details the role that racism has played in stifling development of a more robust family support system in the United States. The third section then enumerates the ways that the US system's absence of family supports disproportionately disadvantages Black families' ability to raise children. While this system expects families to use market earnings or family wealth to provide for children's needs, a range of structural disadvantages make this task far more difficult for Black families than for their white counterparts. Finally, the fourth section traces out the deleterious effects of this system on the circumstances in which Black children are raised in their early years. The predictable result is that Black children experience high rates of poverty and trauma, low-quality paid caretaking, and lower quality of parental caretaking than other children. I close by pointing out that when US Black children do not manage to escape the predictable effects of their circumstances, the absence of the family support system is ignored; instead, Black children's failures are attributed to their supposed intrinsic worthlessness, thereby reinforcing the racism that underlies this system.

This chapter's focus on the many hurdles that our family-support system places in the path of Black families in no way denies the tremendous resilience that a great many families exhibit in the face of these disadvantages and the multitude of coping strategies and workarounds that they have adapted to promote their children's well-being.[11] Black parents, though, should not have to exhibit extra and extraordinary resilience to ensure that their children can thrive. Accordingly, developing a system of government supports that counteracts the effects of systemic racism is an important project for justice, as well as for the well-being of Black children and their families.

The US Family Support System Versus Other Wealthy Democracies' Support Systems

Families are recognized by all contemporary Western countries as central to ensuring that children get the resources, caretaking, and human development they need to do their best. However, how market societies best ensure that parents can deliver the conditions children need to thrive is a subject of contention. Two very different models of the government's role in supporting families have emerged. The United States has generally embraced a laissez-faire vision of the role of government that I have elsewhere called "free-market family policy."[12] The idea behind it is that families do better when they negotiate what they need privately through markets. If markets are strong, this theory has it, then every family will get a big enough slice of the pie to satisfy their needs privately. In this model, it is the job of workers to bargain with employers over the hours they will work and their time at home. Parents will purchase goods and services on the open market that their children need to do their best. They will also provide child care themselves or arrange and pay for child care. Government aid programs are minimal, often targeted at poor families who must prove financial need before receiving benefits, and terminate when families get back on their feet.

In contrast, most other wealthy Western countries have adopted a vision of family supports that I call "pro-family policy." Like free-market policy, pro-family policy recognizes the importance of work, markets, and a strong economy. But it combines this recognition with the belief that families do better when the government actively supports them.

So, while pro-family policy considers the market an important tool for distributing many of the resources that families need to thrive, it also insulates family life from particular market pressures and actively supports families in getting children important resources they need.

Pro-family policies can take a number of forms. Some seek to reduce market inequality and insecurity in ways that improve families' well-being, for example, through laws or policies providing a relatively high minimum wage or mandating regular work schedules. Others significantly "decommodify" conditions that benefit families, for example, ensuring publicly paid family leave and high-quality day care to young children regardless of their family's income. Still others come from the state acting as a "traffic cop" to ensure that the market stays in its lane when it comes to ensuring that paid work does not encroach on family life. These include laws that guarantee workers adequate time with their families by establishing the maximum number of hours employees can be made to work, requiring employers to give workers paid vacation and holiday time, and allowing reduced work hours for parents of young kids. Countries with pro-family policy also supplement private income with a stream of public funding to families, including regular checks called "child benefits" and the paid family leave mentioned earlier. During routine times in families' economic lives, the cash support from paid family leave and child benefits, along with the provision of high-quality child care, raises the "ceiling" on the resources that families could otherwise afford to spend privately on their children. When families experience economic disruptions, such as when parents lose their jobs or their hours at work are cut back, these public funds establish a "floor" for resources that the child will not fall below, even in tough times.

The distinctions I make between free-market and pro-family policy are between ideal types; no countries are perfect exemplars of either of these policies. However, the United States comes closer than any other wealthy country to a system of pure free-market policy. It tolerates far more market inequality than other wealthy democracies do.[13] It is also the only wealthy country that does not provide any paid parental leave whatsoever.[14] It has not developed any large-scale system to provide, subsidize, or even regulate day care for quality.[15] Further, the United States stands apart from other countries in having few to no laws that help parents balance jobs with family responsibilities—no limits on mandatory work hours, no legal option for parents to work part-time, and no required paid (or even unpaid) vacation leave.[16] Unlike most other wealthy democracies, the United States does not provide parents child benefit checks to help ensure that children's needs for steady economic support are consistently met.[17]

Most of the minimal support that families receive from the US government is provided through tax policy. The Child Tax Credit (CTC) gives most US families a yearly tax credit of up to $2,000 a year.[18] Because the CTC is not fully refundable, though, the lowest-earning families—including nineteen million children—do not get the full benefit of the credit.[19] Meanwhile, the Earned Income Tax Credit (EITC) is specifically aimed at low-income families. Yet its primary purpose is to give low- to moderate-income earners an incentive to work. That means the program does not provide any benefits to the poorest American kids whose parents do not have earned income.[20]

Given the absence of other parenting supports, US safety-net programs have a large gap to fill. But the main safety-net family program, Temporary Assistance for Needy Families (TANF), was designed primarily to promote parents' economic independence through incentivizing paid work. Accordingly, the program's eligibility requirements are strict and its disqualifications harsh.[21] The result is that only twenty-three out of one hundred poor families in the nation receive TANF benefits.[22] The few families declared eligible for benefits will not get much: In 2020, the maximum TANF benefit for a family of three in every state fell at or below 60 percent of the poverty line; in eighteen of these states, maximum benefits fell below 20 percent of the poverty line—far too little to provide children with decent lives.[23]

Racism and the Weakness of the US Family Support System

Scholars have traced the large role played by racism in restricting safety-net benefits to US families.[24] Less noted has been how racism played a role in restricting the development of robust routine supports for all families in the United States. As this section describes, the critical turning point came in the early 1970s with the failure of the Comprehensive Child Development Act of 1971 (CCDA), which would have constructed a national network of federally funded child-care centers, along with other strong supports for children and families.[25]

Around the time the CCDA was being considered, most industrialized nations were beginning to adjust and supplement existing family supports. Earlier family-support systems had been constructed on the assumption that families would contain a male breadwinner and a female caretaker. As women increasingly entered the workforce beginning in the 1960s and remained there after having children, countries began to update their welfare models to adapt to the reality of increasing numbers of two-earner families and therefore the need for providing child care and other supports for working families.[26] Of course, in the United States, Black women had always been expected to work outside the home; no attempts had been made to adjust policy supports until white women entered the workforce in large numbers.

In the early 1970s, when the CCDA began to move through Congress, it looked like the United States would join these other countries. Significant popular support for such government measures existed: Polls showed 68 percent of women and 59 percent of men supported federally provided child-care centers.[27] President Nixon also seemed on board with the general project: Soon after he assumed office in 1969, he asserted a "national commitment to providing all American children an opportunity for healthful and stimulating development during the first five years of life."[28] A few months later, he reaffirmed, "there is no single ideal to which this administration is more firmly committed than to the enriching of a child's first 5 years of life."[29]

Notably, the proposed legislation did not simply construct a day-care program to serve the children of the poor mothers increasingly expected to work for pay. Instead, it sought to provide "a full range of health, education and social services" necessary for US children to develop their full capabilities. The bill's preamble stated its ambitious mission: "It is the purpose of this Act to provide every child with a fair and full opportunity to reach his full potential by establishing and expanding comprehensive child development programs and services designed to assure the sound and coordinated development of these programs, to recognize and build upon the experience and success gained through Head Start and similar efforts, to furnish child development services for those children who need them most, with special emphasis on preschool programs for economically disadvantaged children, and for children of working mothers and single parent families."[30]

Along with early childhood education, nutritious meals for enrolled children would have been provided. So would medical care, psychiatric services, programs for disabled children, and family planning and maternity care.[31] Enacting the CCDA would have gone a great way toward ensuring that American families had the government support they needed to raise flourishing children.

US families came close to getting these supports. The bill, which had been written by a coalition of labor, civil rights, welfare rights, women's rights, and educators groups, was introduced in both congressional chambers by a bipartisan group of legislators.[32] It subsequently passed both chambers with bipartisan support.[33] Yet two large controversies arose during its passage, each of which implicated race.[34]

The first concerned the population of children who would be served by these centers. The coalition's goal was universal child care. As a stepping-stone toward this end, the group supported a relatively high income-cutoff level at which parents would begin to pay for day care and, above that point, a very gradual increase of fees as parents' income rose. Broad inclusiveness, the coalition believed, not only would better ensure funding and quality day care over time but would ultimately benefit the children and society. As one commentator explained, a broad mix of children and parents from different races and classes, who "will all come into regular contact with each other," would "bring a new cohesion to the social fabric."[35]

Conservatives were amenable to providing day care for mothers receiving public benefits but were less sanguine about including middle-class families.[36] Some of their resistance rested on implicit bias about the worthiness of mothering by Black mothers.[37] Middle-class mothers (coded white in the popular view) were needed at home to do the critically important work of raising children; social policy that subsidized day care for this population did these children and society a disservice. In contrast, day-care supports for poor mothers (coded as Black in the popular view) were acceptable because the parenting provided by poor Black mothers was far less worthy, and these mothers were the ones in danger of establishing a "culture of dependency"—never mind that the middle-class mothers who stayed home needed to rely on their hus-bands for income support.[38]

Some objections to universal coverage from both conservative Re-publicans and Southern Democrats were more overtly racist. Republican Representative John Ashbrook of Ohio said the quiet part out loud when he worried that the bill created the frightening specter that the "socio-economic and race mix of students would reach its greatest potential."[39] Democratic Representative John Rarick of Louisiana railed that the act would constitute a foot in the door for the federal government to impose the kind of forced busing and integration policies on young white chil-dren that it was currently forcing on children in grade schools:

> The intrusion of the Federal Government into local public education through liberally interpreted Federal laws and bureaucratic edicts backed up by Federal judges under the emotion of compelling racial balance has turned the once-prevailing atmosphere of order in our schools into disor-der and chaos. Acceptance of integration as a status quo in turn called for the next step—busing to achieve racial balance. The busing of schoolchil-dren away from their neighborhood, a practice approaching ethnic and cultural genocide, is also a training program for the parents to condition them to accept future things to come by teaching them to yield to gov-ernmental paternalism.[40]

The second controversy concerned which entities were eligible to re-ceive federal funding to run day-care systems or, in the language of the bill, could be designated as "prime sponsors." The coalition had sought to define the term broadly to allow localities and nonprofits to run these systems, thereby enabling them to receive federal money directly, by-passing state government. This strategy mirrored one that Presidents Kennedy and Johnson had used in antipoverty programs, which not only assured that funds could reach needy Black communities even when states were recalcitrant to pass these funds through but also em-powered these communities in the process by investing them with sig-nificant control over the organizations that dispersed these funds.[41] As Sheila Morgan noted, "The Great Society was not to be simply a set of cash-distributing programs; it was a movement to help disadvantaged people take control of their lives and their communities. With the help of federal funding, many of them did just that. Community action dollars often poured into civil rights and other activist organizations that used these resources to challenge local white power structures."[42] (The opposite strategy was used in systems providing unemployment benefits and welfare benefits; federal benefits for these programs ran through the states, allowing states considerable power to cut off poor families rather than building power within their communities.)[43]

Conservatives in both parties fought this broad definition of prime sponsorship.[44] Much of this was opposition to empowering poor Black communities. In the memorable words of Louisiana Democratic Senator Russell Long, "Why should I pay poor people to stir up trouble when I can't find anyone to iron my shirts?"[45] A few years before, similar funding for Mississippi Head Start centers had angered white political leaders, causing Democratic Senator John Stennis from Mississippi to accuse the program of fomenting racial agitation and to block funding for the Office of Economic Opportunity (OEO), the agency overseeing the Head Start program.[46]

Support for the bill was significantly weakened by these racially infused controversies. Ultimately, although the bill passed both houses of Congress, it did so without Southern Democrat and conservative Republican support.[47] In fact, even some moderate Republicans voted no on the version of the bill that cleared the reconciliation process.[48]

Nixon, who had played his cards close to the vest during the bill's passage in Congress, ultimately vetoed the bill.[49] His reasons remain debated. It is unlikely that the first controversy provoked the veto: By the time the bill cleared Congress, legislators had complied with the administration's request to reduce the income cutoff for free child care considerably.[50] Several informed observers, though, surmise that the veto was made inevitable by the second controversy, given the final draft's broad definition of prime sponsorship, which allowed localities with a population of five thousand or more to serve as prime sponsors.[51] Nixon was later to write that, as the bill was constructed, he viewed it as more of a community-empowerment program than an effort to meet the childcare needs of mainstream America.[52] It did not help that the program was supposed to be administered by the OEO and was attached to a bill extending the life of the OEO, which Nixon was seeking to close because of its efforts to empower local civil rights groups.[53] Ultimately, the president's veto statement recognized "the needs . . . for day care, to enable mothers, particularly those at the lowest income levels, to take full-time jobs." Yet, the statement contended, the act as passed would make the CCDA "the most radical piece of legislation to emerge from the Ninety-second Congress."[54]

Following Nixon's veto, a conservative pressure campaign called on federal legislators to sustain the veto in Congress. As one commentator described it, the campaign took aim at the CCDA's animating belief "that children 'learn better' in programs with a socioeconomic mix of families." That belief, conservatives argued, "was one of the arguments used to justify integrated schools. . . . Conservatives threatened that the federal government would soon begin forcing children into day care centers, just as the government forced desegregation of schools and instituted busing. . . . The threat was that parents would no longer have authority to raise their children in their own way and teach their own values. Rather, upper middle class professionals, who were sympathetic to radicals, blacks, and the poor, would take over childrearing."[55]

Ultimately, the campaign was successful: Thirteen Senate Republicans who had voted for the conference bill switched their votes.[56] The final vote was fifty-one to thirty-six, with twenty-nine Republicans and seven southern Democrats voting the bill down. Nixon's veto was therefore sustained. The politics of race were inextricably interwoven into these results.

Although the coalition tried to reassemble support the subsequent year, the "subtle racism" of the Nixon administration combined with the conservative turn of the country defeated the effort.[57] Instead, the country turned to the tax law described in the first section to support families, instituting a system far less robust than serves families best. A generation later, legislative sponsors of the Family and Medical Leave Act of 1993 did not even try to insert paid leave into the bill, knowing it would have no prayer of success.[58] The defeat of the CCDA and the political realignment it signaled were so decisive that no other significant family supports made serious progress in Congress for another half century.

It took the widespread economic crisis that accompanied the CO-VID-19 pandemic to spur suspension of the United States' free-market family philosophy. In March 2021, Congress temporarily made the Child Tax Credit fully refundable and raised the credit to $3,600 for children younger than age six and $3,000 for those between the ages of six and seventeen.[59] Half these benefits were paid out in monthly benefit checks of $300 per child under six and $250 for children between the ages of six and seventeen.[60] Expansion of the Child Tax Credit was transformative for US households with children. Monthly child benefit payments reached sixty-one million children—roughly 84 percent of all US children.[61] The Center on Poverty and Social Policy at Columbia University calculated that the first payment lifted 3 million children out of poverty—representing a 25 percent cut in the monthly child poverty rate.[62] After the second payment, the number of households with children that did not have enough to eat fell by one-third, or nearly 3.3 million.[63]

The most striking result of the COVID-19 benefits is not that they eased the poverty of the many families in economic crisis during the pandemic but that they lowered child poverty rates *significantly below prepandemic rates*. A Center on Budget and Policy Priorities (CBPP) analysis showed that child poverty fell sharply in 2021, reaching a record low of 5.2 percent, as measured by the Supplemental Poverty Measure (SPM).[64] That figure, the CBPP found, is the lowest figure on record back to 1967. In comparison, in 2018, 13.7 percent of children fell below the SPM poverty line. CBPP concluded that the year-to-year decline in the child poverty rate was the largest ever on record. The significance of such a steep reduction of poverty within a year to the well-being of US children is, as the Brookings Institution put it, "hard to overstate."[65] The drop in the poverty rate for Black children was particularly stunning: In 2018, nearly 25 percent of children lived in families below the poverty line; in 2021, fewer than 10 percent did.[66]

Yet Congress allowed the child-benefit checks to expire at the end of 2021.[67] While almost all Democrats and the Biden administration wanted to continue these checks, Democrat Senator Joe Manchin III (D-WV) refused, and the measure failed to come to a vote in an equally divided Congress. The reasons reported for Manchin's refusal sound in the same racist arguments used in the welfare reform debate in the 1990s: that benefits must include a work requirement (since such subsidies would cause mothers prone to dependency to drop out of the workforce and potentially to seek drugs).[68] Conservative organizations used similar race-influenced tropes. The right-wing American Enterprise Institute argued that continuing child-benefit checks would "fit[] the definition of welfare, with large increases in benefits focused on low-income households and the cost for many borne entirely by other taxpayers."[69] The AEI warned that "the millions of checks that will flow for the first time to parents who don't work at all[] recall[] the worst of former welfare policies" and would "effectively turn the IRS into America's number one welfare benefit-paying agency."[70] After the benefit checks ended, almost four million children fell back into poverty. In January 2022, by the Center on Poverty and Social Policy's estimate, there was a 41 percent increase in child poverty, with Latino and Black children experiencing the highest increases (7.1 percentage points and 5.9 percentage points, respectively).[71]

How the US Family Support System Undermines Cash Support for Black Children

The expectation that families will get what they need from the market without help from the government negatively impacts families of all races. But it visits its harshest effects on Black families because structural racism systematically disadvantages Black workers' and families' access to the economic resources they need to raise sound children.

The income gap between the median Black and white household has lingered at about 60 percent for decades.[72] That is partly because unemployment rates of Black workers have remained roughly double those of white workers since 1970 for workers at every level of education and during both boom and bust economies.[73] And even when Black workers find jobs, the median Black worker earns almost 25 percent less than the median white worker does.[74] Some of the earnings gap comes from racism in hiring and promotion.[75] Some comes from disparities in education, due mainly to the fact that, in the United States, college costs must generally be borne privately; Black families are less able to shoulder this burden. The result is that, while about one-quarter of white workers earn less than fifteen dollars an hour, almost half of Black workers do, leaving them unable to provide basic necessities for a family, even while working full-time.[76]

Black families headed by single mothers must also deal with the gender income gap. Women as a group make eighty-two cents for every dollar men make.[77] For Black women, that figure drops to sixty-two cents.[78] A full half of working women of color earn less than fifteen dollars an hour across states; in half of states, at least 60 percent of Black women do.[79]

African American families are also much less likely than white families to be able to dip into family wealth or receive help from family members to make up shortfalls in income in order to provide for children. The median wealth gap between white households and Black households is nine to one.[80] Experts attribute this gap to the vestiges of segregation, including government "redlining" that made Black families ineligible for home mortgages and therefore unable to build wealth.[81] Families of color also bear the brunt of high levels of economic insecurity: nearly six out of ten Black families live in a household with moderate or high levels of insecurity.[82] Further, just over one-third of Black families have sufficient money put away to cover three months of expenses in case of sickness, job loss, economic downturn, or other emergencies.[83]

Free-market family policy means that far fewer US children of all races generally receive the consistent cash support they need to do their best compared to children in other wealthy countries. A 2017 comparative study concluded that the United States had by far the highest rate of children living in relative poverty of the sixteen wealthy countries that were compared: 21 percent.[84] Nearly half of US single-mother families were poor.[85] Even when comparing poverty rates based on an absolute poverty standard (a standard that defines deprivation without taking the wealth of the country into account), the United States fared poorly, dropping only to a 14 percent poverty rate for young children—a startlingly high rate for the world's wealthiest country.[86] Black families disproportionately bear the burdens of poverty in the US system.[87] Overall, 30 percent of Black children in the United States lived below the federal poverty line in 2022.[88]

The developmental effects of poverty are significant and their consequences lifelong. Children exposed to poverty in early childhood have been shown in grade school to have less brain matter in areas that affect academic achievement, stress regulation, and emotional processing.[89] This helps explain not only why poor children miss more school and do worse in school in the short term than do other children but also why they have poorer health, lower educational achievement, lower earnings, and higher mortality when they grow up.[90] Given the permanent harm that poverty causes children, countries with pro-family policy go to great lengths to ensure that kids from low-income families get the material support they need. The goal of these policies is to make sure that kids do not slip into poverty in the first place. The United States has no such policy supports.

And it is not just the families who fall below the poverty line who cannot afford the resources children need. When researchers from the Economic Policy Institute calculated how much it would actually cost families to meet basic needs at a decent but modest level, including housing, food, child care, transportation, health care, other necessities, and taxes, they determined that families generally need an income of about twice the official poverty level. By this measure, more than three times as many families fall below basic family budget levels as fall below the official poverty line.[91] More than half of African American families cannot meet a basic family budget, compared to one in five white families.[92]

Why Black Children Cannot Get the Caretaking They Need Under US Family Policy

The absence of US family supports makes it not only more difficult for Black families to provide children the basic material resources they need—a decent roof over their head and three square meals on the table—but also far more difficult for them to provide the caretaking that helps children do their best. Abundant research demonstrates the critical importance of children's first five years to their long-term well-being and development. This science shows that children do their best only when they receive high-quality caretaking and nurturing in their early years. If children do not get these circumstances, it affects the basic wiring of their brains. It is exceedingly hard to repair these shortfalls later down the road. Free-market family policy, though, ensures that most Black parents must engage in paid work to put food on the table while their children are young. Meanwhile, structural racism means most will not be able to ensure their children receive the high-quality caretaking they need during these same years.

To simplify a vast amount of research, we know that four caretaking circumstances during children's first years help them flourish: (1) parental caretaking for up to the child's first year; (2) after the parent returns to work, high-quality day care; (3) in the year or two before kindergarten, attendance at a high-quality prekindergarten; and (4) throughout early childhood, high-quality time with a nurturing parent. Countries with pro-family policies by design make it easy for parents to give young kids the conditions that benefit them. These countries provide paid parenting leave during the first year or so after a child is born or adopted.[93] And when parents return to work, these countries make high-quality caretaking available that is either free or heavily subsidized.[94] They also provide universal, high-quality prekindergarten to children for the year or two before formal schooling starts.[95] These policies mean that parents do not have to trade off financially supporting their family with getting kids the care they need. The result is that almost all kids get the circumstances that will help them do best. In the United States under free-market family policy, families can get children what they need only if they can privately muster the resources to do so. The economic challenges that result from structural racism make this significantly more difficult for Black families than for other families.

To begin with, consider parents' ability to stay home with a child during the child's first month, which "is associated with decreased low-birth-weight births and infant mortality, increased breastfeeding, and improved maternal mental health."[96] Such leave from work is particularly important to African American families because of the Black maternal mortality crisis—Black mothers are more than three times as likely to die from pregnancy-related causes as white women—and the fact that Black infant mortality is twice that of white infants.[97] Leaves also give parent and child time to bond and to establish a sound parent-child relationship, both of which have developmental payoffs for children.[98] Yet under the federal Family and Medical Leave Act (FMLA), workers simply have their jobs protected for twelve weeks of unpaid leave.[99] To make matters worse, four in ten US workers are not even covered by the FMLA because of its strict eligibility requirements.[100] All this means that parental leave is truly available only as long as parents have access to paid leave from their employer or can afford to take time off without pay.

Unfortunately, fewer than one in five of US workers have access to paid leave through work.[101] This access is disproportionately skewed toward white workers; and even the few Black workers who get paid leave tend to get less time than white workers who do.[102] Absent paid leave, few families with young children will have the savings necessary to afford more than a few weeks of time off.[103] Here too, Black families are disadvantaged by their fewer economic resources. One study of California mothers suggested that before implementation of state paid parental leave, Black mothers took only an average of one to two weeks leave from work because they could afford no more.[104] (Leave periods rose considerably after the implementation of publicly paid leave.)

Once parents return to work, Black children are also significantly disadvantaged with regard to the quality of day care they receive. Much of the day care available in the United States is of startlingly low quality. The title of *The New Republic*'s exposé on US day care, *The Hell of American Daycare*, aptly sums up the situation. As its author, Jonathan Cohn put it, "We lack anything resembling an actual child care system. Excellent day cares are available, of course, if you have the money to pay for them and the luck to secure a spot. But the overall quality is wildly uneven and barely monitored, and at the lower end, it's Dickensian."[105] Across all day-care situations, experts rate the majority of day care provided to US children as "fair" or "poor." Less than 10 percent of care is rated very high quality.[106]

African American children receive the worst of this care, both because their families cannot afford better and because, in our segregated housing system, high-quality day care is geographically not as available to Black families.[107] The National Institute for Early Education Research reported that although 36 percent of white children in center-based day care experienced high-quality education (a startlingly low number itself), only 25 percent of Black children did.[108] Non-center-based daycare delivered even more alarming quality: "While only [30 percent] of homebased care attended by white children received 'low' ratings, more than half of those attended by black children . . . [53 percent] were rated as 'low.' Low- and medium-quality settings made up the full range of home-based settings for black children, with [0 percent] of centers they attended rated as 'high.'"[109] All this is despite the fact that excellent caretaking at home or in day care provides outsized and lifelong benefits to kids.

Turning to the third circumstance, while Black and white children have roughly equal rates of preschool enrollment—just shy of half attend—Black children tend to be enrolled in significantly lower-quality programs compared to white children.[110] Again, economics and geographic availability drive these disparities. Even when prekindergarten is publicly provided through the Head Start program, Black children still receive lower-quality education compared to white children, probably because they live in comparatively resource-poor and segregated neighborhoods.[111] A National Institute for Early Education Research assessment concluded that "one year of universal high-quality pre-K could practically eliminate the Black-White reading skills gap at kindergarten entry—from nearly seven months to almost zero—and cut the math skills gap almost in half—from about nine months to five months."[112] Instead, the poor-quality pre-K that Black children receive widens this gap.

Finally, free-market family policy also puts Black families at a disadvantage with respect to the fourth circumstance: high-quality time with a parent. The quality of care children receive from their parents matters tremendously; it is a far better predictor of children's outcomes than their day-care experience.[113] The most important factor driving the quality of care, in the neuroscientist Michael Meaney's words, "is the mental and physical health of the mother."[114] Here, free-market family policy combined with the continued effects of racism places Black mothers well behind the starting block.

A large part of the problem is the economic stress our system puts on Black families. Remember that a full half of Black women earn fifteen dollars an hour; many of them are the sole breadwinner. As the Princeton sociologist Matthew Desmond has noted, low-wage workers are much less healthy for a combination of reasons that could be improved by a simple infusion of cash: These reasons include having more unmet medical needs because they cannot pay for care; the inability to afford healthy food; the chronic stress associated with poverty, which "has been linked to a wide array of adverse conditions, from maternal health problems to tumor growth"; and the diminished psychological capacity to eat well or take measure to look after themselves like quitting smoking because of the stress of grinding poverty.[115] The Black maternal mortality crisis, which is driven by a combination of economic disparities, differential access to health-care coverage, and racism, is only the most obvious marker of the grossly disproportionate gaps in health between Black and white mothers.[116]

The free-market family system also takes a significant toll on Black parents' mental health. Economic and other forms of chronic stress, we know, cause rates of mental illness to mushroom.[117] And even when they do not rise to the level of causing diagnosable mental illness, increased stress associated with being a single parent, financial stress and insecurity, and work-related stress, including the stress that comes from working evening and night shifts and unstable work hours, negatively affects parents' mental states.[118] Black parents are far more subject to such increased stresses than are white parents in our system. A disproportionate number of Black parents have the stress of working rotating shifts, or unstable hours.[119] Further, largely because of economic circumstances, a disproportionate number of Black families are single parents, which increases time and economic distress since there is generally only one breadwinner and primary caregiver providing for the child.[120] The toll these factors take on parents has been shown to decrease the quality of parents' interactions with their children.[121]

On top of all this, free-market policy greatly increases the likelihood that Black children will experience the profoundly scarring events that physicians and scientists have come to call "adverse childhood experiences," or ACEs. The basic idea is that when children experience significant trauma, like family chaos, bullying, living with someone with mental illness or substance abuse, or living in foster care, the stress creates a significant physiological response. If this stress response is severe and prolonged enough, it disrupts the development of the wiring in children's brains. Increased ACE exposures drastically and cumulatively affect children's lifetime outcomes. By ensuring that three in ten Black children grow up in poverty, free-market family policy practically guarantees that considerable numbers of Black children will be exposed to ACEs. Parental neglect, domestic violence, substance abuse, and homelessness are all ACEs driven up by poverty.[122] Further, because free-market family policy so greatly constrains parents' economic options, it decreases their ability to remove their children from these stressors when they occur. The removal of Black children into foster care is another ACE disproportionately visited on Black children.[123] Almost one in ten will be removed for some period by the time they reach age eighteen.[124] Adults who experience more ACEs as children have much higher odds of developing alcoholism, substance abuse, or depression; of attempting suicide; of engaging in criminal behavior; and of having an early death.[125]

To sum all this up, free-market family policy demands that parents rely on private economic resources to raise young children. Because structural racism has straitened Black families' wealth, as well as constrained their incomes and the chances that they will receive paid family leave, most Black parents with young children must work. Yet their limited income and the neighborhoods they live in mean that they will not be able to give children the high-quality day care and prekindergarten their children require to do well. And the unequal stressors and burdens this system places on Black families make it far more difficult for them to give their children the parenting that serves them best.

Given what we know about how important children's early circumstances are to their sound development, the results of free-market family policy on the outcomes of African American children are unsurprising. At nine months of age, differences between Black and white children's mental development are extremely small, only a sliver of the racial gap that will be seen later.[126] By age two, though, the racial gap has widened considerably. And by the time Black children reach kindergarten, they are, on average, about nine months behind white children in mathematics and seven months behind in reading.[127] Controlling for factors associated with race in conditions of systemic racism—economic status, family education, and so forth—causes the gaps to disappear.[128]

These early gaps in achievement have persistent effects. Studies show that the achievement gap between Black and white US teens is not a product of their formal education—indeed formal education generally helps reduce the achievement gap. Instead, the achievement gap is either largely or entirely set by the time children reach ages four or five, meaning that children's early circumstances drive these later disparate outcomes.[129]

Conclusion

The absence of a routine system of family supports in the United States was a product of racial fissures half a century ago. The system it created now magnifies the effects of economic inequality that are the product of structural racism and thereby locks racial hierarchy into the next generation. Ironically, when African American youth demonstrate outcomes that are expected given the circumstances to which our social policy subjects them, they are then written off as undeserving and unworthy. These outcomes are then attributed to the cultural dysfunction of Black families or to too-generous government programs, rather than to the systemic racism that caused them.[130]

NOTES

1 Devon W. Carbado, "Critical What What," *Connecticut Law Review* 43, no. 5 (July 2011): 1608.
2 James Forman, *Locking Up Our Own: Crime and Punishment in Black America* (Farrar, Straus and Giroux, 2017); Michelle Alexander, *The New Jim Crow* (New Press, 2012).
3 Michael J. Klarman, "The Degradation of American Democracy—And the Court," *Harvard Law Review* 134, no. 1 (November 2020): 1–264; Keith G. Bentele and Erin E. O'Brien, "Jim Crow 2.0? Why States Consider and Adopt Restrictive Voter Access Policies," *Perspectives on Politics* 11, no. 4 (December 10, 2013).
4 Dalton Conley, *Being Black, Living in the Red: Race, Wealth, and Social Policy in America* (University of California Press, 2009); Donna L. Franklin, *Ensuring Inequality: The Structural Transformation of the African American Family* (Oxford University Press, 1997).
5 Mehrsa Baradaran, *The Color of Money: Black Banks and the Racial Wealth Gap* (Harvard University Press, 2017); Richard Rothstein, *The Color of Law* (Norton, 2018); Ta-Nehisi Coates, "The Case for Reparations," *The Atlantic*, June 2014.
6 Erika K. Wilson, "The New White Flight," *Harvard Law Review* 134, no. 7 (2021): 2382–2448.
7 Thomas Brock, "Young Adults and Higher Education: Barriers and Breakthroughs to Success," *Future of Children* 20, no. 1 (2010): 109–32; Andre M. Perry, Marshall Steinbaum, and Carl Romer, "Student Loans, the Racial Wealth Divide, and Why We Need Full Student Debt Cancellation," Brookings, June 23, 2021, www.brookings.edu.
8 Matthew Desmond, *Evicted: Poverty and Profit in the American City* (Crown, 2017).
9 Dorothy Roberts, *Shattered Bonds: The Color of Child Welfare* (Civitas Books, 2002); Dorothy Roberts, *Torn Apart: How the Child Welfare System Destroys Black Families—and How Abolition Can Build a Safer World* (Basic Books, 2022).
10 US Department of Health and Human Services, "Major Provisions of the Personal Responsibility and Work Opportunity Reconciliation Act of 1996 (P.L. 104-193)," December 16, 1996, www.acf.hhs.gov; Bridgette Baldwin, "Stratification

of the Welfare Poor: Intersections of Gender, Race, and 'Worthiness' in Poverty Discourse and Policy," *Modern American* 6, no. 1 (2010); Ife Floyd, Ladonna Pavetti, Laura Meyer, Ali Safawi, Liz Schott, Evelyn Bellew, and Abigail Magnus, "TANF Policies Reflect Racist Legacy of Cash Assistance," Center on Budget and Policy Priorities, August 4, 2021, www.cbpp.org; Richard C. Fording, Joe Soss, and Sanford F. Schram, "Distributing Discipline: Race, Politics, and Punishment at the Frontlines of Welfare Reform," University of Kentucky Center for Poverty Research, November 2008.

11 Leslie D. Hollingsworth, "Resilience in Black Families," in *Handbook of Family Resilience*, ed. Dorothy S. Becvar (Springer, 2013); Tonya D. Dibbs, "Leading with Racial Equity: Promoting Black Family Resilience in Early Childhood," *Journal of Family Social Work* 22, nos. 4–5 (2019): 315–32, https://doi.org/10.1080/10522158.2019.1635938.

12 Maxine Eichner, *The Free-Market Family: How the Market Crushed the American Dream (and How It Can Be Restored)* (Oxford University Press, 2020, 19–42.

13 Thomas Blanchet, Lucas Chanel, and Amory Gethin, "Why Is Europe More Equal than the United States?" *American Economic Journal: Applied Economics* 14, no. 4 (2022): 480–518, https://doi.org/10.1257/app.20200703.

14 "The Family and Medical Leave Act of 1993, as Amended," Pub. L. No. 103-3, 107 Stat. 6 (codified as amended at 29 U.S.C. § 2601-654 (2012)); Ellen Francis, Helier Cheung, and Miriam Berger, "How Does the U.S. Compare to Other Countries on Paid Parental Leave? Americans Get 0 Weeks. Estonians Get More than 80," *Washington Post*, November 11, 2021, www.washingtonpost.com.

15 Eichner, *Free-Market Family*, 106–15; Jonathan Cohn, "The Hell of American Day Care: An Investigation into the Barely Regulated, Unsafe Business of Looking After Our Children," *New Republic*, April 15, 2013, https://newrepublic.com.

16 Eichner, *Free-Market Family*, 22–23.

17 Eurostat, "Composition of Family/Children Expenditure," in "Social Protection Statistics—Family and Children Benefits," Statistics Explained, May 2023, https://ec.europa.eu; UNICEF, *Towards Universal Social Protection for Children: Achieving SDG 1.3 ILO-UNICEF Joint Report on Social Protection for Children* (UNICEF, 2019).

18 Child Tax Credit (CTC), 26 U.S.C. § 24(h)(2) (2021).

19 CTC, 26 U.S.C. § 24(h)(2) (2021); Elaine Maag, "Options to Improve the Child Tax Credit for Low-Income Families: An Update," Tax Policy Center, November 29, 2023, www.taxpolicycenter.org; Robert Greenstein, Elaine Maag, Chye-Ching Huang, Emily Horton, and Chloe Cho, "Improving the Child Tax Credit for Very Low-Income Families," US Partnership on Mobility from Poverty (USPOMFP), April 5, 2023, 1–2.

20 Earned Income, 26 U.S.C. § 32 (2018); Center on Budget and Policy Priorities, "Policy Basics: The Earned Income Tax Credit," April 8, 2023, www.cbpp.org.

21 Elissa Cohen, Sarah Minton, Megan Thompson, Elizabeth Crowe, and Linda Giannarelli, *Welfare Rules Databook: State TANF Policies as of July 2015*, OPRE

Report 2016-67 (US Department of Health and Human Services, Administration of Children and Families, 2016), 158, 183–94; Elizabeth Lower-Basch and Stephanie Schmit, *TANF and the First Year of Life Making a Difference at a Pivotal Moment* (CLASP: The Center for Law and Social Policy, 2015), 1, 12; Ladonna Pavetti and Ali Zane, "TANF Cash Assistance Helps Families, but Program Is Not the Success Some Claim," Center on Budget and Policy Priorities, August 2, 2021, www.cbpp.org.

22 Center on Budget and Policy Priorities, "Policy Basics: Temporary Assistance for Needy Families," March 1, 2022, 6–7, www.cbpp.org.

23 Pavetti and Zane, "TANF Cash Assistance Helps Families."

24 Desmond, *Evicted*; Roberts, *Shattered Bonds*; Roberts, *Torn Apart*.

25 US Congress, Senate, *Comprehensive Child Development Act of 1971: Joint Hearings Before the Subcommittee on Employment, Manpower, and Poverty, and the Subcommittee on Children and Youth of the Committee on Labor and Public Welfare*, 92nd Cong., 1st sess. (US Government Printing Office, 1971).

26 Ann Shola Orloff and Jonah D. Levy, "From Maternalism to 'Employment for All': State Policies to Promote Women's Employment Across the Affluent Democracies," in *The State After Statism: New State Activities in the Age of Liberalization*, ed. Jonah D. Levy (Harvard University Press, 2006).

27 "Poll Supports Aid to Child Centers: Gallup Says 64% Back Use of Government Funds," *New York Times*, July 13, 1969, 32; Kimberly J. Morgan, "A Child of the Sixties: The Great Society, the New Right, and the Politics of Federal Child Care," *Journal of Policy History* 13, no. 2 (2001): 223.

28 Richard Nixon, "Special Message to the Congress on the Nation's Antipoverty Programs, February 19, 1969," American Presidency Project, www.presidency.ucsb.edu.

29 Richard Nixon, "Address to the Nation on Domestic Programs," August 8, 1969, American Presidency Project, www.presidency.ucsb.edu.

30 Comprehensive Child Development Act (CCDA), S. 1512, 92nd Cong., 1st sess. (1971).

31 CCDA, § 501(a)(2)–(4), § 514(2).

32 Morgan, "Child of the Sixties," 239; "A Sense of Urgency: Profile of Marian Wright Edelman," *New Yorker*, March 27, 1989, 48, 67.

33 Jack Rosenthal, "President Vetoes Child Care Plan as Irresponsible," *New York Times*, December 10, 1971.

34 Edward F. Zigler, Katherine Marsland, and Heather Lord, "A Golden Moment Squandered: The Inside Story of the Critical 1971 Comprehensive Child Development Act," in *The Tragedy of Child Care in America* (Yale University Press, 2011): 30; William Roth, *The Politics of Daycare: The Comprehensive Child Development Act of 1971* (Institute for Research on Poverty, University of Wisconsin–Madison, 1976).

35 Sheila M. Rothman, "Other People's Children: The Daycare Experience in America," *Public Interest* 60 (Summer 2024): 12, www.nationalaffairs.com.

36 *Congressional Record*, 92d Cong., 1st sess., 1971, vol. 117, part 29: 38170 (Statement of Hon. Thomas M. Pelly).

37 Dorothy E. Roberts, "The Value of Black Mothers' Work," *Connecticut Law Review* 29 (1994): 871, 873–875.

38 Roberts, "Value of Black Mothers' Work."

39 *Congressional Record*, 92d Cong., 1st sess., 1971, vol. 117, part 32: 41890 (statement of Rep. John Ashbrook).

40 *Congressional Record*, 92d Cong., 1st sess., 1971, vol. 117, part 24: 32410 (statement of Rep. John Rarick).

41 Morgan, "Child of the Sixties," 228; Jill Quadagno, "Fostering Political Participation," in *The Color of Welfare: How Racism Undermined the War on Poverty* (Oxford University Press, 1996).

42 Morgan, "Child of the Sixties," 226.

43 Richard A. Cloward and Frances Fox Piven, "The Weight of the Poor: The Strategy to End Welfare," *The Nation*, May 2, 1966.

44 Roth, *Politics of Daycare*, 20.

45 Edward Zigler and Susan Muenchow, *Head Start: The Inside Story of America's Most Successful Educational Experiment* (Basic Books, 1994), 110.

46 "Sense of Urgency," 48, 67; Morgan, "Child of the Sixties," 227.

47 Morgan, "Child of the Sixties," 230.

48 Morgan, "Child of the Sixties," 229–31.

49 Richard M. Nixon, *Public Papers of the Presidents: Richard M. Nixon, 1971* (US Government Printing Office, 1971), 1176–78.

50 Morgan, "Child of the Sixties," 224.

51 Zigler and Muenchow, *Head Start*.

52 Morgan, "Child of the Sixties," 232. Nixon's handwritten notes on William Shannon article in *Papers of the Nixon White House. Part 6, The President's Office Files, Series A, Documents Annotated by the President, 1969–1974* (Congressional Information Service, 1990), 218–231.

53 Morgan, "Child of the Sixties," 232–33.

54 Nixon, *Public Papers of the Presidents*, 1176–78.

55 Frederika Randall, "The Hand That Rocks the Cradle: A Study of the Comprehensive Child Development Act of 1971" (master's thesis, MIT, May 11, 1973).

56 "To Override Presidential Veto of S. 2007 (Two-Thirds Not Having Voted in the Affirmative, the Veto Was Upheld)," December 10, 1971, GovTrack, www.govtrack. us.

57 "Sense of Urgency," 48, 67.

58 Deborah Dinner, "Feminism Lost: Law, Sex Equality, and the Origins of Neoliberal America" (unpublished manuscript, 2024), chap. 7.

59 American Rescue Plan Act of 2021 (ARPA), Pub. L. No 117-2, § 9611, 135 Stat. 4.

60 ARPA of 2021, § 9611; White House, "The Child Tax Credit," accessed 2024, www. whitehouse.gov.

61 US Department of the Treasury, "Treasury and IRS Disburse Sixth Monthly Child Tax Credit to Families of 61 Million Children," December 15, 2021, https://home.treasury.gov.

62 Zachary Parolin, Sophie Collyer, Megan A. Curran, and Christopher Wimer, "Monthly Poverty Rates Among Children after the Expansion of the Child Tax Credit," *Poverty & Social Policy Brief* 5, no. 4 (2021).

63 Claire Zippel, "After Child Tax Credit Payments Begin, Many More Families Have Enough to Eat," Center on Budget and Policies Priorities, August 30, 2021.

64 Sharon Parrott, "In Pandemic's Second Year, Government Policies Helped Drive Child Poverty Rate to a Record Low, Cut Uninsured Rate, New Census Data Show," Center on Budget and Policy Priorities, September 13, 2022, www.cbpp.org.

65 Christopher Pulliam and Richard Reeves, "New Child Tax Credit Could Slash Poverty Now and Boost Social Mobility Later," Brookings, March 11, 2021.

66 Pulliam and Reeves, "New Child Tax Credit."

67 ARPA of 2021, § 9611.

68 Hans Nichols, "Scoop: Manchin's Red Lines," *Axios*, October 17, 2021, https://axios.com.

69 Matt Weidinger, "Child Allowances Make the IRS America's Number One Welfare Agency," American Enterprise Institute, June 9, 2021, www.aei.org.

70 Weidinger, "Child Allowances."

71 Zachary Parolin, Sophie Collyer, and Megan A. Curran, "Absence of Monthly Child Tax Credit Leads to 3.7 Million More Children in Poverty in January 2022," Center on Poverty and Social Policy at Columbia University, February 17, 2022, https://povertycenter.columbia.edu.

72 Valerie Wilson, "Racial Disparities in Income and Poverty Remain Largely Unchanged amid Strong Income Growth in 2019," *Working Economics Blog*, September 16, 2020, www.epi.org.

73 Valerie Wilson and William Darity, "Understanding Black-White Disparities in Labor Market Outcomes Requires Models That Account for Persistent Discrimination and Unequal Bargaining Power," Unequal Power Project, Economic Policy Institute, March 25, 2022, www.epi.org.

74 Wilson and Darity, "Understanding Black-White Disparities"; Valerie Wilson and William M. Rodgers III, "Black-White Wage Gaps Expand with Rising Wage Inequality," Economic Policy Institute, September 19, 2016.

75 Wilson and Darity, "Understanding Black-White Disparities"; Marianne Bertrand and Sendhil Mullainathan, "Are Emily and Greg More Employable Than Lakisha and Jamal? A Field Experiment on Labor Market Discrimination," *American Economic Review* 94, no. 4 (September 2004): 991–1013, www.aeaweb.org.

76 Kaitlyn Henderson, "The Crisis of Low Wages in the U.S.," Oxfam America, March 21, 2022, www.oxfamamerica.org.

77 Robin Bleiweis, "Quick Facts About the Gender Wage Gap," Center for American Progress, March 20, 2020, www.americanprogress.org.

78 Bleiweis, "Quick Facts."

79 Bleiweis, "Quick Facts"; Henderson, "Crisis of Low Wages."

80 Rakesh Kochhar and Mohamad Moslimani, "Wealth Gaps Across Racial and Ethnic Groups," Pew Research Center, December 4, 2023, www.pewresearch.org.

81 Kathryn Edwards, *Accounting for Black-White Wealth Differences* (RAND, December 2022), www.rand.org.

82 Robert P. Jones, Daniel Cox, and Juhem Navarro-Rivera, "Economic Insecurity, Rising Inequality, and Doubts About the Future," Public Religion Research Institute, September 23, 2014, www.prri.org; Jacob S. Hacker, Philipp Rehm, and Mark Schlesinger, "Standing on Shaky Ground: Americans' Experiences with Economic Insecurity," Institution for Social and Policy Studies at Yale, December 2010, https://isps.yale.edu; Jacob S. Hacker, "Understanding Economic Insecurity: The Downward Spiral of the Middle Class," *Communities and Banking* 22, no. 4 (2011): 25–28.

83 Khadijah Edwards, "Most Black Americans Say They Can Meet Basic Needs Financially, but Many Still Experience Economic Insecurity," Pew Research Center, February 23, 2023, www.pewresearch.org.

84 Janet Gornick and Emily Nell, "Children, Poverty, and Public Policy: A Cross-National Perspective" (LIS Working Paper Series, No. 701, Luxembourg Income Study, May 2017), www.lisdatacenter.org.

85 Gornick and Nell, "Children, Poverty."

86 Gornick and Nell, "Children, Poverty," 9, table 1.

87 Amanda Fins, "National Snapshot: Poverty Among Women and Families," National Women's Law Center, December 2020.

88 Annie E. Casey Foundation, "Children in Poverty by Race and Ethnicity in United States," 2023, https://datacenter.aecf.org.

89 Joan Luby, Andy Belden, Kelly Botteron, Natasha Marrus, Michael P. Harms, Casey Babb, et al., "The Effects of Poverty on Childhood Brain Development," *JAMA Pediatrics* 167, no. 12 (December 2013): 1135–42, https://doi.org/10.1001/jamapediatrics.2013.3139; Nicole L. Hair, Jamie L. Hanson, Barbara L. Wolfe, and Seth D. Pollak, "Association of Child Poverty, Brain Development, and Academic Achievement," *JAMA Pediatrics* 169, no. 9 (September 1, 2015): 822–29, https://doi.org/10.1001/jamapediatrics.2015.1475.

90 Ajay Chaudry and Christopher Wimer, "Poverty Is Not Just an Indicator: The Relationship Between Income, Poverty, and Child Well-Being," *Academic Pediatrics* 16, no. 3 (April 2016), https://doi.org/10.1016/j.acap.2015.12.010.

91 James Lin and Jared Bernstein, "What We Need to Get By," , October 29, 2008, www.epi.org.

92 Lin and Bernstein, "What We Need to Get By."

93 Eichner, *Free-Market Family*, 97–102.

94 Eichner, *Free-Market Family*, 103.

95 UNESCO, *Right to Pre-Primary Education: A Global Study* (UNESCO, 2021), https://doi.org/10.54675/NWYU4732.

96 Julia M. Goodman, Connor Williams, and William H. Dow, "Racial/Ethnic Inequities in Paid Parental Leave Access," *Health Equity* 5, no. 1 (October 1, 2021): 738–49, https://doi.org/10.1089/heq.2021.0001.

97 CDC, "Pregnancy Mortality Surveillance System," March 23, 2023, www.cdc.gov; CDC, "Infant Mortality," September 13, 2023, www.cdc.gov.

98 Natalie H. Brito, Denise Werchan, Annie Brandes-Aitken, Hirokazu Yoshikawa, Ashley Greaves, Maggie Zhang, "Paid Maternal Leave Is Associated with Infant Brain Function at 3 Months of Age," *Child Development* 93, no. 4 (April 4, 2022): 1030–43, https://doi.org/10.1111/cdev.13765.

99 "The Family and Medical Leave Act of 1993, as Amended," Pub. L. No. 103-3, 107 Stat. 6 (codified as amended at 29 U.S.C. § 2601-654 (2012)).

100 National Partnership for Women and Families, *A Look at the U.S. Department of Labor's 2012 Family and Medical Leave Act Employee and Worksite Surveys* (National Partnership for Women and Families, February 2013), https://national-partnership.org.

101 Barbara Gault, Heidi Hartmann, Ariane Hegewisch, Jessica Milli, and Lindsey Reichlin, *Paid Parental Leave in the United States* (Institute for Women's Policy Research, March 2014), https://iwpr.org.

102 Goodman et al., "Racial/Ethnic Inequities."

103 Eichner, *Free-Market Family*, 102–6.

104 Eichner, *Free-Market Family*, 1; Linda Houser and Thomas P. Vartanian, *Pay Matters: The Positive Economic Impacts of Paid Family Leave for Families, Businesses and the Public* (Rutgers Center for Women and Work, 2012).

105 Cohn, "Hell of American Day Care."

106 National Institute of Child Health and Human Development, *The NICHD Study of Early Child Care and Youth Development* (US Department of Health and Human Services, 2006), www.nichd.nih.gov.

107 Bruce Fuller, Sharon L. Kagan, Gretchen L. Caspary, and Christiane A. Gauthier, "Welfare Reform and Child Care Options for Low-Income Families," *Future of Children* 12, no. 1 (2002): 96–119, https://pubmed.ncbi.nlm.nih.gov.

108 Steve Barnett, Megan Carolan, and David Johns, "Equity and Excellence: African-American Children's Access to Quality Preschool," National Institute for Early Education Research, November 2013, https://nieer.org.

109 Barnett et al., "Equity and Excellence."

110 Erin Hardy and Rebecca Huber, "Neighborhood Preschool Enrollment Patterns by Race/Ethnicity," diversitydatakids.org, January 2020, www.diversitydatakids.org; Rachel Valentino, "Will Public Pre-K Really Close Achievement Gaps? Gaps in Prekindergarten Quality Between Students and Across States," *American Educational Research Journal* 55, no. 1 (September 20, 2017): 79–116, https://doi.org/10.3102/0002831217732000; Daphna Bassok and Eva Galdo, "Inequality in Preschool Quality? Community-Level Disparities in Access to High-Quality Learning Environments," *Early Education and Development* 27, no. 1 (September 4, 2015): 128–44, https://doi.org/10.1080/10409289.2015.1057463.

111 Marianne M. Hillemeier, Paul L. Morgan, George Farkas, and Steven A. Maczuga, "Quality Disparities in Child Care for At-Risk Children: Comparing Head Start and Non-Head Start Settings," *Maternal and Child Health Journal* 17, no. 1 (March 4, 2012): 180–88, https://doi.org/10.1007/s10995-012-0961-7.

112 Allison Friedman-Krauss and Steven Barnett, "Access to High-Quality Early Education and Racial Equity," National Institute for Early Education Research, June 2020, https://nieer.org.

113 Jay Belsky, Deborah Lowe Vandell, Margaret Burchinal, K. Alison Clarke-Stewart, Kathleen McCartney, and Margaret Tresch Owen, "Are There Long-Term Effects of Early Child Care?," *Child Development* 78, no. 2 (March 23, 2007): 681–701, https://doi.org/10.1111/j.1467-8624.2007.01021.x.

114 Liz Warwick, "Dr. Michael Meaney: More Cuddles, Less Stress!," Centre of Excellence for Early Childhood Development, 2024, www.researchgate.net.

115 Matthew Desmond, "Dollars on the Margin," *New York Times Magazine*, February 23, 2019, www.nytimes.com.

116 United Nations Population Fund, *Maternal Health of Women and Girls of African Descent in the Americas* (United Nations Population Fund, July 2023), www.unfpa.org.

117 Sarah Khan and Rafeeq Khan, "Chronic Stress Leads to Anxiety and Depression," *Annals of Psychiatry and Mental Health* 5, no. 1 (2017), https://doi.org/10.47739/2374-0124/1091.

118 Regarding single parenthood, see Lori S. Anderson, "Predictors of Parenting Stress in a Diverse Sample of Parents of Early Adolescents in High-Risk Communities," *Nursing Research* 57, no. 5 (September 2008): 340–50, https://doi.org/10.1097/01.nnr.0000313502.92227.87.

119 Adam Storer, Daniel Schneider, and Kristen Harknett, "What Explains Racial/Ethnic Inequality in Job Quality in the Service Sector?," *American Sociological Review* 85, no. 4 (June 19, 2020): 537–72, https://doi.org/10.1177/0003122420930018.

120 Elizabeth M. Caucutt and Nezih Guner, "Incarceration, Unemployment, and the Racial Marriage Divide" (BSE Working Paper 1300, Barcelona School of Economics, November 2021).

121 W. Jean Yeung, Miriam R. Linver, and Jeanne Brooks-Gunn, "How Money Matters for Young Children's Development: Parental Investment and Family Processes," *Child Development* 73, no. 6 (2002): 1861–79, https://doi.org/10.1111/1467-8624.t01-1-00511; Rashmita S. Mistry, Elizabeth A. Vandewater, Aletha C. Huston, and Vonnie C. McLoyd, "Economic Well-Being and Children's Social Adjustment: The Role of Family Process in an Ethnically Diverse Low-Income Sample," *Child Development* 73, no. 3 (2002): 935–51, https://doi.org/10.1111/1467-8624.00448.

122 A. J. Sedlak, J. Mettenburg, M. Basena, I. Petta, K. McPherson, A. Greene, and S. Li, *Fourth National Study of Child Abuse and Neglect (NIS-4): Report to Congress, Executive Summary* (Office of Planning, Research, and Evaluation, Administration for Children and Families, US Department of Health and Human Services, 2010); Neal Halfon, Kandyce Larson, Michael Lu, Ericka Tullis,

and Shirley Russ, "Life Course Health Development: Past, Present and Future," *Maternal and Child Health Journal* 18 (2014): 344–65; Tammie Y. Kwong, "Adverse Childhood Experiences (ACEs) and Their Influence on Social Connectedness," School of Public Health, Yale University, January 2014, https://doi.org/10.13140/RG.2.2.24973.84964.10; Roy Wade, Judy A. Shea, David Rubin, and Joanne Wood, "Adverse Childhood Experiences of Low-Income Urban Youth," *Pediatrics* 134, no. 1 (July 2014), https://doi.org/10.1542/peds.2013-2475.

123 Roberts, *Shattered Bonds*; Roberts, *Torn Apart*.

124 Elisa Minoff and Alexandra Citrin, *Systemically Neglected: How Racism Structures Public Systems to Produce Child Neglect* (Center for the Study of Social Policy, 2022).

125 National Scientific Council on the Developing Child, *The Science of Early Childhood Development: Closing the Gap Between What We Know and What We Do* (National Scientific Council on the Developing Child, 2007); Jack P. Shonkoff and Andrew S. Garner, "The Lifelong Effects of Early Childhood Adversity and Toxic Stress," *American Academy of Pediatrics* 129, no. 1 (January 2012): 236, https://doi.org/10.1542/peds.2011-2663.

126 Ronald G. Fryer and Steven D. Levitt, "Testing for Racial Differences in the Mental Ability of Young Children," *American Economic Review* 103, no. 2 (2013): 981–1005, https://doi.org/10.1257/aer.103.2.981.

127 Friedman-Krauss and Barnett, "Access to High-Quality Early Education."

128 Helen F. Ladd, "Education and Poverty: Confronting the Evidence," *Journal of Policy Analysis and Management* 31, no. 2 (2012): 203–27, https://doi.org/10.1002/pam.21615; Richard Rothstein, *Class and Schools: Using Social, Economic, and Educational Reform to Close the Black-White Achievement Gap* (Teachers College Press, 2004).

129 Joseph J. Merry, "Tracing the U.S. Deficit in PISA Reading Skills to Early Childhood: Evidence from the United States and Canada," *Sociology of Education* 86, no. 3 (January 10, 2013), https://doi.org/10.1177/0038040712472913.

130 Charles Murray, *Losing Ground: American Social Policy, 1950–1980* (Basic Books, 2015).

11

Prison Family Law

PRISCILLA ALOYO OCEN

A few years ago, I visited the California Institution for Women (CIW) in Chino, California, as part of a legal team organized by the California Coalition for Women Prisoners and the Lawyers Committee for Civil Rights. At the time, CIW was one of the largest women's prisons in the world.

As we were being processed into the prison in the sparse waiting room, I noticed a bulletin board with ten to fifteen old, faded photos of white women with infants. The women were dressed in prison gowns and the babies in bonnets. The photos were taken in the 1950s, when CIW opened, housing largely white women who were convicted of non-violent felonies. These photos, with their displays of white women with smiling faces engaged in maternal bonding, stood in stark contrast to the women of color whom I would later encounter, who struggled to see their children after being caught up in a rapidly expanding prison system, where they were isolated and caged.

Inside of the cold, drab visiting room, incarcerated women asked me questions about how to get in touch with their children, described horrific neglect experienced by pregnant women, and told of the rumors of "baby stealing." I wondered what these photos I had encountered in the prison waiting room suggested about the structure and purpose of this prison and others like it. The photos suggested that this place was not built solely for punishment. Indeed, I later learned that the prison was founded with the mission of restoring "fallen" white women into the domestic sphere of marriage and motherhood.

Similar questions emerged during another visit, at the Valley State Prison for Women in Chowchilla, California, located in the middle of a largely white, rural community, four hours north of Los Angeles. During this visit, I met with "Kim," a Black woman in her late thirties. She was an unmarried mother who gave birth while incarcerated. Kim wanted to speak with me about issues she experienced with pregnancy, childbirth, and child custody.

During our conversation, Kim described a horrific birthing process in which she was told by prison guards, rather than her own body, when she would give birth as she was scheduled for a C-section delivery. When in transport to the hospital, at nearly nine months pregnant, she was shackled. Within forty-eight hours of giving birth, she was separated from her son. In an effort to avoid foster care, Kim assigned a volunteer family from a local church to be her son's guardian until she was released four months later. Kim was concerned about this arrangement, and she wanted to speak with me about ensuring that her parental rights were protected.

Kim and the other women I met with were among the approximately 1.9 million people in federal, state, and local carceral facilities in the United States. Studies estimate that over 60 percent of people in prison and nearly 80 percent of people in jails are parents to minor children. Kim's son was among the roughly 2.6 million children who have an incarcerated parent and 4.5 million children who have had a parent incarcerated at some point in their lives.[1]

Like Kim, people in prisons have multiple familial identities. Indeed, prisons not only hold parents of children but also warehouse children, spouses, siblings, and people capable of pregnancy or who are otherwise of reproductive age who may or may not wish to be parents. As Kim's story demonstrates, the impact of incarceration extends beyond the individual. Children lose parents; parents lose children; spouses are separated; extended family suffer the loss of grandchildren, cousins, aunts, and uncles; and kinship networks are torn apart. Families, in other words, are deeply impacted by incarceration.

Like Kim and her son, incarcerated people and their families are disproportionately poor and Black. Indeed, one out of every three people in prison are Black, and one out of every eight Black children have had a parent in prison. While Black men constitute 40 percent of incarcerated parents, increasingly, like Kim, incarcerated parents are Black and Latina women.

These families are subject to an entirely different regime of family law than their nonincarcerated counterparts are. They enjoy fewer protections and more regulation. Indeed, while state regulations of the family are traditionally subject to heightened scrutiny, in *Turner v. Safley*, the Supreme Court held that similar regulations governing the intimate family lives of incarcerated people are subject to rational basis review because prison administrators, and not courts, are to make the difficult judgments concerning institutional operations.[2] Under this form of review, the administrative interests of prison officials, not the lives and relationships of incarcerated people, are of paramount concern. This decision, in effect, means that people in prison are subject to a constitutional regime that is distinct from the one governing the "free world," and as such, prisons can more easily regulate the familial associations of the millions of people like Kim who are in jail or prison.

Moreover, the impacts of incarceration are intergenerational, as trauma of separation facilitated by prisons reverberates beyond the individual to families and kinship communities. Children of incarcerated parents, for example, experience a range of "health problems, emotional difficulties, behavioral problems, low school engagement and grade retention." Children of incarcerated parents often have subsequent involvement with the criminal legal system, as their trauma is subject to criminalization rather than care.[3] In addition, the elderly parents of incarcerated people often take on caretaking responsibilities, often causing stress, health problems, or premature death. As I argue in this chapter, these examples demonstrate the ways in which prison separates generations of families, constituting a form of what the sociologist Orlando Patterson described as "natal alienation."[4]

Yet, the impact of incarceration on family life, particularly Black family life, is almost completely ignored by family law casebooks and courses. As Kimani Paul-Emile and Jennifer Gordon have noted about family law's treatment of race more broadly, "Family law addressed issues of race in ways that can only be described as tokenistic" or ignored those issues outright.[5] This chapter aims to fill this discursive gap by examining the constitutional, statutory, and regulatory regime governing incarcerated people like Kim and their families. These constitutional rules and statutory regulations constitute a form of what this chapter calls "prison family law," which is distinct from the traditional family law that is taught in most law schools.

Prison family law determines when and how incarcerated people can communicate with their children, spouses, and other family members. It establishes the legal standards for child removal and termination of parental rights. Prison family law authorized a prison denial of an incarcerated person's request to participate in in vitro fertilization with his wife, despite the fact that the request posed no risk of danger and would not cost the state anything. It sets the parameters for when and how incarcerated people who are pregnant will give birth and how long they can spend with their child after the child is born. In sum, prison family law governs almost every facet of family life for incarcerated people and their families.[6] Under this regime, prisons have become a racialized space of family regulation that impacts millions of people, a significant number of whom are Black.

The chapter argues that "prison family law" should be understood as a parallel form of family law and taught as such in family law curricula. While scholars such as Andrea Dennis and Dorothy Roberts have persuasively argued that mass incarceration and criminalization are part of a broader system of racialized family regulation, few family law casebooks include material about the impact of policing and incarceration on families in poor communities of color.[7] In one leading casebook, "incarceration" is mentioned only 32 times, mostly in relation to penalties for nonpayment of child support. The word "prison" is mentioned 72 times, mostly in in the context of Turner v. Safley and the right to marry. By comparison, the casebook mentions "abortion" 296 times, "marriage" 1,000 times, "in vitro fertilization" 40 times, "divorce" 788 times, and "surrogate" 34 times.[8]

This erasure occurs despite the fact that the number of people incarcerated in US jails and prisons nearly matches the 2.6 million people who marry each year and far exceeds the six hundred thousand divorces that are filed each year.[9] This disparity in treatment is, as Robin Lenhardt has observed, part of a broader lack of engagement with race within family law.[10] Engagement with "prison family law" is critical to our broader understanding of the ways in which race, poverty, and social control shape family regulation in the United States.

In addition to showing why prison family law should be included as part of the family law canon, the chapter provides a roadmap—an easy way of incorporating prison family law into a family law course. By exposing some of the ways that prison intersects with and acts as family law, the chapter provides key groundwork for critical learning and discussion in any family law course.

A (Brief) History of the Relationship Between Prisons and Family Regulation

Most family law classes and casebooks are structured around the legal regulation and cultural significance of familial relations and intimate association. Through this lens, family law courses tend to focus on the ways in which the government regulation of the institution of marriage and the liberalization of divorce mediate these familial relations and intimate choices.

Indeed, family law examines how both individual privacy and state regulation often collaborate and collide in various ways to shape family life in the United States. It does so by interrogating how individual privacy and state regulation are mediated within the context of marriage, divorce, and sexuality. Additionally, family law examines questions regarding the ways in which familial associations constitute a form of private dependency by serving as a mechanism for support, care, and economic stability within the confines of the nuclear family instead of the state. At the same time, family law courses and casebooks often interrogate the central role of the state in shaping private familial and intimate choice. As the authors of one of the leading casebooks put it, "Family law today reflects a fundamental tension between respect for family privacy and deference to state authority."[11]

While family law courses and casebooks purport to explore how private family life shapes public institutions and vice versa, they rarely examine the ways in which social and political institutions primarily regulate economically marginalized communities of color in places like prisons and jails. This is probably due to the narrow ways that prisons and jails are understood to function in legal scholarship and in law courses more broadly.

In law school curricula, prisons, to the extent they are discussed, are generally covered in courses such as criminal law, criminal procedure, or specialty seminars. They are framed as places where people are sent to be punished, incapacitated, or rehabilitated after they have been convicted of a crime. This framing, however, obscures the gendered and racialized history of prisons and their relationship to family regulation. Given this narrow framing of the function and history of prisons, it is unsurprising that the family law canon fails to appreciate the role of prisons in shaping family life.

We often discuss prisons as if they have always been a fixture in the US landscape, performing relatively similar punitive functions over time. This is simply not the case. Instead, as the historian Adam J. Hirsh notes, "the wholesale incarceration of criminals is in truth a comparatively recent episode in the history" in the United States.[12] Driven by evolving political, economic, and ideological realities, imprisonment shifted from a rarely imposed sanction to a system of punishment that was used to police racial boundaries, define gender norms, and regulate family life.

The First Wave of Prisons in the United States

During the "colonial era," prisons performed a function more akin to contemporary jails, housing people charged with but not yet convicted of a crime. Punishments, such as fines, shaming, banishment, or torture, were largely imposed outside of a carceral setting.[13] Following a Quaker-led reform campaign against corporal punishment, Pennsylvania became the first state to operate a prison that used incarceration as a sanction nearly twenty years after the ratification of the Declaration of Independence.[14] By 1830, several Northern states built prisons to incarcerate people convicted of crimes as a form of punishment.[15] This first wave of prisons set the stage for the use of incarceration to regulate gender norms and family life in the United States.

The regulatory trend set by the first wave of prisons continued in the mid-nineteenth century, as urban centers expanded and jails and prisons in the North and West were populated by white men who were from poor rural or European-immigrant backgrounds.[16] These men, many of whom were unmarried laborers, were perceived to be a threat to social order. As the historian Kelly Lytle Hernandez notes, in this era, "many white social leaders fiercely believed that the bedrock of US society was the enfranchised white male citizen who held a steady job, owned a home, and headed a nuclear family."[17] White men who failed to meet this standard were targeted for arrest under broad vagrancy laws and incarcerated in local jails or sentenced to hard labor.[18]

In the South, most prisons were not established until after the Civil War, probably because most of the Black population was subject to the unchecked private violence and punishment imposed under chattel slavery.[19] Following the abolition of slavery, Southern states quickly enacted a series of Black Codes that targeted Black people for criminalization, incarceration, and hard labor in convict leasing camps or on chain gangs.[20] The criminalization of Black people in the post–Civil War era was done in an effort to prop up the Southern economy by replacing "slave labor" with "prison labor."[21] By 1885, nearly 90 percent of people in Southern prisons were Black.[22]

While the motivation for these Black Codes was the exploitation of Black labor, the laws also prescribed norms for sexual intimacy, barring interracial marriage, adultery, interracial sex, prostitution, and vagrancy. Many Black women were prosecuted and incarcerated for offenses such as feticide and inducing abortions, while others were imprisoned despite obvious pregnancies.[23] Additionally, Black Codes further regulated intimate family life by permitting children to be removed from their parents and "apprenticed out" if their parents were deemed "unfit" or unavailable for any reason, including incarceration. Black people who were subject to this racialized system of punishment were deemed to be "slaves of the state" by the Virginia Supreme Court, which enabled people in prison to be stripped of all manner of rights, including their rights to family.[24]

Gender, Women's Prisons, and the Regulation of Family Life

For much of US history, white women were largely excluded from public forms of punishment, viewed as too delicate and frail for incarceration.[25] The few women who were subject to incarceration were cast as irredeemable, "fallen women" and were housed in segregated units within men's prisons.[26] In these improvised spaces, they were subject to all manner of violence, sexual abuse, and deprivation. In addition, they were forced to perform domestic labor for prisons, such as cleaning, washing, and sewing.[27] Appalled by the shabby conditions confronting women in men's prisons, progressive reformers began to push for the creation of separate women's prisons in the late nineteenth century to accommodate the growing number of incarcerated white women.[28]

The Indiana Reformatory Institution for Women and Girls opened in 1873 as the first state-run prison for women.[29] These prisons, which were called "reformatories," were designed to rehabilitate "fallen women" and to restore their ability to occupy the domestic spheres of marriage and motherhood.[30] Women were housed with their children in prisons like New York's Bedford Hills.[31] Many of these facilities used "the parent-child bond . . . as a natural incentive" for white women in the newly formed women's prisons to participate in rehabilitative programming. At the California Institution for Women, which was founded in 1933, white women were required to take homemaking classes as part of their custodial sentence.[32] Not all women, however, benefited from the feminist push to create "reformatories" for "fallen women."

Criminalized and incarcerated Black women were often placed in segregated units in women's facilities or sent to men's prisons. In these spaces, Black women were viewed as irredeemable and unsuited for marriage or child rearing. According to the historian Talithia LeFlouria, incarcerated Black women were physically abused, sexually assaulted, and forced to work on chain gangs or on prison operations.[33] Black women activists such as Mary Church Terrell highlighted the ways in which Black women were left out of the white feminist vision for prison reform, noting that "although children are born to the colored women in these camps by the score, one reads of no indignant protest made by the enlightened Christian white women of the South."[34] This gendered and raced model of punishment dominated the penal landscape for much of the early twentieth century, as prisons were governed by the dictates of Jim Crow justice.

Prison Family Law: Imprisonment as a Racialized System of Family Law

Since the inception of prisons in the mid-nineteenth century, they have grown in size and scope from a rarity in the US landscape to an institution that houses a population that is one of the largest in the world. Driven by the "war on crime," millions of people from poor Black and Brown communities have been targeted for criminalization and warehoused in jails and prisons. Over the past fifty years, prisons have supplanted de jure segregation as a mechanism for regulating and maintaining the racialized boundaries that have kept Black people subordinate since the founding of the United States. At the same time, mass incarceration is now capturing more and more women, who now constitute the fastest growing prison population in the country.

While prisons have evolved over time, the regulation of gender and family life as a core part of punishment remains, often facilitated by constitutional jurisprudence. Indeed, as prison populations have grown, the Supreme Court has routinely applied a less protective standard of review when faced with challenges to prison rules that limit familial connections and intimate associations of incarcerated people. In *Turner v. Safley*, for example, the Court rejected the strict scrutiny analysis that typically applies when fundamental liberty interests are burdened by government policy.

While recognizing that "prison walls do not form a barrier separating prison inmates from the protections of the Constitution," the Court found that "courts are ill-equipped to deal with the increasingly urgent problems of prison administration and reform."[35] As a result of the "difficulties" of judicial oversight of jails and prisons, the Court held that "when a prison regulation impinges on inmates' constitutional rights, the regulation is valid if it is reasonably related to legitimate penological interests."[36] The Court went on to say that this reduced, rational basis standard of review was necessary because "prison administrators, and not the courts, are to make difficult judgments concerning institutional operations."[37]

The prevailing doctrine of deference to prison officials has served, as Sharon Dolovich notes, as a "catch-all justification for curtailing both the burden on prison officials to ensure constitutional prisons and prisoners' prospects for recovery."[38] Under this deferential posture, courts often fail to rigorously examine the safety or administrative rationales put forward by prison officials as justification for restrictions of familial rights.

As I argue in the sections that follow, under this less restrictive means of family regulation, matters related to marriage and divorce, child-parent relationships, and reproductive autonomy (a) are primarily structured around institutional policy rather than constitutional rules, (b) are enforced through prison officials rather than courts or judges, and (c) elevate the administrative interests of the prison over critical familial rights. Prison family law stands in stark contrast to the ways in which family law is traditionally understood as a system that is structured by the federal Constitution in disputes mediated through courts and under legal rules that elevate individual and familial rights over state interests.

Under prison family law, fundamental liberty interests of incarcerated people are routinely subject to less protection than those of their counterparts in the "free world." As a result, prison regulations have become more restrictive and have intruded into more and more of the areas of family life that are critical to rehabilitation and human flourishing. Given that Black people are disproportionately incarcerated, this means that Black families are disproportionately regulated by prison family law.

Prison Family Law and the Regulation of Marriage and Divorce

Marriage

Marriage is one of the few areas where incarcerated people figure into family law, as the Court's recognition that incarcerated people have the right to marry has become foundational to the broader constellation of marriage cases. In *Turner v. Safley*, the Court considered a suit brought by people incarcerated by the Missouri Division of Corrections challenging a regulation that prohibited marriage unless an incarcerated individual could demonstrate a "compelling reason" for the marriage. In finding the marriage restriction unconstitutional, the Court noted, "The right to marry, like many other rights, is subject to substantial restrictions as a result of incarceration. Many important attributes of marriage remain, however, after taking into account the limitations imposed by prison life."[39]

Indeed, marriage has many benefits for incarcerated people: emotional support, assistance with transitions once released from prison, government benefits, property rights, and stronger ties to children, among others. Such relationships also offer incarcerated people stability and long-term support, which may enable people to better survive the trauma of incarceration. Moreover, as the sociologist Katherine Beckett notes, "romantic partnerships contribute to desistance from crime."[40] In recognizing these benefits and the constitutional significance of marriage in the prison context, *Turner* represented one of the rare instances in which the Court placed the rights of incarcerated people on par with those of their nonincarcerated peers.

While the formal right to marry may exist, as a practical matter, many incarcerated people face significant barriers to marriage. This was undisturbed by *Turner*, as the Court stated that "it is undisputed that Missouri prison officials may regulate the time and circumstances under which the marriage ceremony itself takes place, such as distance or licensing fees."[41]

Incarceration means that people are housed at significant distances from their partners, which makes it difficult to visit or to plan for a wedding. Moreover, couples may have difficulty communicating due to the cost of phone calls or the lag time involved with corresponding via traditional mail. As a result of these challenges, incarcerated people are less likely to get married, particularly those in men's prisons. One study found that incarcerated men are 70 percent less likely to marry than their nonincarcerated counterparts are. For individuals serving life sentences, lower federal courts have upheld restrictions barring them from marrying.[42]

Divorce

People who were married when incarcerated are more likely to separate or divorce their partners due to physical distance, communications challenges, and the psychological toll of incarceration itself. Studies have found that men in prison were three times more likely to divorce than their nonincarcerated counterparts were.[43] The study found that the length of the individual sentence increased the likelihood of divorce. Given the racial disparities in sentencing, this means that imprisonment is more likely to impact the marriages of people of color, as Black and Latinx communities often receive the harshest sentences.

Similarly, under *Boddie v. Connecticut*, incarcerated people have the right to access courts to seek a divorce, yet the practical challenge of incarceration often makes it difficult for incarcerated people to obtain a divorce.[44] Paying fees or obtaining waivers, filling out forms, serving notice, and traveling to court are all barriers that prevent people in prison from obtaining a divorce. In some states, such as California, incarcerated people do not have the right to attend divorce proceedings. As one commentator noted, "thorny civil and domestic matters, like child custody or divorce, are hard enough to navigate for someone on the outside; they are near impossible for the average prisoner who has neither the power to compel transportation to court nor the money to hire an attorney."[45]

The inability to access divorce disproportionately imposes hardships on incarcerated women, who are more likely than their male counterparts to have experienced gender-based violence at the hands of a romantic partner. Such abuse is often directly related to the crimes for which women are incarcerated. If incarcerated women are unable to divorce their abusive partners, it can undermine other legal matters. For example, parole panels may inquire about what a woman has done to change the circumstances that led to the criminal offense that landed her in prison. If an incarcerated woman is still married to an abusive partner that contributed to the criminal offense, that can be held against her, keeping her locked both in prison and in a toxic marriage.

Prison Family Law and the Regulation of Parental Rights

Approximately 1.9 million adults are in state, local, and federal prisons or jails. More than half of these individuals are parents of minor children, with approximately 19 percent of those children age four or younger.[46] Over the past few decades, this number has grown significantly because of the significant increase in the women's prison population. According to one study, "more than 58 [percent] of women in state and federal prison and nearly 80 [percent] of women in local jails have children who are minors."[47]

These children, like their incarcerated parents, are disproportionately Black. Even though a majority of people in prison and jail are parents, criminal courts rarely consider child-care responsibilities when sentencing people to terms of incarceration. The failure to consider the parent-child relationship impacts millions of children, undermining their attachment to their parent and their overall development. For these children and their parents, incarceration not only means prolonged separation and emotional harm but also creates a mechanism for a unique form of state control over their relationships, on the basis of a penal legal regime that does not apply to families outside the prison context.

In traditional family law, the state presumes parents to be fit, unless proven otherwise. For the state to intervene in such a parent-child relationship, there must be a compelling state interest, and the policy advancing that interest must be narrowly tailored. This standard is grounded in a series of cases beginning with *Meyer vs. Nebraska* and *Pierce vs. Society of Sisters*, in which the Court held that parents have a fundamental liberty interest in directing the care, custody, and upbringing of their children.[48] As the Court stated in *Prince v. Massachusetts*, "It is cardinal with us that the custody, care and nurture of the child reside first in the parents, whose primary function and freedom include preparation for obligations the state can neither supply nor hinder."[49]

The right to the care and upbringing of one's child is not limited to custodial parents. Under the Uniform Marriage and Divorce Act, there is a strong presumption in favor of visitation for a noncustodial parent. According to the act, the "parent not granted custody of the child is entitled to reasonable visitation rights unless the court finds . . . that visitation would endanger seriously the child's physical, mental, moral, or emotional health."[50]

The constitutional right to direct the care and upbringing of children and to have access to visitation is not absolute. A family court may alter legal and physical custody based on the best interest of the child. In addition, parents may lose these rights if there is sufficient proof that a child has been abused or neglected. The legal standards that apply to incarcerated people and their children, however, are far less protective of their fundamental liberty interests than those of their "free world" counterparts, which makes it more likely for their families to be highly regulated and permanently separated.

Child Custody and Visitation

The state, which is responsible for parental incarceration, places no obligation on itself to ensure that parents are entitled to reasonable visitation. Instead, the state's interest in safety and security is placed above the interests of parents and their children when it comes to visitation, and caregivers are responsible for ensuring that parents can see their children, which is an often-arduous process.

On average, caregivers must travel at least one hundred miles to reach remote prisons. This means putting up the money for gas or a bus trip, not to mention the significant amount of time that it takes to travel. This means taking time from work, school, or other obligations. Unsurprisingly, caregivers report that distance is the most significant barrier to visiting a loved one in prison.[51] As a result of these and other barriers, only a third of incarcerated parents in prisons have contact with their children.[52]

When caregivers are able to facilitate visits between children and their incarcerated parents, they are subject to numerous indignities that often discourage real connection between incarcerated parents and their children. For example, the California Department of Corrections and Rehabilitation admonishes visitors that they are "subject to continuous surveillance."[53] Visitors must undergo intrusive searches upon arrival. They confront arbitrary rules that can result in visits being cut short or canceled outright.

Moreover, state and federal prisons restrict the quality of contacts during in-person visits. In *Overton v. Banzetta*, the Supreme Court upheld a Michigan prison regulation that limited visits by minors, including a prohibition on visits from a child if a parent's rights have been terminated.[54] Since *Overton*, visitation restrictions have proliferated. New York State, for example, limits visits to one hour, and only two children can visit at a time. Georgia permits two-hour visits only on weekends. The Cook County Jail does not allow toys or touching. According to the California Department of Corrections and Rehabilitation, "Visitors may briefly embrace their loved one while masked upon greeting and again upon exiting the visiting room," and anything beyond that is "considered excessive."[55]

Given the challenges associated with in-person visits, many families are left to use video visits or phone calls to maintain contact between parents and children. While convenient, video visitation is not cheap, costing up to one dollar per minute, according to one study. This does not include the cost of the hardware or internet necessary to use video visitation software. According to a report from the Marshall Project, many users complained of "grainy images, poor audio quality, unsynced video and audio or videos that disconnect before their allotted time."[56]

Termination of Parental Rights

Visitation, however, is only the tip of the iceberg when it comes to the way in which prison family law regulates and restricts parental rights. Many incarcerated parents are threatened with the loss of their parental rights entirely due to the absence associated with imprisonment. In these cases, children may be placed in the custody of a family member or the state through foster care.

In *Santosky v. Kramer*, the Supreme Court held that "the fundamental liberty interest of natural parents in the care, custody, and management of their child does not evaporate simply because they have not been model parents or have lost temporary custody of their child to the State." As a result, "when the State moves to destroy weakened familial bonds, it must provide the parents with fundamentally fair procedures."[57] Under this traditional constitutional standard, when a child is removed from a parent, the state has the burden of proving that a parent is unfit and that it is in the child's best interest for parental rights to be terminated.

The federal Adoption and Safe Families Act supplements the constitutional standard announced by the Court in *Santosky* by requiring that a family court order the termination of parental rights if a child has been in foster care for fifteen of twenty-two months. The timeline is even faster if a child is under three years old. During this time, parents are required to follow a reunification plan, which may include classes, drug testing, or supervised visitation. At the end of the reunification period, parental rights may not be terminated absent a showing of parental unfitness by clear and convincing evidence.

In 2021, approximately four hundred thousand children were in foster care. As the scholarship of Dorothy Roberts and others has extensively documented, Black families are disproportionately surveilled and policed by the foster care system, otherwise known as the family policing system. Black children make up 14 percent of all children but 22 percent of all children are in the foster care system. According to the American Bar Association, over 10 percent of Black children are removed from their homes and placed in foster care, which is twice the rate of their white counterparts. Incarceration exacerbates this trend, as studies estimate that incarceration is the reason for between 7 and 12 percent of all foster care admissions.

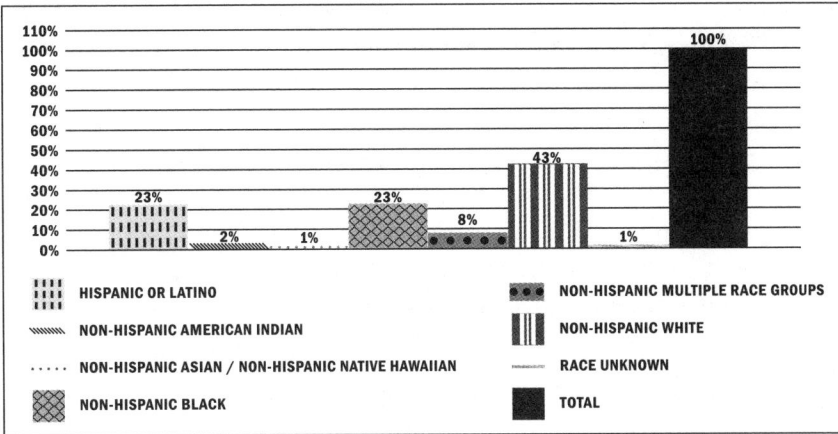

Figure 11.1. Children in foster care by race and Hispanic origin (percentage), 2021. (Anne E. Casey Foundation)

Incarcerated parents do not enjoy procedural protections to the same degree as their nonincarcerated counterparts. While parents in dependency court proceedings are entitled to basic due process protections such as notice and an opportunity to be heard, these rights often elude incarcerated parents. Recent reporting by news outlets such as the Marshall Project have found that incarcerated parents are often not notified about important court dates, nor are they able to attend hearings due to the vagaries of prison regulations.[58] Incarcerated parents often cannot comply with court orders and have difficulty maintaining connections with their children, which is a consideration in parental termination proceedings.

Given all of the challenges facing incarcerated parents, it is unsurprising that they are more likely than their nonincarcerated counterparts to lose their parental rights when their child is in foster care. Indeed, approximately twenty states explicitly allow incarceration to be used as a basis for the termination of parental rights. For example, under Texas law, a parent who has a child in foster care may have their rights terminated if they have been convicted of a crime that will result in "confinement or imprisonment and inability to care for the child" for two or more years.[59] In other states, the absence caused by incarceration is used as evidence of neglect. As I have noted elsewhere, "In these states, courts rely on incarceration or incarceration-related limitations as justification for the termination of parental rights."[60] As a recent study by the Marshall Project found, "incarcerated parents are more likely to lose their parental rights than those who physically or sexually assault their kids."[61]

In sum, under a regime of prison family law, the Court elevates the state's interests in punishment over the parent-child bond, which is generally protected by law. As a result, incarcerated parents, who are disproportionately Black, are routinely separated from their children by prisons that are more interested in administrative efficiency than in protecting the integrity of marginalized families.

Prison Family Law and the Regulation of Reproductive Autonomy

The Supreme Court has recognized the fundamental right to procreate in a series of cases, including *Skinner v. Oklahoma* and *Cleveland Board of Education v. LaFleur*. In these cases, the Court held that procreation "involves one of the basic civil rights of man" that constitutes "a basic liberty."[62] In *Skinner*, for example, the Court struck down a state law that required men convicted of certain offenses to be sterilized. In reaching this conclusion, the Court found that "marriage and procreation are fundamental to the very existence and survival of the race."[63] In *LaFleur*, relying on *Skinner*, the Court struck down a regulation that limited how long pregnant women could teach and under what conditions they could return to school. There, the Court reaffirmed the right to procreate, noting that there is a right "to be free from unwarranted governmental intrusion into matters so fundamentally affecting a person as the decision whether to bear or beget a child."[64]

This traditional doctrine is covered in nearly all family law casebooks and is covered in one form or another in family law courses across the country. Yet prisons and jails routinely flout these "basic rights" in the name of administrative efficiency, most often with the blessing of federal courts. Indeed, prisons have legally denied incarcerated people access to in vitro fertilization with partners on the outside and often limit choices that pregnant people may make while incarcerated. This means that prisons and jails routinely restrict the ability of incarcerated people, who are disproportionately Black, from procreating or exercising meaningful choice regarding the "decision to bear or beget a child."

Procreation

In *Gerber v. Hickman*, an *en banc* panel of the Ninth Circuit considered a petition by a California state prisoner who was serving a life sentence. Gerber and his wife desired to have children and could only do so via assisted reproductive technology, as he was not permitted to have conjugal or familial visitation. Gerber stipulated that he and his wife would bear the full cost of the process and had arranged for their attorney to transport the petitioner's semen out of the prison for purposes of the insemination procedure.

Applying the deferential standard articulated in *Turner v. Safley*, the *en banc* court noted, "Incarceration, by its very nature, removes an inmate from society," separating the prisoner "from his spouse, his loved ones, his friends, family, and children."[65] The court asserted that prisoners have no right to conjugal visits or privacy given the basic nature of incarceration. For similar reasons, the court concluded that procreation was incompatible with the objectives of imprisonment (i.e., retribution and incapacitation) and thus does not survive incarceration. In reaching this conclusion, the *en banc* panel privileged the minor administrative costs to the state over the significant infringement of Gerber's reproductive rights.

Pregnancy and Childbirth

Pregnancy is treated in various ways by family law and in family law courses, depending on the context. In some cases, it is treated as a fundamental liberty interest that is rooted in the decision to "bear or beget a child." In other cases, pregnancy is treated as a disability that requires employers to make "reasonable accommodations" for pregnant employees or as a basis on which pregnant people can seek family medical leave. In the prison context, by contrast, pregnancy is treated as a "serious medical need" that requires prisons to provide adequate medical care. Very rarely, however, do family law courses grapple with the treatment of incarcerated pregnant people as part of a broader examination of the law's regulation of pregnancy.

The questions raised by the treatment of incarcerated pregnant people are by no means a small set of concerns. At any given time, pregnant people constitute up to 10 percent of the population in women's jails and prisons, representing thousands of people who are pregnant behind bars. In these spaces, pregnant people seldom enjoy the constitutional, medical, or statutory rights afforded to their counterparts in the "free world." Instead, pregnant people are routinely subjected to inhumane conditions that punish them for carrying a pregnancy to term, enabled by a regime of prison family law that disproportionately impacts Black families.

Under this regime, and contrary to best practices for care and support during pregnancy, incarcerated pregnant people routinely experience what Carolyn Surfin calls the "material deprivation" of incarceration: "uncomfortable beds, food at only scheduled mealtimes, close living quarters, and in general, inconsistent and substandard prenatal care."[66] Indeed, according to a report by the US Department of Justice, only half of all pregnant women receive any kind of prenatal care at all.

The lack of care that pregnant people experience during their pregnancies extends to their birthing experience. In federal lawsuits across the country, incarcerated pregnant people have described the failure of carceral institutions to provide medical care during labor and delivery, resulting in people giving birth in isolated cells. Even when care is provided, dignity and autonomy are withheld, as pregnant people are often coerced into cesarean deliveries. Given all of the neglect experienced by incarcerated pregnant people, it is unsurprising that they disproportionately experience negative birthing outcomes, such as low birth weight, preterm birth, and stillbirth.[67]

Courts have generally affirmed the rights of pregnant incarcerated people in the rare cases when lawsuits are filed. Unlike other areas of prison family law, the treatment of pregnant women has been deemed unconstitutional. Nevertheless, the problem continues because of a woeful underenforcement of critical rules of family law, which is enabled by a culture of disregard of basic tenets of law that are routinely valued and applied outside of the prison context.

Prison Family Law's Impact on Black Family Life and Family Law

From the legal rules regarding marriage and divorce to limits on procreation and parental rights, prison family law constitutes an alternative system of family law that disproportionately regulates Black families. The failure of family law scholars and courses to grapple with the role that prisons play in regulating family life generally and Black family life specifically means that we do not meaningfully understand or critique how these institutions function or the justifications for the systemic family separation that they produce. Several harms to both the field and Black families flow from the failure of family law scholars and practitioners to adequately grapple with the system of prison family law.

First, prison family law causes the separation of families and produces intergenerational trauma. When a person is imprisoned, they not only are deprived of their freedom and caged in a cell but also lose critical familial connections. Spouses are separated from each other, and parents are denied access to their children on the basis of the whims of prison officials who implement constitutionally sanctioned family separation policies.

The harms of incarceration-induced family separation are well documented and long standing. Incarcerated people suffer from depression and isolation, which decreases their motivation while inside and increases the likelihood of rearrest once released. Spouses of incarcerated people are forced to shoulder additional caretaking burdens in the absence of their incarcerated loved one. Children of incarcerated parents experience psychological distress, behavioral problems, attachment challenges, and an increased risk of criminalization, thus continuing the cycle of incarceration and family separation.[68]

Second, prison family law reinforces isolation, stigma, and racial subordination. When incarcerated people are subjected to systematic family separation as a matter of law, it suggests that they are undeserving of basic human rights. Not only does this isolate them from their peers outside of prison, but it also stigmatizes their families and communities of origin. The dehumanization of prison family law disproportionately affects Black families, further entrenching the racially subordinate status that leads to vulnerability to incarceration in the first place.

Third, the failure to engage prison family law obscures the relationship between the family law canon and social inequality. Family law scholarship and curricula have long been criticized for failing to meaningfully engage race and the role of family law in perpetuating racial inequality. Indeed, the legal scholar Jill Hasday has argued that family law's canon frames family law as an institution that no longer contributes to inequality.[69] According to Hasday, the family law canon "both overstates the changes that have occurred in family law over time and understates the distinctions that family law currently draws between families."[70]

One way that family law understates the distinctions drawn between Black and non-Black families is through the erasure of prison family law in scholarship and courses. Prison family law is premised on inequality, as Black people are disproportionately stopped, arrested, prosecuted, and incarcerated by a system that uses punishment as a response to broader social problems. Prisons, in turn, reinforce inequality, by isolating people away from their families and imposing exclusions that make it difficult for formerly incarcerated people to meaningfully participate in social life.[71]

Conclusion

Prison family law impacts millions of incarcerated people and their families every day. Every day, the interests of prison administrators in punishment and security are elevated over the fundamental human rights and liberty interests of people impacted by the criminal legal system. Yet, the stories and legal systems confronted by people like Kim are seldom engaged by family law scholars and advocates.

While prisons are wholly absent from the family law canon and classrooms, they are all too present in the lives of millions of parents, children, spouses, and others. Family law scholars fail to appreciate and students do not learn about the devastating impact of prisons on intimate family choice, the parallel legal regime that governs families impacted by incarceration and that provides little protection for constitutionally protected rights, or what lawyers and policy makers can do to protect racialized families that are regulated by what Alexis Karteron calls a "shadow system of family separation."[72]

As legal scholar Robin Lenhardt has observed, "Family law scholars who are serious about theorizing and offering solutions for the problems faced by 21st Century families must begin to grapple with race in earnest."[73] In order to this, we must address the ways in which prisons and prison family law regulate Black families by engaging questions of race and carcerality in the family law canon.

NOTES

1 Bryan L. Sykes and Becky Pettit, "Mass Incarceration, Family Complexity, and the Reproduction of Childhood Disadvantage," *Annual of American Academy of Political and Social Science* 654 (July 2014): 127–49; Anne E. Casey Foundation, *A Shared Sentence: The Devastating Toll of Parental Incarceration on Kids, Families, and Communities* (Anne E. Casey Foundation, 2016), 1.

2 Turner v. Safley, 482 U.S. 78 (1987).

3 *Turner*, 482 U.S. at 78.

4 Orlando Patterson, *Slavery and Social Death: A Comparative Study* (Harvard University Press, 1982), 5, 7 (Patterson defines natal alienation as "alienation of the slave from all formal, legally enforceable ties of blood" and "all rights and claims of birth.").

5 Kimani Paul-Emile and Jennifer Gordon, "Celebrating a Lasting Legacy: Robin Lenhardt," *Fordham Law Review Online* 89 (2020): 16.

6 While I focus on prisons in this chapter, the arguments advanced here may be applied with equal force to jails and juvenile and immigrant detention centers, as well as forms of community supervision such as probation and parole.

7 Dorothy Roberts, *Torn Apart: How the Child Welfare System and How Abolition Can Build A Safer World* (Basic Books, 2022); Dorothy Roberts, "Prison, Foster Care, and the Systemic Punishment of Black Mothers" *UCLA Law Review* 59 (2012): 1474–1500; Andrea L. Dennis, "Criminal Law as Family Law," *Georgia State University Law Review* 33 (2017): 285–375; Jeanie Suk, "When Criminal Law Comes Home," *Yale Law Journal* 119 (2006): 2 ("the home is becoming a space in which criminal law deliberately reorders and controls private rights and relationships in property and marriage.").

8 D. Kelly Weisberg and Susan Frelich Appleton, *Modern Family Law: Cases and Materials*, 8th ed. (Aspen, 2024). In citing this casebook, I do not mean to single out this particular casebook or its authors, as the trend I observed is not limited to this casebook.

9 According to the National Center for Health Statistics, approximately two million people married and six hundred thousand people divorced in 2023. See National Centers for Health Statistics, "Provisional Number of Marriages and Marriage Rate: United States, 2000–2023 and Provisional Number of Divorces and Annulments and Rate: United States, 2000–2023," accessed April 26, 2025, www.cdc.gov.

10 Robin Lenhardt, "Color of Kinship," *Iowa Law Review* 102 (2017): 2071–2107; R. A. Lenhardt, "Marriage as Black Citizenship?," *Hastings Law Journal* 66 (2015): 1317–64.

11 Weisberg and Appleton, *Modern Family Law*, 15.

12 Adam J. Hirsch, *The Rise of the Penitentiary: Prisons and Punishment in Early America* (Yale University Press 1992), xi.

13 Hirsch, *Rise of the Penitentiary*, 3–12.

14 Matthew W. Merkell, "An American Resolution: The History of Prisons in the United States from 1777 to 1877," *Stanford Law Review* 51 (1999): 841–47.

15 Merkell, "American Resolution," 849.
16 Kelly Lytle Hernandez, "Hobos in Heaven: Race, Incarceration, and the Rise of Los Angeles, 1880–1910," *Pacific Historical Review* 83 (2014): 413–15.
17 Hernandez, "Hobos in Heaven," 413.
18 Hernandez, "Hobos in Heaven," 413.
19 Christopher R. Adamson, "Punishment After Slavery: Southern State Penal Systems, 1865–1890," *Social Problems* 30 (1983): 555–56.
20 Douglas Blackmon, *Slavery by Another Name: The Re-enslavement of Black Americans from the Civil War to World War II* (Anchor Books, 2009).
21 Sarah Haley, *No Mercy Here: Gender, Punishment, and the Making of Jim Crow Modernity* (University of North Carolina Press, 2019).
22 Nikki Brown, "Keeping Black Motherhood Out of Prison: Prison Reform and Woman Saving in the Progressive Era," *Journal of African American History* 104 (2019): 13.
23 Sarah Haley, "'Like I Was a Man': Chain Gangs, Gender, and the Domestic Carceral Sphere in Jim Crow Georgia," *Signs: Journal of Women in Culture and Society* 39, no. 1 (2013): 53, 65; Priscilla A. Ocen, "Punishing Pregnancy: Race, Incarceration, and the Shackling of Pregnant Prisoners," *California Law Review* 100 (2012): 1266–68.
24 Ruffin v. Commonwealth, 62 Va. 790, 796 (1871).
25 Estelle B. Freedman, *Their Sisters' Keepers: Women's Prison Reform in America, 1830–1930* (University of Michigan Press, 1984), 15.
26 Freedman, *Their Sisters' Keepers*, 15–16.
27 Freedman, *Their Sisters' Keepers*, 14–16.
28 Freedman, *Their Sisters' Keepers*, 40–42.
29 Freedman, *Their Sisters' Keepers*, 51.
30 Freedman, *Their Sisters' Keepers*, 40–45.
31 Miriam Van Walters, "Incentive and Penalty in Education," *Journal of Correctional Education* 46, no. 2 (1995): 80.
32 Kathleen A. Cairns, *Hard Time at Tehachapi: California's First Women's Prison* (University of New Mexico Press, 2009), 66–68.
33 Talitha LeFlouria, *Chained in Silence: Black Women and Convict Labor in the New South* (University of North Carolina Press, 2015), 12–13.
34 Brown, "Keeping Black Motherhood Out of Prison," 7.
35 Turner v. Safley, 482 U.S. 78, 84 (1987).
36 *Turner*, 482 U.S. at 89.
37 *Turner*, 482 U.S. at 89.
38 Sharon Dolovich, "Forms of Judicial Deference in Prison Law," *Prison Legal News*, January 15, 2013, www.prisonlegalnews.org.
39 *Turner*, 482 U.S. at 95.
40 Katherine Beckett and Allison Goldberg, "The Effects of Imprisonment in a Time of Mass Incarceration," *Crime and Justice* 51 (2022): 369.
41 *Turner*, 482 U.S. at 99.

42 Butler v. Wilson, 365 F. Supp. 377 (SDNY 1973).

43 National Research Council, *The Growth of Incarceration in the United States: Exploring Causes and Consequences* (National Academies Press, 2014), 265.

44 Boddie v. Connecticut, 401 U.S. 371 (1971).

45 Kim Bellware, "It's Almost Impossible for Inmates to Get a Divorce," *The Atlantic*, September 1, 2017, www.theatlantic.com.

46 Leah Wang, "Both Sides of the Bars: How Mass Incarceration Punishes Families," Prison Policy Initiative, August 11, 2022, www.prisonpolicy.org.

47 Erica Bryant, "More than 5 Million Children Have an Incarcerated Parent," Vera Institute of Justice, May 7, 2021, www.vera.org.

48 Meyer vs. Nebraska, 262 U.S. 390 (1923); Pierce vs. Society of Sisters, 268 U.S. 510 (1925).

49 Prince v. Massachusetts, 321 U.S. 158, 166 (1944).

50 Uniform Marriage and Divorce Act § 407(a) (1973).

51 Lindsay Cramer, Margaret Goff, Bryce Peterson, and Heather Sandstrom, *Parent-Child Visiting Practices in Prisons and Jails: A Synthesis of Research and Practice* (Urban Institute, 2017): 15. Brae Young and Jillian Turanovic, "Spatial Distance as a Barrier to Visitation for Incarcerated Youth and Why Families Overcome It," *Justice Quarterly* 39 (2022): 354–78.

52 Bernadette Rabuy and Daniel Kopf, "Separation by Bars and Miles: Visitation in State Prison," Prison Policy Initiative, October 20, 2015, www.prisonpolicy.org.

53 California Department of Corrections and Rehabilitation, "In the Visiting Room," accessed April 25, 2025, www.cdcr.ca.gov ("Incarcerated people and visitors are subject to continuous surveillance.").

54 Overton v. Banzetta, 539 U.S. 126 (2003). Restrictions included bans on visits from younger siblings, nieces, nephews, and other minors.

55 California Department of Corrections and Rehabilitation, "In the Visiting Room."

56 Beatrix Lockwood and Nicole Lewis, "Can You Hear Me Now?," Marshall Project, December 19, 2019, www.themarshallproject.org.

57 *Santosky v. Kramer*, 455 U.S. 745, 753–54 (1982).

58 Eli Hagar and Anna Flagg, "How Incarcerated Parents Are Losing Their Children Forever," Marshall Project, December 2, 2018, www.themarshallproject.org.

59 Tex. Fam. Code § 161.001(b)(1)(Q)(ii) (2017).

60 Priscilla A. Ocen, "Incapacitating Motherhood," *University of California Davis Law Review* 51 (2018): 2191.

61 Hagar and Flagg, "How Incarcerated Parents Are Losing."

62 *Skinner v. Oklahoma ex rel. Williamson*, 316 U.S. 535, 541 (1942).

63 *Skinner*, 316 U.S. at 541.

64 Cleveland Board of Education vs. LaFleur, 414 U.S. 632, 640 (1974).

65 Gerber v. Hickman, 291 F.3d 617, 620–21 (2002).

66 Caroline Surfin, *Jailcare: Finding the Safety Net for Women Behind Bars* (University of California Press, 2017), 123.

67 Surfin, *Jailcare.*

68 Eric Martin, "Hidden Consequences: The Impact of Incarceration on Dependent Children," *National Institute of Justice Journal*, March 1, 2017, https://nij.ojp.gov.

69 Jill Elaine Hasday, "The Canon of Family Law," *Stanford Law Review* 57, no. 3 (December 2004): 830 ("By canon, I mean the ways of thinking about family law that are widely shared by legal scholars and especially by legal authorities, like legislators and judges"; "the family law canon classifies almost every inequality in family law as part of the past rather than the present").

70 Hasday, "Canon of Family Law," 830.

71 Joshua M. Price, *Prison and Social Death* (Rutgers University Press, 2015) (noting that prisons in the United States are natally alienating, drawing on Orlando Patterson's work examining the critical link between enslavement and generational separation).

72 Alexis Karteron, "Family Separation Conditions," *Columbia Law Review* 122 (2022): 649.

73 Lenhardt, "Color of Kinship," 2097.

12

Breaking Women Free of the Prison Industrial Complex

MICHELLE S. JACOBS

Almost $300 billion annually is spent in the United States on the criminal legal system, including not only policing but also the prison industrial complex (PIC).[1] Some scholars conclude that the total costs of spending on the criminal legal system is over $1 trillion.[2] Buried within those figures are the 2.2 million people incarcerated in the United States. The number swells to 4.5 million if people on probation or parole are included.[3] The number of people incarcerated is larger than the population of fifteen states, and the average annual cost of incarcerating one individual is now $134,000.[4] State and municipal budgets are captured by spending on police, to the disadvantage of spending on social needs. A study examining the budgets of fifty cities highlights the percentage of the city budgets that were devoted to policing. Cities can spend up to and over one-third of their entire budgets on policing.[5]

After the death of George Floyd in 2020, a group of researchers created a new index, the Carceral Resource Index, to measure the degree to which municipalities prioritize police spending over supporting social needs, to see if data showed whether race and income inequality correlated with the prioritization of carceral spending. The data showed that cities perversely chose carceral funding over health and social support. The authors observed a correlation between race and economic inequality: "When race and class disparities were considered jointly, cities only prioritized health and social support when high income White residents strongly outnumbered low-income Black residents. When the proportion of these two groups was more balanced, or when low-income Black residents outnumbered high income White residents, we observed a shift towards carceral funding."[6]

The great majority of the 2.2 million people incarcerated are men, and a disproportionate number of them are Black and Latine. But the

"War on Drugs" combined with punitive drugs laws and mandatory sentencing schemes dramatically increased the number of women being incarcerated. Women's levels of incarceration increased over 500 percent between 1980 and 2021.[7] As the impacts of mass incarceration became clear, activists advocated for the repeal of harsh drug penalties and mandatory sentencing schemes. This advocacy began to have a real effect in 2020, when numbers of women, specifically Black and Latina women in prisons and jails, were decreasing in the period prior to the COVID-19 pandemic. However, data now show that numbers of women being incarcerated are increasing again.[8]

As of 2016, the last year for which federal data are available, over 172,000 women were incarcerated in prisons and jails. The federal prisons hold the smallest number, at 14,000, while state prisons held 72,000 and local jails held 76,000.[9] The total today is closer to 225,000.[10] As the number of incarcerated women grew, so too did the number of children impacted by having a parent incarcerated. More women than men entering prison report that they are the parent of a child under the age of eighteen. In addition, more women than men are the custodial parent of the children and/or are the head of a single-parent household. Overall, 1.5 million children have a parent who is incarcerated, with 1.25 million of those children having a parent incarcerated in state prisons.[11] Frighteningly, the number of children who have a parent who is incarcerated in state prisons *equals* the number of state prisoners.[12] If the number of parents who are under correctional supervision (parole or probation) is added in, the total number of children impacted by carceral systems rises to 8.3 million.[13] The Bureau of Prisons does not routinely update available data on women prisoners, and it does not adequately analyze data based on the race of female inmates. But state statistics do shed light here. Black women are incarcerated at a rate 1.6 times that of white women, and Latinas are incarcerated at a rate 1.3 times that of white women.[14] Women's population in jails is also a critical factor, as they are the largest growing incarcerated population.[15]

A child suffers devastating consequences when a parent, particularly the mother of the child, is taken away from them through incarceration. African American and Hispanic children were 7.5 times and 2.3 times more likely, respectively, than white children to have an incarcerated parent.[16] Children of incarcerated parents are themselves 6 times more like to become incarcerated themselves. This can be shown in the data of the women who are in state prisons, where 32 percent of them report that they had a parent who was incarcerated.[17] Having a parent incarcerated is recognized as an adverse childhood experience (ACE), a kind of trauma that has negative impact on a child's development, and the negative consequences continue into adulthood.[18] In addition to the trauma of losing the parent, the child may also suffer housing instability as the family adjusts to find a place for the child to live. Instability in housing renders children vulnerable to sexual and physical abuse. It is important to note that many women in prison report that they were victims of abuse before the age of sixteen. Economic instability can also occur as households are forced to stretch already-limited resources to cover another household member. In the case of foster care, there is the potential trauma of being separated from siblings and extended family members.[19] Children experiencing multiple traumas caused by parental incarceration can develop depression and anxiety and can begin to "act out" and otherwise engage in antisocial behavior. These are mental health issues for which there are few resources within the community that can be accessed to help the children. They can begin to self-medicate to deal with trauma, and that exposes them to the possibility of developing substance abuse disorders. Incarceration of mothers tears the fabric of a community in many ways.

Women's Pathways to Incarceration

What causes women to become ensnared in carceral systems? Scholars agree that women and men have different pathways into offending. Although most literature on inmates focuses on men, a body of research devoted to incarcerated women is spreading across the fields of sociology, psychology, criminology, and law. No matter what field or the language used to express these pathways, they can be reduced to four to five: The women are (1) overwhelmingly from poor and marginalized communities; (2) suffer from substance abuse disorders; (3) were treated for past or current mental health disorders; (4) have been physically or sexually abused (often before the age of sixteen); and (5) experienced trauma in intimate relationships.[20] Women experience these five factors in significantly higher percentages than do men entering carceral control. Other formulations of the factors combine mental health and trauma and substitute pressures of raising and maintaining a family as the fifth factor. Women who come under carceral control experience many of the same challenges that lead families to fall under the surveillance of family court outside of carceral environments. And indeed, women with children who are sentenced to repeated periods of incarceration may already be involved in proceedings with family court systems, particularly if they have histories of substance abuse or are in need of mental health treatment.

Poverty and Marginalization

Poverty is a key factor shaping opportunities women have in life. Nearly half of the women in prison come from families that were on welfare or receiving other public benefits.[21] Lack of safe, stable, and affordable housing is a key factor in maintaining stability for women and their children. Lack of housing can force women into homelessness or leave them dependent on relatives and others for shelter. This in turn can lead to women's (and their children's) victimization, as those providing shelter may demand sexual favors in return for providing shelter.[22] Alternatively, women, may have to settle for shelter in a place where drug use is open. For a woman who may already be struggling to stay clean, this can be a problem. Social services can also use the instability of housing to bring petitions for neglect against a mother, thereby increasing her already enormous number of stressors. Bureau of Justice statistics show that 26 percent of women experienced homelessness within a year of the arrest that leads to incarceration.[23]

Economic instability affects housing stability. Communities that experience organized abandonment have inadequate supplies of safe and affordable housing.[24] These communities also suffer from a lack of employment opportunities that can provide a livable wage, which in turn impacts a woman's ability to find safe and stable housing. However, to obtain employment that provides a livable wage, there must be employment opportunities available in the community, and women need to have the skills to obtain higher-paying jobs. Prison data show that 53 percent of women in prison do not have a high school diploma, making it unlikely they can qualify for higher-paying jobs. In fact, data show that compared to male inmates, women enter prison in a lower economic state. Over half of the women in prison were without a job in the month before the arrest that led to incarceration.[25] Women who do not have sufficient legal means to earn income will by necessity resort to illegal means to supplement income for them and their families. This could include engaging in survival sex work, selling drugs, or theft.

Substance Abuse and Mental Health Issues

Women who enter prisons and jails are traumatized, and their trauma starts when they are children, often before the age of sixteen. The women report that almost 20 percent of them experienced time living in foster care as children.[26] Approximately 60 percent of women inmates have been victims of sexual or physical abuse, and those numbers increased to 94 percent in state facilities and jails.[27] As noted earlier, early trauma can lead to substance abuse disorder and mental health issues. The data on prisons and jails show the degree to which substance abuse disorders and untreated mental health issues drives women's entry into prison and jails. In some cases, up to 82 percent of women in jails have substance abuse disorders, but even in state prisons, the number of women suffering from substance abuse is well over half. Diagnosable mental health disorders touch 76 percent of women held in state institutions. The women often have multiple mental health disorders, while prisons and jails have limited tools both to assess their disorders and to provide treatment.[28] Women in jails as opposed to prisons are offered even fewer services because they are detained for shorter periods of time than when sentenced to prison. A woman can be repeatedly sent to jail and detained, sometimes for up to a year, and never receive any substance abuse treatment or mental health assistance.[29]

The shameful aspect of these numbers is the fact that the factors are mostly all avoidable if a state or municipality was invested in the safety and stability of all of its residents. Universal basic income projects all over the country and the world repeatedly show that a guaranteed basic income benefit helps stabilize housing and gives women the opportunity to continue or finish school and obtain jobs that pay a livable wage, thereby allowing them to stabilize their families. Homelessness is solvable. It is possible to catch people who did not complete high school and help them acquire the education they need. Mental health issues can be treated if there is a variety of levels of trained mental health professionals available within a community. The failure to thrive is not as a result of individual action of a so-called justice-involved woman but rather because of the state's apathy toward the difficulties of its most vulnerable residents.

The Trauma of Survivors

Sexual and physical abuse are traumas that create pathways to incarceration for women. However, the trauma of domestic violence should be mentioned separately. Criminalized survivors of domestic violence are women who experienced violence in both family and interpersonal abuse.[30] These are women who become incarcerated because they were trapped in violent relationships, where they either dared to survive and killed or maimed violent partners or were coerced to engage in crime by the abuser. First, a family member or intimate partner abuses her. If she calls for help and the police *actually* come, the police do not believe the woman or take her complaints seriously.[31] When the antiviolence movement aligned with law enforcement and supported mandatory arrests, survivors were treated as perpetrators, to excuse the police from making initial aggressor determinations.[32] Or, due to racist stereotyping of Black women in particular, the police saw the woman as the initial aggressor.[33]

Survived and Punished Project, an advocacy group for criminalized survivors of domestic violence, argues that the law divides women into two categories: "good victim" and "nonvictim criminal."[34] The organization argues that the divide has been created by antiviolence advocates partnering with police and district attorneys. Good victims are those who cooperate with the police and help lock up perpetrators. But not everyone is considered a "good victim." "Survivors are criminalized for being Black, undocumented, poor, transgender, queer, disabled, women or girls of color, in the sex industry, or for having a past 'criminal record.' Their experience of violence is diminished, distorted, or disappeared, and they are instead simply seen as criminals who should be punished. . . . The institutionalization of this racialized 'good victim/criminal' dichotomy has left a huge portion of survivors, overwhelmingly Black women, unsupported and unaccounted for by the anti-violence movement."[35] The consequences of the divide are devastating for Black and Brown women, who are criminalized for surviving their abuse.[36]

Criminalized survivors find no relief in the courts, as the courts do not hear or value these women's lives or their stories of abuse, and as a result, they do receive any consideration of their horrid experiences of abuse at trial or when they are being sentenced. Courts rarely hear their experiences and efforts to survive abuse as self-defense. Consequently, they are sentenced for the crimes with no mitigation or excuses available to them. When they enter the carceral system, they are exposed to another wave of violence from correctional employees, which can include beatings and sexual assault.

Again, the factors that cause women to be at risk of incarceration are not easily disaggregated. For example, studies of women seeking substance abuse treatment report high levels of intimate partner violence.[37] In addition to using drugs to self-medicate, an abusive partner can coerce the use of drugs to assert control.[38] Intimate partner violence can also lead to women experiencing posttraumatic stress disorder (PTSD) or otherwise aggravating existing mental health issue. If a woman is employed, it can cause her to lose employment and create instability in housing. The abuser can coerce the woman into committing crimes, or she may commit crimes as a mechanism of survival. The criminal legal system, however, does not perceive her as a victim, merely as a criminal offender, and she will be sentenced accordingly. The victim of abuse then becomes the victim of the criminal legal system. According to the Sentencing Project, at "every stage of the criminal legal process, survivors confront obstacles that lead to severe and long-term punishment for offenses connected to the victimization they experienced."[39] The number of women who report that they are victims of intimate partner violence can depend on which kind of carceral facility in which they are held. Federal prisons might report 40 percent, while the percentage in state prisons and jails is higher, with 77 percent of women in jails reporting they have been victims of partner violence.[40] Until recently, however, prisons did not have clear programmatic policies to address the needs of women inmates. Basically, the institutions were driven by policies adopted for men.

Mothers Who Come Under Carceral Control

The ability of poor women of color to have and maintain families is subject to overbearing scrutiny from family courts and child welfare workers. Recent studies confirm that many child welfare services per-petuate racially biased decision-making when dealing with mothers of color.[41] Those difficulties are of course magnified when prison authori-ties are added into the mix. Not all women in prisons and jails have children, but the majority do. There are four categories of women with children who may be under carceral control: women who have children but lose custody in family court proceedings before entering prison; women who have custody of their children upon entering prison; women who are pregnant when entering prison; and women who are not pregnant but are raped after entering prison and become pregnant. All four categories of women face significant challenges to maintaining ties with their children and preserving their family units while incarcer-ated and after reentry.

Women with Children upon Entry into Custody

The first two groups of women with children share common barriers to maintaining ties with their children, and those barriers can be in place regardless of whether the children are in foster care with strangers or placed with family members. However, it should be noted that for some women who lose custody of their children prior to entering prison, the court may have terminated their custodial rights. They will not be able to maintain ties. When the child is in the custody of another, the cus-todial "parent," whether foster or relative, will determine whether the child will have contact with their mother. If the custodial persons do not desire it, it will be difficult for the mother to stay in contact with her children, other than through writing letters.[42] When the child is very young, writing letters is not a strong means of maintaining contact.

In the event, however, that the custodial caregiver does not object to the child maintaining ties with their mother, there is the question of distance, particularly if the mother is in a federal prison. A woman may be serving her sentence far away from the community she comes from. The costs of traveling to see the mother in person may be prohibitive. The First Steps Act of 2018 contained a provision requiring the federal government to house its inmates no more than five hundred driving miles from their home community.[43] But five hundred driving miles is a ten-hour trip and requires visitors to have an overnight stay.[44] Costs for such a visit can rapidly spiral out of the ability of a family to make those visits happen.[45] In fact, over 50 percent of formerly incarcerated women reported that they had not had a single visit from their children during the course of their incarceration.[46] When visits are not possible, the mother may have to rely on phone calls to stay in touch with her children. But, in a capitalist society where everyone stands in line to earn money off caged bodies, the telecommunication companies are no exception. Families with loved ones in prison are charged exorbitant amounts of money to receive collect phone calls.[47]

If the woman's children are in foster care and her sentence is longer than fifteen months, she also runs the risk of having her parental rights terminated under the Adoption and Safe Families Act of 1997 (ASFA).[48] ASFA was one of several pieces of legislation signed by President Bill Clinton that had a disastrous impact on Black women and their families.[49] The act incentivized the states to begin termination of parental rights for any children who remained in foster care for fifteen months out of twenty-two months.[50] There was bipartisan support for the bill because proponents believed it would be beneficial for children, as it would quicken the adoption process and give them the stability that their birth families could not provide. Legislators failed to take into account that Black, Brown, and developmentally delayed children are not easily adopted out.[51] Congress was warned that the timelines established under the bill were insufficient to give poor mothers an opportunity to fight for custody and would create a category of children known as legal orphans, but the bill passed anyway.[52] ASFA provisions can be triggered even if the woman serves several short sentences if their children were involved with social services and family courts prior to their incarceration. While they are incarcerated, mothers often do not have the information on how to fight the parental termination proceedings and may not even know they have taken place.[53] Scholars argue that the ASFA was racially motivated legislation.[54] Now twenty-five years later, data conclusively demonstrate that there are now more children than ever in foster care and that the burden of the statute falls disproportionately on Black and Brown children and their families.[55] A multiyear, multiorganization effort is afoot to have ASFA repealed, but as of now, it remains the law.[56]

Survivors and Their Children

Mothers who are survivors of intimate partner violence that led to their incarceration also have significant barriers to maintaining ties with their children while incarcerated. The father of the children may be the person whom the woman killed or seriously injured during her struggle to save her own life. When she enters prison, her children may be with the family of the deceased partner, and they may object to the mother maintaining ties to the children, particularly if the partner's family is in denial about the violence he perpetrated in the household. Even if the children are placed with the woman's family, her own family may be conflicted about the fact that she killed the children's parent.

The children have their own emotional struggle to deal with. If they are aware of the abuse, they may wonder why their mother stayed with the abusing father. They also have to deal with the trauma of losing both parents—one to incarceration and the other to death. Children and their nonincarcerated relatives may feel cultural pressure to keep ties with the father, if he is alive.[57] If the mother manages to maintain contact with her children, the dynamics of intrafamily violence may make it difficult to rebuild relationships after release from incarceration.

Pregnant in Prison

Women who enter prison pregnant and women who are raped in prison and become pregnant are in the most vulnerable position for creating and maintaining ties with their children. Approximately fifty-eight thousand pregnant women enter US prisons and jails each year. However, relatively little data have been collected on their experiences of having children while incarcerated. The Bureau of Prisons (BOP) data on pregnant women were last collected in 2004 and have not been significantly updated since then. The First Step Act directed BOP to collect data on pregnant inmates. In 2024, BOP reported that it did have the capacity to collect the data, but to date, no collected data have been published.

In addition to women entering prison pregnant, there are women who are raped by prison staff while they are incarcerated. Again, the US government does not regularly collect data about sexual victimization in prisons and jails. The Prison Rape Elimination Act of 2003 (PREA) was passed to address the issue of rampant sexual violence within prisons and jails.[58] The bill included a mandate that BOP collect and maintain data with regard to sexual victimization of inmates and to adopt policies and guidelines to identify risk of abuse and procedures to process complaints.[59] The most recent report available on sexual victimization published by BOP was issued in 2013. However, the US Senate conducted hearings in 2022 in response to disturbing lawsuits brought by female prisoners alleging that they had been raped while in federal custody. The committee's final report was issued in December 2022 and found that "BOP employees sexually abuse women in their custody in at least two thirds of the BOP facilities where women were held."[60] They also found that BOP had not followed the PREA policies established and in many cases did not punish officers who were the perpetrators of sexual violence.[61] Raping female prisoners was not isolated to the BOP but occurred in state prisons and jails from California to New York. The stories of these women are now being heard in litigation, including stories of women who became pregnant because of rape.

In the absence of reliable data produced by BOP, the Advocacy and Research on Reproductive Wellness of Incarcerated People Center of John Hopkins School of Medicine conducted the first comprehensive study of pregnant incarcerated women, called Pregnancy in Prison Statistics (PIPS) Project, to collect statistics about pregnant inmates. The data were collected from twenty-two state prisons, six jails, and all federal prisons over the year 2016–17. In total PIPS-collected data on 3,000 women; 396 were pregnant admissions in US prisons, or 4 percent of the prison population. The jails admitted 1,622 pregnant females. A total of 753 live births in prison and 144 live births in jails were documented. The study recorded other outcomes as well, including eleven abortions in prisons and thirty-three in jails. The most striking data were the placement numbers. While placement with families accounted for the most births, at 186, no placement information was available for an almost equal number—183 births. There were twenty-nine foster care placements, twenty-one to designated non-family members and fifteen to adoption, which equaled the number of children who had prison nurseries as an available placement option.[62]

Pregnant incarcerated women may want to consider abortion as an option; however, there is no consistent policy regarding reproductive health rights for women inmates. Under *Roe v. Wade*, inmates had the legal right to access abortions, but only four states and the federal government had laws regulating access to abortion for incarcerated persons.[63] Carolyn Sufrin, one of the principal investigators in the PIPS study, stated that access to abortion can vary from prison to prison in the *same* state and even in states where abortion is legal.[64] The policies of the particular institution govern whether inmates will have the option. Sufrin pointed out that often these rules may be unwritten policy, and inmates are not always informed about their options.[65] They may not know, for example, that abortion is an option that is available to them.[66] The Supreme Court overturned the *Roe* decision in *Dobbs v. Jackson Women's Health Organization*.[67] What impact this will have on inmates is unclear, according to Sufrin. Because of the inconsistent nature of reproductive health care, Sufrin thought that the repeal of *Roe* might have some impact but that, in some situations, it would have no impact.[68]

Finally, there is the issue of shackling. At least thirty-seven states have laws limiting the shackling of pregnant inmates. The limitations can go as far as banning shackling throughout the pregnancy as well as during labor delivery and the postpartum recovery period, although not all states go that far. The federal government bars the use of shackling on pregnant persons as of 2018.[69] A corollary study using the PIPS data examined shackling policies for pregnant inmates. It found that although the majority of states have laws restricting the use of shackling during childbirth, the practice is still used, even in facilities that acknowledge that state law prohibited it.[70] And in many cases, the women remained shackled in the postpartum period. The use of restraints on pregnant and postpartum people is medically dangerous and violates international standards of care. It remains to be seen whether the First Step Act will have a significant impact on shackling. The move toward state restrictions on shackling is good, but only as far as compliance with the laws is monitored and enforced. Whether this will be so remains unclear.

Placement of Children After Birth

There are limited options available for an incarcerated mother and her newborn to bond and to maintain ties after birth. For a small number of women, there may be an option to stay in a prison-based nursery with their child or be allowed to reside in a community-based residential program. Seven states have prison-based nursery programs in which an inmate can stay with her newborn child for a finite period of time.[71] The time can run from the shortest period of thirty days to programs that allow children to remain with their mothers for up to eighteen months.[72] But whatever the time duration, it is finite. At the end of the specified period, the child and mother are separated, and the child is transferred to the designated caregiver. The opportunities to reside in a prison-based nursery are extremely limited due both to the size of the units housing them and to the qualifications for being eligible to participate. The women must be low-level offenders and not have any previous charges of neglect or child abuse.[73] If the prison has no nursery option available, children are usually taken away from their mothers within forty-eight to seventy-two hours of birth, leaving no time for proper bonding with the child.[74] In that event, women must make the same decision that women entering prison with children must make regarding finding a family member or nonfamily person who will accept responsibility for the child. If none is available, the state will take the child and place them in foster care, with a high probability that the child will be adopted out.

Community-based residential parenting programs, on the other hand, allow the mother to serve her time outside the prison in a program run by a nonprofit that has partnered with correctional services.[75] Mothers live in a home-like setting, with a private sleeping space for the woman and her children. In most programs, a child can stay with the mother until the child reaches school age.[76] Eligibility is similar to the prison-based nursery. The woman must be a low-level offender, but women with substance abuse issues are also admitted and can receive treatment while in the programs.[77]

But not all community-based residential parenting programs are equal. Some have close connections with corrections departments, where agents surveil the woman and their children and can establish policies that can be more restrictive than even what the women endure in prison.

When Women Return to the Community

Web on Return

The United States releases approximately six hundred thousand inmates a year back to their communities. Of those, seventy-eight thousand are women.[78] In addition, 1.8 million women are released from jails. Women's successful reentry depends on programming that is gender responsive, and yet, despite the remarkable growth of incarcerated women, gender-responsive reentry programming has not seen a similar growth.[79] Gender-responsive programming acknowledges that women's problems are unique and require specific trauma-based approaches to helping their reentry. Studies have shown that the failure to address the specific needs of women who are reentering contributes to increased risk of recidivism.[80]

Women also do not receive the same kind of community support when they return as men do. Men expect support from their wives, mothers, and family upon reentering because they were not caregivers before they were incarcerated. Most women, on the other hand, were caregivers, and the community may expect them to return to the caregiving function when they are released. The women may have high expectations for themselves to care for their families, including parents and children. They may feel shame and guilt for having engaged in activity that deprived their families of their help.[81] But there are barriers to their being able to return to caregiving functions. They are not always in good physical health because of years of little or no adequate health care in the prisons.[82] They must find a job and secure housing that will be safe for them and their children and can pass inspection by child welfare authorities. And above all, they need time to stabilize themselves emotionally and learn to navigate in the outside world.

Failure to satisfy conditions of release in any of the factors just discussed can lead to a parole or probation violation, which can send the woman back to a penal institution. The same factors that led to the woman's incarceration in the first place put her constantly at risk of violating probation or parole.

The barriers exist because women detained in prisons are released to halfway houses. If a woman is lucky, she may be placed in a halfway house that has a relationship with employers who are willing to hire persons with a felony conviction. Even in this instance, however, employment opportunities are usually low-wage jobs and are often a long distance away from the living space, which makes it difficult for the woman to meet drug testing or counseling schedules and to maintain regular check-ins with probation or parole officials, all of which interferes with attempted renewed parental duties. Women who are released from jails rarely have halfway house opportunities available to them and are left to find whatever meager support is available on their own.

Even when women are released from prison or jail, they are not free from the criminal legal system but rather transitioned to institutions of social control: substance abuse treatment centers, mental health counselors, and child welfare agencies. As one scholar puts it, they are trapped in "an endless tautology of recycling clients back and forth from one so-called help system to another," in an ever widening net of social control.[83] This exists on top of interaction with the ongoing formal control of parole or probation.

Reestablishing Ties with Children

Women who have been away from their children while incarcerated are highly motivated to reestablish ties with them and, when possible, to regain custody. Recidivism studies show that women who maintain strong ties with their children and families are less likely to recidivate. Yet, reestablishing relationships are extremely difficult legally as well as socially. If a child is in foster care, the mother needs to find a way to activate a review of her case in the family courts. In order to have the best results, she will need a lawyer; but lawyers are not usually available, and the mother will not have the funds to pay for counsel. A petition to regain custody brings social services workers back into her life, with the racially biased apparatus that comes with child protective services and family courts. Parole and probation officers can be particularly disruptive to the process of regaining children if they set conditions of supervision so intense that the mother cannot comply with child welfare requirements.[84]

Persons who have served as primary custodians of the child can also be obstacles to a formerly incarcerated woman reuniting with her children, even if they are family members. Women report that sometimes their children's caregivers do not believe the mother should be trusted with her children when she gets out. They may object to visits, and in some cases, the family will report the mother to parole or probation or child welfare authorities for any perceived infraction, whether real or not. There is also the issue of disruption of custodial authority, as the child becomes confused as to which "mother" has the right to discipline or control the child. This also produces resentment from the custodial parent, who can feel threatened by the mother's return.[85]

Why Shoot for Failure Repeatedly?

All the materials on women's incarceration and reentry state the same conclusions: Women's pathways to incarceration are different. Women are economically marginalized. They suffer significant substance abuse and mental health problems, and they are overwhelmingly victims of trauma that includes physical and sexual abuse from strangers, family members, and intimate partners. All recommendations state that women prisoners need to have trauma-informed treatment, both while they are incarcerated and when they are released. And yet there are relatively few services available to women in prison or when they are released that follow the recommendations. While more data are always helpful to understand women's challenges, the solutions to successful reentry are known, as has been demonstrated by the nonprofits founded and run by formerly incarcerated women. Why, then, is so little still being done?

One argument suggests that no economic incentive exists for government to fund successful approaches to reducing and eliminating mass incarceration, particularly of people of color. The Prison Policy Initiative created a comprehensive listing of all of the entities that earn money from Black and Brown bodies remaining incarcerated.[86] The criminal legal system, including the prison industrial complex, provides billions of dollars to private businesses and government workers. Everyone feeds at the table of incarceration: Construction companies build prisons; agencies staff prisons; private companies are paid to feed prisoners. Telecommunication companies are paid to provide phone and internet, and agricultural entities get next to free prison labor, as do some high-end fashion brands.[87] States receive congressional representation based on prison populations in their state, despite the fact that prisoners in most cases do not have the right to vote while incarcerated.[88] Rather than seeing the reentry process as broken, perhaps it is just working as intended.[89]

Free Women and Disrupt the Prison Industrial Complex

The Abolition Agenda

Abolitionists believe the prison industrial complex and all its associated tentacles must be dismantled for marginalized communities to be free from racial capitalism and state surveillance.[90] For decades, scholar-activists such Ruth Wilson Gilmore, Angela Davis, and James Kilgore have advocated for prison abolition. New voices have joined them as the language of abolition inches closer to mainstream. Gilmore describes abolition as a "long game" and an "evolutionary process."[91] There is no one way to achieve prison abolition, and the coalition of activists strive to move the process forward without getting in each other's way.[92] As Davis has stated, "Abolitionist strategies are especially critical because they teach us that our visions of the future can radically depart from the present."[93]

Prison abolitionists work from three pillars: (1) support moratoriums on the creation of new prisons and jails; (2) decarcerate those who are already locked up; and (3) excarcerate, meaning stop sending people to prison.[94] Women prisoners need to be decarcerated as quickly as possible, and equally as important, they need to be adequately supported so that they do not go back to prison. In order for decarceration to be successful, new approaches to reentry, with an eye toward eliminating the web of supervision and control, are critical. There are programs that work that need to be replicated and expanded.

Wraparound Services

Community-based programs with wraparound services work. The concept of wraparound services is *not* new, and it has been used successfully for women returning to the community.[95] There are programs around the country that provide wraparound services, but there are too few. Three are highlighted here.

A New Way of Life Reentry Project (ANWOF), founded by Susan Burton, is the gold standard and has been helping women for twenty-four years.[96] In its 2022 annual report, ANWOF reported that it served 132 women residents and their children, with 83 in residence across its eleven homes. Of the total residents, 99 percent stayed free from reincarceration, and 99 percent met with conditions of probation or parole.[97] The project provides housing with no time limits to its residents, assists with finding substance abuse and mental health treatment, and provides workforce training. As part of the project's wraparound services, it helps women to obtain new identity documents. The project has two teams of lawyers. One team works to obtain expungement of criminal records and to obtain occupational licenses. A separate legal team provides pro bono services to residents who have family court appearances or are petitioning to increase visitation with their children or regain custody. To help expand options for women, ANWOF created the Sisterhood Alliance for Freedom and Equality (SAFE) network, a collective of formerly incarcerated individuals whom ANWOF trains to replicate wraparound services. The network has authorized SAFE locations in eighteen states and four countries. Services in SAFE include gender-sensitive services for trans women and nonbinary individuals returning from incarceration. But ANWOF reaches only a small fraction of the 2,888 women California released from prisons in 2019 in alone.

Hour Children is one of the New York programs for women who were formerly incarcerated.[98] It supports women who are reentering as well as those still serving time. Family reunification is a critical component of Hour Children's philosophy. As part of its prison-based services, it provides children in New York State who have mothers in prison an opportunity to visit their mothers once a month by organized bus trips.[99] Some children can enjoy multiday visits when host families provide overnight accommodations. Hour Children has six communal residences in Queens, New York. When its members are ready to move to permanent housing, the organization works with area builders to get housing units. New York State made a commitment to provide six thousand units of housing for formerly incarcerated individuals, and Hour Children was able to secure twenty-six units of housing for its women.[100] The organization reports that 96 percent of its women have stayed free, and 90 percent had successful reintegration with their families. New York released 1,421 women from prison in 2019 and 30,049 from jails.[101]

Finally, Marian House in Baltimore, Maryland, is a nonprofit organization with a religious background. It was founded by Sisters of Mercy and the School Sisters of Notre Dame in response to the conditions the nuns saw at the Women's Detention Center in Baltimore.[102] Many of the incarcerated women in detention were long-term substance abusers, yet 67 percent were not directed to reentry services when released.[103] Marian House was opened to assist them in recovery, but unlike traditional recovery programs, the women are not required to leave in thirty or sixty days. Residents can stay for up to two years. Counseling for substance abuse and mental health issues is handled in-house. The organization also helps women get educational assistance and prepare them for work reentry. Over the years, Marian House has expanded its capacity from fourteen to fifty-three women. Maryland released 649 women from prison in 2019 and 15,464 from jails.[104] A transitional housing program was created to help residents prepare to move into permanent housing. The organization also purchased an apartment building where Marian House graduates and other low-income women who cannot afford to enter the regular housing market can live. The program has a forced savings provision, such that when the women are ready to leave, they have both a savings and a checking account already established with funds from the women's work during the time they are residents.

Alternatives to Incarceration (ATIs)

Alternatives to incarceration (ATIs) represent the effort to excarcerate—to stop the flow of women to prisons and jails. Women at risk of becoming incarcerated will suffer less harm in community-based alternatives to carceral control. ATIs can help keep families intact and reduce intergenerational trauma, thereby breaking the carceral cycle.[105] The phrase, however, includes many concepts, some of which are still harmful to women and their families, such as electronic monitoring and drug courts.[106] Community-based nurseries are an example of ATIs that have gained wider acceptance in states, particularly those with large numbers of incarcerated women. But as just noted, some of these programs also resemble incarceration.[107] The best approaches to ATIs are programs that support and encourage the human development of a woman at risk, rather than threaten her with punishment and more state violence. One of the nine perspectives of abolitionist work is that women must remain nonmembers of the established prison system.[108] When done well, ATIs are a powerful tool that not only frees women but saves money. An ATI placement costs about 12 percent of what it costs to incarcerate.[109]

Conclusion

Abolitionists understand that the state will never allow its system to be reformed in a meaningful way; therefore, the only way marginalized people can survive and thrive in healthy and safe communities is to build a radically different system.[110] While that system is being built, efforts must be made to reduce the harm caused by the existing system. To support models that work, monies must be taken from carceral entities and redirected to community-based programs with holistic treatment. Funding community-based programs is not without pitfalls, as the lure of access to money can lead some nonprofits to become co-opted and enter into power relationships with law enforcement.[111] The solutions that prevent the destruction of women of color and their families are known and achievable. Abolitionists work to create a world where that can happen.

NOTES

1 Tara O'Neil Hayes, "The Economic Costs of the Criminal Justice System," American Action Forum, July 16, 2020, www.americanactionforum.org.

2 Institute for Advancing Justice Research and Innovation, "The Economic Burden of Incarceration in the U.S." (Working Paper #AJI072016, October 2016), www.prisonpolicy.org.

3 Lauren-Brook Eisen, "The Federal Funding That Fuels Mass Incarceration," Brennan Center for Justice, June 7, 2021, www.brennancenter.org.

4 Peter Wagner and Bernadette Rabuy, "Following the Money Prison of Mass Incarceration," Prison Policy Initiative, January 2017, www.prisonpolicy.org.

5 Vera Institute of Justice, "What Policing Costs: A Look at Spending in America's Biggest Cities," accessed June 18, 2024, www.vera.org. Milwaukee, Wisconsin, spends a remarkable 58 percent of its budget on policing.

6 Britt Skaathum, Francesca Maviglia, Anh Vo, Allison McBride, Sarah Seymour, Sebastian Mendez, et al., "Prioritization of Carceral Spending in U.S. Cities; Development of the Carceral Resource Index (CRI) and the Role of Race and Income Inequality," PLOS One, December 15, 2022.

7 Niki Monazzam and Kristen M. Budd, "Incarcerated Women and Girls: Report," Sentencing Project, July 24, 2024, www.sentencingproject.org.

8 Monazzam and Budd, "Incarcerated Women and Girls."

9 Aleks Kajstura and Wendy Sawyer, "Women's Mass Incarceration: The Whole Pie 2023," March 1, 2023, www.prisonpolicy.org.

10 Monazzam and Budd, "Incarcerated Women and Girls," 2.

11 Leah Wang, "Both Sides of the Bar: How Mass Incarceration Punishes Families," Prison Policy Initiative, August 11, 2022, www.prisonpolicy.org.

12 Wang, "Both Sides of the Bar."

13 ACLU, "The Prison Rape Elimination Act of 2003 (PREA)," April 2011, www.aclu.org.

14 Monazzam and Budd, "Incarcerated Women and Girls," 2.

15 Elizabeth Swavola, Kristi Riley, and Ram Subramanian, "Overlooked: Women in Jails in an Era of Reform," Vera Institute of Justice, August 2016, www.vera.org.

16 Wang, "Both Sides of the Bar."

17 Wang, "Both Sides of the Bar."

18 CDC, "Adverse Trauma Experiences (ACEs): Preventing Childhood Trauma to Improve Adult Health," Vital Signs, November 2019, www.cdc.gov. Many women prisoners had multiple ACEs in their childhood. Melissa S. Jones, Meredith G. F. Worthen, Susan F. Sharp, and David A. McLeod, "Life as She Knows It: The Effects of Adverse Childhood Experiences on Intimate Partner Violence Among Women Prisoners," *Child Abuse & Neglect* 85 (2018): 68–79.

19 Shubert Center for Child Studies, "Children of Incarcerated Parents: An Overview," Issue Brief, October 2014, https://case.edu.

20 Beth Richie, "The Social Impact of Mass Incarceration of Women," in *Invisible Punishment: The Collateral Consequences of Mass Incarceration*, ed. Marc Mauer and Meda Chesney-Lind (New Press, 2002); Wendy Sawyer, "The Gender Divide, Tracking Women's State Prison Growth," Prison Policy Initiative, January 2018, www.prisonpolicy.org; Correctional Association of New York, *It Reminds Us of How We Got Here* (Correctional Association of New York, 2020).

21 Prison Policy Initiative, "Women's Mass Incarceration: The Whole Pie 2024," June 18, 2024, www.prisonpolicy.org; Kajstura and Sawyer, "Women's Mass Incarceration."

22 National Sexual Violence Research Center, "Statistics," accessed June 18, 2024, www.nsvrc.org/statistics.

23 Kajstura and Sawyer, "Women's Mass Incarceration."

24 Ruth Wilson Gilmore, "Organized Abandonment w/ Ruth Wilson Gilmore (10/06/22)," *Death Panel*, Soundcloud, October 6, 2022, www.deathpanel.net.

25 Kajstura and Sawyer, "Women's Mass Incarceration."

26 Kajstura and Sawyer, "Women's Mass Incarceration."

27 ACLU, "Prison Rape Elimination Act of 2003."

28 Swavola et al., "Overlooked."

29 Yosha Gunasekra, "How One Woman's Sexual Abuse Resulted in Years Behind Bars," *Marie Claire*, May 2018, www.marieclaire.com.

30 Liz Komar and Alexandra Bailey, *Sentencing Reform for Criminalized Survivors: Learning from New York's Domestic Violence Survivors Justice Act* (Sentencing Project, April 19, 2023), www.sentencingproject.org.

31 Andrea J. Ritchie, *Invisible No More: Police Violence Against Black Woman and Women of Color* (Beacon, 2017); Mariame Kaba and Andrea J. Ritchie, "Tricks and Tensions," in *No More Police: A Case for Abolition* (New Press, 2022), 77.

32 Beth Richie, *Arrested Justice: Black Women, Violence, and America's Prison Nation* (New York University Press, 2012), 118–19.

33 B. Richie, *Arrested Justice.*

34 Survived and Punished Project, "Analysis and Vision," 2016, https://survivedandpunished.org.

35 Survived and Punished Project, "Analysis and Vision."

36 B. Richie, *Arrested Justice.*

37 Komar and Bailey, *Sentencing Reform.*

38 Komar and Bailey, *Sentencing Reform.*

39 Komar and Bailey, *Sentencing Reform*, 8.

40 Swavola et al., "Overlooked."

41 Children's Rights and Columbia Law School Human Rights Institute, "Racial (In) Justice in the U.S. Child Welfare System," July 2022, www.childrensrights.org.

42 Wang, "Both Sides of the Bar."

43 First Step Act, Public Law 115-339, 115th Congress.

44 Beatrix Lockwood and Nicole Lewis, "The Long Journey to Visit a Family Member in Prison," Marshall Project, December 18, 2019, www.themarshallproject.org.

45 B. Richie, "Social Impact," 139.

46 Stephanie S. Covington, "A Woman's Journey Home: Challenges for Female Offenders and Their Children," ASPE, November 30, 2001, https://aspe.hhs.gov.

47 "Families Spend 'Exorbitant Rates' to Call Their Incarcerated Loved One. A New Bill Aims to Change That," *PBS News*, February 3, 2023, www.pbs.org (discussing the plight of families with incarcerated loved ones and a new bill, the Martha Wright Reed Just and Reasonable Communications Act, signed by President Joe Biden in 2023). Aleks Kajstura, "Evading Regulation, Some In-State Phone Calls from Jails Costs over $1.50 Per Minute," Prison Policy Initiative, January 19, 2017, www.prisonpolicy.org.

48 Adoption and Safe Families Act of 1997, Pub. L. No. 105-89.

49 Dorothy Roberts, "The Clinton-Era Adoption Law That Still Devastates Black Families Today," *Slate*, November 21, 2022, https://slate.com.

50 ASFA, Sec. 103 (a)(3).

51 David Crary, "Many Say Now Is the Time to Fight Racial Bias in Foster Care," *AP News*, April 14, 2021, https://apnews.com.

52 Crary, "Many Say Now Is the Time."

53 Michael Fitzgerald and Kate Gonzales, "Advocates and Officials Press Case for Overhauling Key Adoption and Child Welfare Law," *The Imprint*, February 21, 2011, https://imprintnews.org.

54 Dorothy E. Roberts, *Shattered Bonds: The Color Of Child Welfare* (Civitas Books, 2002); Martin Guggenheim, "How Racial Politics Led Directly to the Enactment of the Adoption and Safe Families Act—The Worst Law Affecting Families Ever

Enacted by Congress," *Columbia Journal of Race and Law* 11, no. 3 (November 18, 2021): 711–32.

55 Mical Raz, "What We've Learned About the Impact of the Adoption and Safe Families Act Twenty-Five Years Later," PolicyLab, Children's Hospital of Philadelphia, February 2023, https://policylab.chop.edu (gathers listing of research on ASFA's consequences).

56 Repeal ASFA, a nonprofit organization fighting for the rights of Black families, accessed June 18, 2024, www.repealasfa.org.

57 Meghan Krausch, "Grassroots Defense Committees Support Criminalized Survivors," *Truthout*, July 9, 2022, https://truthout.org.

58 PREA, Pub. L. No. 108-79.

59 PREA, Secs. 3 and 4.

60 US Senate, *Sexual Abuse of Female Inmates in Federal Prisons: Staff Report, Permanent Subcommittee on Investigations* (US Senate, December 2022), www.hsgac.senate.gov.

61 US Senate, *Sexual Abuse*, 18; "'Every Woman's Worse Nightmare': Lawsuit Alleges Widespread Sexual Abuse at California Prisons for Women," *Los Angeles Times*, January 19, 2024, www.latimes.com; Quinn Owen, "Former Female Inmates Speak About Widespread Sexual Abuse by Prison Staff," *ABC News*, December 13, 2022, https://abcnews.go.com.

62 ARRWIP, "Pregnancy in Prison Statistics (PIPS) Project," accessed June 18, 2024, https://arrwip.org; Michael Fitzgerald and Kat Gonzales, "Advocate and Officials Press Case for Overhauling Key Adoption and Child Welfare Law," *The Imprint*, February 21, 2022, https://imprintnews.org.

63 Roe v. Wade, 410 U.S. 113 (1973).

64 Joshua Sharfstein, "Jailed and Pregnant: What the Roe Repeal Means for Incarcerated Persons," Johns Hopkins Bloomberg School of Public Health, September 21, 2022, https://publichealth.jhu.edu.

65 Sharfstein, "Jailed and Pregnant."

66 Carolyn B. Sufrin, Ashley Devon-Williamston, Lauren Beal, Crystal M. Hayes, and Camille Kramer, "'I Mean I Didn't Really Have a Choice of Anything': How Incarceration Influences Abortion Decision-Making and Precludes Access in the United States," *Perspectives on Sex Reproductive Health* 55, no. 3 (2023): 165–77.

67 Dobbs v. Jackson Women's Health Organization, 597 U.S. 215 (2022).

68 JIWC, "Abortion Access for Incarcerated People in the U.S.," Center for Leadership Education in Maternal and Child Public Health, May 2023, https://mch.umn.edu/abortion/.

69 First Step Act.

70 Camille Kramer, Karenna Thomas, Ankita Patil, Crystal M. Hayes, and Carolyn B. Sufrin, "Shackling and Pregnancy Care Policies in U.S. Prisons and Jails," *Maternal and Child Health Journal* 27 (2023): 186–96.

71 Women's Prison Association, *Mothers, Infants and Imprisonment: A National Look at Prison Nurseries and Community-Based Alternatives* (Institute on Women and

Criminal Justice, May 2009), 5, www.prisonlegalnews.org. The report identifies nine states that have prison-sponsored nurseries: California, Illinois, Indiana, Ohio, Nebraska, New York, South Dakota, Washington, and West Virginia.

72 Women's Prison Association, *Mothers, Infants and Imprisonment*, 9.

73 Women's Prison Association, *Mothers, Infants and Imprisonment*, 9.

74 Substance Abuse and Mental Health Services Administration, *After Incarceration: A Guide to Helping Women Reenter the Community* (US Department of Health and Human Services, 2020), 19, https://store.samhsa.gov.

75 Women's Prison Association, *Mothers, Infants and Imprisonment*.

76 Women's Prison Association, *Mothers, Infants and Imprisonment*.

77 Women's Prison Association, *Mothers, Infants and Imprisonment*, 5.

78 Holly Ventura Miller, "Female Reentry and Gender Responsive Programing," National Institute of Justice, May 19, 2021. Prison Policy initiative puts the number of women at eighty-one thousand. Leah Wang, "Since You Asked: How Many Women and Men are Released from Each State's Prisons and Jails Every Year?," Prison Policy Initiative, February 28, 2024, www.prisonpolicy.org.

79 Miller, "Female Reentry."

80 New York Women's Foundation, *Women Injustice: Gender and the Pathway to Jail in New York City* (New York Women's Foundation, 2023), https://justiceandopportunity.org.

81 Andrea M. Leverentz, *The Ex-Prisoner's Dilemma: How Women Negotiate the Competing Narratives of Reentry and Desistance* (Rutgers University Press, 2014), 177–78.

82 Tanya Telfair LeBlanc, Laurie Reid, Hazel D. Dean, and Yvonne Green, "Introduction: Health Equity Among Incarcerated Female Adolescents and Adult Women: Infectious and Other disease Morbidity," *Women Health* 54, no. 8 (2022): 687–93.

83 Madonna R. Maidment, *Doing Time on the Outside: Deconstructing the Benevolent Community* (University of Toronto Press, 2006), 128.

84 Margaret Oot Hayes, "Mothering After Imprisonment," on *Interrupted Life Experiences of Incarcerated Women in the United States*, ed. Rickie Solinger, Paula C. Johnson, Martha L. Raimon, Tina Reynolds, and Ruby C. Tapia (University of California Press, 2010), 390.

85 Hayes, "Mothering After Imprisonment," 389.

86 Peter Wagner and Bernadette Robury, "Following the Money of Mass Incarceration," Prison Policy Initiative, January 25, 2017, www.prisonpolicy.org.

87 Robin McDowell and Margie Mason, "Prisoners in the U.S. Are Part of a Hidden Work Force Linked to Hundreds of Popular Food Brands," *AP News*, January 29, 2024, https://apnews.com; Isabella Rosengren, "The Fashion Labels Whose Clothes Are Made by Prisoners," *BBC News*, July 6, 2020, www.bbc.com.

88 Sam Levine, "2020 Census Will Continue to Count Prisoners Where They Are Incarcerated," *HuffPost*, February 8, 2018, www.huffpost.com.

89 Jennifer M. Ortiz and Hayley Jackey, "The System Is Not Broken, It Is Intentional: The Prisoner Reentry Industry as Deliberate Structural Violence," *Prison Journal* 99, no. 4 (2019): 484–503.

90 Cherisse Burden-Stelly, "Modern U.S. Racial Capitalism," *Monthly Review*, July 2020. The term "racial capitalism" is credited to Cedric Robinson's *Black Marxism: The Making of the Black Radical Tradition* (Zed Press, 1983), in which he described it as "the development, organization, and expansion of capitalist society pursued essentially racial directions."

91 "Ruth Wilson Gilmore: 'Where Life Is Precious, Life Is Precious,'" *On Being with Krista Tippett*, March 30, 2023, https://onbeing.org.

92 Kaba and Ritchie, "Tricks and Tensions."

93 Angela Y. Davis, "Believe in New Possibilities," in *Abolition for the People*, ed. Colin Kaepernick (Kaepernick, 2021), 22.

94 Prison Research Education Action Project, *Instead of Prisons: A Handbook for Abolitions* (Prison Research Education Action Project, 1976), chap. 3, Prison Policy Initiative, www.prisonpolicy.org.

95 Stephanie Covington, "A Woman's Journey Home: Challenges for Female Offenders and Their Children" (working paper prepared for the "From Prison to Home" Conference, January 30–31, 2002), ASPE, https://aspe.hhs.gov.

96 Susan Burton and Cai Lynn, *Becoming Ms. Burton: From Prison to Recovery to Leading the Fight for Incarcerated Women* (New Press, 2019).

97 A New Way of Life Reentry Project, *2022 Annual Report* (A New Way of Life Reentry Project, 2023), https://anewwayoflife.org.

98 Hour Children, "A Time to Come Home," April 7, 2021, https://hourchildren.org.

99 Hour Children, "Prison-Based Family Services Programs," accessed June 18, 2024, https://hourchildren.org.

100 Hour Children, "Time to Come Home."

101 Wang, "Since You Asked."

102 Marian House, "History," accessed June 18, 2024, www.marianhouse.org.

103 Marian House, "Incarceration," accessed June 18, 2024, www.marianhouse.org. The stories of the formerly incarcerated women show clearly the failure of state-sponsored reentry support for women, or the lack thereof. These women faced repeated periods of incarceration with little to no help offered upon release.

104 Wang, "Since You Asked."

105 Women and Incarceration Project, Center for Women's Health and Human Rights, Suffolk University, "Women & Imprisonment Project," accessed June 18, 2024, https://sites.suffolk.edu.

106 Coletta Youngers and Corina Ginacomello, "Electronic Monitoring: A New Form of Punishment for Many Women," WOLA, December 13, 2022, www.wola.org.

107 Tess Domb Sadof, "Alternatives to Incarceration Aim to Strengthen Families," Vera Institute of Justice, August 10, 2015, www.vera.org (noting that some programs in Washington State have privatized electronic monitoring of mothers).

108 Prison Research Education Action Project, *Instead of Prisons*, chap. 3.

109 Caroline Bushe and Adam Schaffer, "JusticeHome: Breaking Barriers & Helping Families via Alternatives to Incarceration," WOLA, October 2020, https://womenanddrugs.wola.org.

110 Ruth Wilson Gilmore and James Kilgore, "Commentary: The Case for Abolition," Marshall Project, June 19, 2019, www.themarshallproject.org; Legal Defense Fund, "Justice in Public Safety Project: Framework for Public Safety," accessed June 18, 2024, www.naacpldf.org/framework-for-public-safety/; Mariame Kaba, *We Do This till We Free Us: Abolitionist Organizing and Transforming Justice* (Haymarket Books, 2021).

111 INCITE! Women of Color Against Violence, *The Revolution Will Not Be Funded: Beyond the Non-Profit Industrial Complex* (Duke University Press, 2017).

13

Ensuring All Families Flourish

CLARE HUNTINGTON

I write this chapter at the close of my twentieth year teaching and writing about family law. For two decades, I have argued that family law should foster strong, stable, positive relationships within families.[1] In this work, I draw on a broad definition of family law. Beyond the direct regulation of family relationships and behavior, I argue that family law also includes seemingly unrelated laws—from zoning regulations to the criminal legal system—that influence family life.[2] Using this broad definition illuminates the many ways the law negatively impacts families, but it also points toward an ambitious agenda that would help all families flourish and redress the deep legacy of racial discrimination in the United States.[3] In this chapter, I revisit this agenda, contending that the government must take a proactive stance toward families and adopt policies that dismantle racial inequality.

We cannot lose sight of this ambitious-but-essential vision. At the same time, I am interested in the art of the possible in the current politically polarized climate. Although there is a yawning divide between the steps the government *should* take and the steps we have taken, as I describe in this chapter, policy makers have done more to assist families, including families of color, than we might recognize. These steps fall far short of what needs to be done, but examining these efforts generates useful insights for broader reform.

A Far-Reaching Vision to Help All Families Flourish and Address Inequality

Overwhelming evidence from multiple disciplines establishes that strong, stable, positive relationships—especially during childhood—are essential for both individual and societal well-being.[4] For most children, especially very young children, the most influential relationships are within the family. But families do not operate in a vacuum, and multiple factors affect the ability of a parent or other primary caregiver to provide a child with a strong, stable, positive relationship. It matters whether the parent has a reliable job that generates sufficient income to care for the child. It matters whether the parent is raising the child in a community with good schools and access to playgrounds. It matters whether the family has health insurance and thus can receive needed care without incurring ruinous debt. And it matters whether the parent has social support from other adults in the community. These factors—and many more—influence family life and child outcomes.

Although it is not always readily apparent, the law plays a significant role in these aspects of family life. Beyond determining who is a family in the first place and the rights and obligations family members owe each other, the law also sets the context for relationships. Consider a few examples of this broader understanding of family law. Zoning laws determine whether neighborhoods contain safe play spaces and encourage interaction among neighbors. Employment laws control work conditions and minimum wages. Criminal laws decide whether the legal system will emphasize incarceration, which, in turn, affects whether a child will have a parent in their daily life. And state investments—in child care, education, affordable housing, health care, public transportation, and much more—impact family functioning.

The problem is that too often the law has a negative impact on families. When directly regulating family relationships, family law can inflict tremendous harm. State laws, for example, often fail to recognize and support a broad range of families, especially those outside the traditional norm. And the family regulation system unnecessarily removes children from the care of their parents. More broadly, family law pays insufficient attention to the context of family life. In many communities, zoning laws do not require developers to build sidewalks and communal areas that would encourage neighborly interactions and give families a safe place to play. Employment laws do not ensure that parents have access to reliable jobs with decent pay. Criminal laws and policies overemphasize incarceration. And the government makes miserly investments in critical resources, including child care, education, affordable housing, health care, and public transportation.

Family law has also created racial inequalities among families. In urban planning and housing policies, for example, scholars have shown that the government deliberately produced and then reinforced racial residential segregation. This segregation deprived Black families of access to high-quality schools, parks, reliable public transportation, and, critically, the housing equity that has been a primary driver of economic prosperity for white families.[5] Similarly, the criminal legal system reflects past and ongoing governmental practices that are borne disproportionally by Black families. Policies such as denying bail and imposing long sentences drive the overincarceration of Black men and women.[6] One of the many harsh consequences is the separation of Black parents and children.

Family law must address both sets of harms: those that affect all families and those that affect families of color. Fostering strong, stable, positive relationships within all families begins with strengthening the relationship between parents and between parents and children. There are numerous ways to do so. Neighborhood-based family relationship centers, for example, can provide family mediation and access to services.[7] And programs like the Nurse-Family Partnership help new parents adjust to the challenges of parenting.[8] Family law must also pay far greater attention to the context of family life.[9] By subsidizing quality child care, the government would help parents work, defray the debilitating cost of child care, and ensure children are in safe, stimulating settings. By investing in universal early childhood education, the government would partner with parents to improve kindergarten readiness and boost academic achievement. By building and maintaining welcoming parks and playgrounds, the government would give parents and children a safe place to spend time together. And by providing universal health care, the government would ensure families have access to the care they need, including treatment for health issues that directly impact the parent-child relationship, like substance use disorder and mental illness.

To address racial inequality among families, family law must take deliberate, focused steps. To redress the legacy of racial residential segregation and underinvestment in Black neighborhoods, for example, policies today must tackle the ongoing effects of past intentional discrimination. The government should make direct investments in Black communities, improve the quality of neighborhood schools, increase access to credit, dismantle barriers to racial integration, and much more. Only intentional efforts will begin to reverse the impact of intentional discrimination. Similarly, policy makers must engage in direct reforms to the criminal legal system at the federal, state, and local level. This is not the place to elaborate these reforms, but it is essential to accelerate the reduction in incarceration and grapple with the harms inflicted on families by the criminal legal system.

In short, there is much work to be done to improve opportunities for all families and especially to redress racial inequality. The question is how to achieve this vision, especially given the polarized nature of our polity.

(Limited) Progress Notwithstanding Political Polarization

Although there is a long way to go to ensure that all families flourish, there have been some steps in the right direction, which is especially notable given the current political climate. Consider a few examples of relatively successful policies: Red states and blue states have expanded prekindergarten, with enormous benefits, especially for Black children. The earned income tax credit (EITC) delivers $64 billion to thirty-one million families annually, with recipients disproportionately Black and Hispanic (although children of immigrant parents are less likely to receive the tax credit).[10] And Medicaid expansion has delivered health care to millions of low-income families, sharply reducing the number of uninsured nonelderly adults in all racial and ethnic groups. Together, these policies—which typically enjoy wide bipartisan support and can be understood as part of a broader trend of what I call pragmatic family law—have led to meaningful change for families.[11] These programs are clearly not enough, and they may sap energy from the systemic change that is desperately needed; but it is still worth considering what has—and has not—been achieved. The remainder of this chapter unpacks the phenomenon of pragmatic family law.

Political Polarization

Polarization is a now-familiar attribute of US law, policy, and society.[12] There are many sites of contestation, from gun control to immigration, but family law is one of the central battlegrounds in a polarized United States. Even casual observers are familiar with the divides around family laws and policies, with familiar fights over reproductive health care, gender-affirming care, and state support for low-income families.

Numerous forces contribute to contestation and polarization in family law. The allocation of decision-making authority—with state laws controlling much of family law—provides multiple opportunities for states to adopt divergent policies. And the subject matter is fertile ground for disagreement. Family law doctrine and policy reflect deeply held values and address issues around bodily autonomy and sexual liberty. And many aspects of family law implicate equality and equity in numerous dimensions, including race, class, gender, sexual orientation, and gender identity. In short, family law issues are not simply policy choices but instead fights over values, identity, and a way of life.[13]

Family law is also subject to broader forces driving polarization more generally. There is a growing divergence between the two main political parties, with limited ideological overlap between Republicans and Democrats.[14] Political affiliation often aligns with other parts of identity, especially race and religiosity, making the divisions especially profound.[15] Further, geographic clustering means Republicans and Democrats are dominant in different states, and the political parties have brought national politics to the state and local level, making these levels of government active sites of contestation.[16] Additionally, advocates and legal actors tend to frame issues in the language of rights, which heightens the sense of division and winners and losers.[17] A final factor driving polarization is growing democratic deficits, including partisan gerrymandering, restrictions on voting, and campaign finance failures.[18]

In sum, both the content of family law and the larger context of polarization in the United States makes it hard to agree on doctrine and policy. But there is more agreement than we might expect, as I describe in the next section.

Progress Despite Polarization

There are numerous programs of state support that defy the dominant pattern of polarization. These programs are directed at low-income families—who are disproportionately Black, Hispanic, and Native American—and the programs enjoy relatively broad and bipartisan support. This support is surprising in light of the historical and ongoing hostility to state support for low-income families, especially families of color. Cash welfare programs are especially contentious, with politicians demonizing recipients and invoking racist stereotypes.[19] And yet three programs—including one that is, in essence, cash welfare—do not provoke this same opposition.

The first example is universal prekindergarten. Red and blue states across the country are investing in early education, following the lead of Oklahoma, which was an early and strong leader.[20] To be sure, progressive states tend to spend more per pupil, but states of all political stripes are investing in the quality of prekindergarten programs.[21] States such as Alabama, Hawaii, Michigan, Mississippi, Missouri, and Rhode Island meet all of the quality benchmarks set by the National Institute for Early Education Research, and another set of politically diverse states meet most of the benchmarks.[22] These investments in quality are critical because abundant research establishes that high-quality programs are far more effective in boosting student outcomes than are lower-quality programs.[23]

The earned income tax credit is a second example of a supportive program that does not elicit widespread political opposition. A casual observer may not understand this program, but what is called a "tax credit" is really a cash transfer tied to work: Low-wage workers typically do not owe federal taxes, but if they file a federal tax return, they receive a check from the government in the amount of the "credit."[24] Adults with children in the home are eligible for a substantial credit: For the 2023 tax year, the maximum credit was $7,430.[25] (Adults without children in the home receive far less: a maximum credit of $600.)[26] The main cash welfare program—Temporary Assistance for Needy Families—provides $3.35 billion in federal cash payments to approximately two million people per month.[27] By contrast, the EITC delivers $64 billion to thirty-one million low-income workers.[28] And notwithstanding its cash nature, the EITC enjoys wide bipartisan support.[29] Indeed, Congress has repeatedly expanded the EITC since the mid-1970s.[30] The child tax credit (CTC) is another "credit" that operates as cash welfare, and the CTC does not have a work requirement. It, too, enjoys wide bipartisan support.[31]

A final example is Medicaid expansion under the Affordable Care Act (ACA).[32] The ACA was highly controversial when first enacted, with conservative leaders claiming that it unleashed federal power on individuals and infringed on states' rights.[33] After the passage of the law, Democrats lost control of the US House of Representatives, hundreds of seats in state legislatures, and many governorships.[34] The ACA also helped spark the creation of the Tea Party.[35] When the Supreme Court struck down the ACA's requirement that states expand Medicaid or lose Medicaid funding entirely, many conservative states celebrated.[36] But soon after the decision, many of the same states changed their position and chose to expand Medicaid; states like Indiana, under then-Governor Mike Pence, led the way.[37] Since then, fifteen conservative states have expanded Medicaid.[38]

This is not an exhaustive list of pragmatic approaches to family well-being. To name one more, state laws providing protections for pregnant workers run the political gamut, and most were enacted in the past decade.[39] Thirty states and the District of Columbia have a pregnant workers fairness act, filling gaps that had been left by federal law until Congress acted in late 2022.[40] These laws typically require employers to make reasonable accommodations for pregnant workers, thus promoting women's access to the workforce—especially for women of color, who are overrepresented in the low-wage workforce and often work jobs that are physically demanding.[41]

I call this approach to family well-being "pragmatic family law." I mean this partly in the colloquial sense of "pragmatic": The programs and policies reflect commonsense solutions. But I also mean it in the philosophical sense of pragmatism: a methodology with a distinct lineage in American thought. Tracing back to the late nineteenth and early twentieth centuries, pragmatism is a method that focuses not on first principles but instead on whether an idea is useful.[42] The early pragmatists asserted that all ideas are tentative and subject to testing and revision based on empirical evidence and experimentation. And they were pluralist in their understanding of knowledge, looking to lived experience as well as more traditional sources of empirical evidence.[43]

Advocates and scholars have long used pragmatism to address social problems. Scholars of race and feminism, for example, use the tools of pragmatism to deepen our understanding of the roles of race and gender in society and to imagine new possibilities for social change. W. E. B. Du Bois began this tradition by arguing that previous pragmatist works had ignored race as an impediment to social experimentation and consensus and that adding this perspective was critical.[44] Working in a Black community in Philadelphia, Du Bois was the first researcher to gather empirical data on the living conditions of Black Americans, documenting the subjectively lived and felt experiences of Black Americans.[45]

Today, scholars of race and advocates for political change continue to look to pragmatism. Cornel West emphasizes the pragmatic method's potential to resist social hierarchy, given its focus on problem solving and collectivity.[46] Similarly, Black feminist scholars such as Patricia Hill Collins, V. Denise James, and Deva Woodly look to pragmatism as a method for social change. Collins, a sociologist, elaborates on the idea of "visionary pragmatism," arguing that social change requires attention to both what *can* be and what *is*—at least today.[47] James, a philosopher, looks to one of the original pragmatists, John Dewey, for his rejection of utopian ideals, embrace of the possible, focus on consequences and outcomes, and treatment of lived experiences as a respectable source of knowledge.[48] James argues that this approach creates a vision for social hope.[49] And Woodly, a political scientist, argues that pragmatism can encourage modern social movements by centering lived experience, asking, "What does it mean to experience justice?" rather than "What constitutes justice?"[50] And the pragmatic method can further social justice by encouraging listening, especially to marginalized voices and those directly affected by systems of discrimination and injustice.[51]

As this summary illustrates, American pragmatism is a vibrant living tradition, adopted in numerous contexts and for varying purposes. Three elements of the living tradition are useful for seeing a methodological link in the programs described earlier: (1) a rejection of abstract ideals and political ideology and, instead, a focus on what works to solve a problem; (2) a commitment to experience-based learning, empirical evidence, and experimentation (this ground-up theory of knowledge especially values lived experience); and (3) the use of contextualized decision-making, because what works in one area and context may not in another.

These elements of pragmatism flow through the programs described earlier. Consider the movement for universal prekindergarten. When seeking to expand access, advocates framed the question in concrete, specific terms focused on child well-being by asking whether prekindergarten improves academic performance during elementary school.[52] This shifted the focus away from more politically contentious questions about state support and instead centered the abundant empirical evidence demonstrating the positive impact of prekindergarten on children's educational outcomes, at least for quality programs.[53] Experimentation was also a core component of the movement, with major foundations providing funding for demonstration projects.[54] Some experimentation in prekindergarten policy was serendipitous. A change in school financing formulas in Oklahoma left some districts with additional money, which they used to fund prekindergarten programs.[55] After parents enrolled their children and saw the benefits firsthand, they began to support prekindergarten by a wide margin, advocating with school districts to continue the program, bringing the lived experience of families to the movement.[56] Finally, the effort to expand prekindergarten relied on context-based decision-making, taking account of local politics and, especially, the resonance of messaging.

Medicaid expansion is another example of the pragmatic method at work. The initial resistance to expansion in conservative states was rooted in political ideology, but politicians soon showed a willingness to focus on the health-care needs of their low-income residents rather than ideology.[57] It helped that states had increased bargaining power in the wake of the Supreme Court decision striking down mandatory expansion, giving states an opportunity to expand Medicaid on their own terms.[58] The Obama administration worked individually with the states resisting expansion, rather than approaching them as a unified group.[59] Experience-based learning also played a significant role in shifting policy. Citizens communicating to government actors their on-the-ground experiences of receiving health care helped fundamentally change the politics of public funding.[60] Indeed, between 2010 and 2017, the politics surrounding the ACA shifted such that cutting back on Medicaid was politically untenable.[61] Put in the language of pragmatism, individuals experienced health care through expanded Medicaid and then insisted that government actors continue the coverage. And in some states where government officials refused to expand Medicaid, citizens took the lead through ballot initiatives, focusing on the concrete need of access to health care.[62]

The Potential of Pragmatic Family Law

Pragmatic family law furthers child well-being generally, and it has made some headway in furthering racial equity. Consider the earned income tax credit. The poverty rate for Black children decreased from 49 percent in 1993 to 18 percent in 2019—a similar percentage decrease as across other racial groups.[63] Many factors played a role in this historic drop, but the EITC was the single biggest government program reducing child poverty.[64] More generally, given the overrepresentation of Black adults in the low-wage workforce, the EITC disproportionately benefits Black and Hispanic families.[65] Other examples of pragmatic family law also address the needs of families of color. Women of color are overrepresented in physically demanding jobs, like home health aide work, and thus especially benefit from pregnant workers fairness acts, which help address pregnancy complications and maternal mortality.[66] Medicaid expansion has increased health-care coverage for nonelderly adults in all racial and ethnic groups. For example, the percentage of uninsured in 2019 dropped from 44 percent in 2010 to 28 percent for American Indian/Alaska Native nonelderly adults, from 32 percent to 22 percent for Hispanic nonelderly adults, and from 20 percent to 12 percent for Black nonelderly adults.[67] And there is early evidence that Medicaid expansion is reducing racial health disparities.[68] Finally, expanded access to prekindergarten has boosted the academic achievement of Black children, who, unlike children in other racial groups, show strong academic gains from prekindergarten even after controlling for quality of the program.[69]

In all these ways, pragmatic family law has improved child well-being for all groups, and it has begun to chip away at some of the racial inequities in the United States. As the next section describes, however, there are good reasons to temper enthusiasm for pragmatism.

The Limits of Pragmatic Family Law

Notwithstanding the gains described in this chapter, pragmatic family law has not—and probably cannot—fundamentally change law or society. Pragmatic family law operates within existing political constraints, and it has not yet led to a sea change in the state's stance toward supporting families. Unlike other wealthy countries, the United States predicates public policy on the assumption that family members will care for each other with limited government support.[70] Ending this privatization of dependency would require fundamental changes to law and policy. And pragmatic family law is not going to usher in a new age of state support.

The EITC, for example, lifts millions of children out of poverty, but only by a marginal amount.[71] And it does not change the broader economic conditions that keep millions of low-wage workers in dangerous jobs earning poverty or near-poverty wages.[72] Moreover, the EITC and related programs do not address other barriers to work and economic stability, such as the need for subsidized child care. In another example, Medicaid expansion helped fill critical gaps; but the United States still does not have universal health care, and nearly one in nine people under age sixty-five remains uninsured, with much higher rates for individuals of color.[73] It is also telling that many of the states that continue to resist Medicaid expansion have a high proportion of Black residents.[74]

Another reason for tempered enthusiasm is the ongoing political division over measures to address racial inequities. It is notable that advocates and policy makers have not framed the pragmatic policies described in this chapter as efforts to address racial inequities. And framing the programs in such terms may well erode support. Polling shows that two-thirds of the American public opposes reparations for descendants of enslaved people.[75] Thus, if advocates restyled the EITC as a racial equity payment program, for example, views on the desirability of the subsidy would probably be polarized, and much support would evaporate.[76] In short, pragmatism in family law should work for all families, but race, racism, and deep divides about whether the United States should do more to address racial inequities are fundamental cleavages in the United States. This makes it significantly harder to use the pragmatic method to dismantle structural racism.

Notwithstanding these challenges for pragmatism in the current political climate, the method still has an important, if perhaps aspirational, role to play in reducing racial equity. As Du Bois, James, West, and other scholars of race have argued, pragmatism's call to learn from lived experience opens the door to understanding the role of race, gender, and other important aspects of identity in that experience. Indeed, one of the core tenets of American pragmatism is listening to those who are most affected by a problem and learning from their experience. This tool has the potential to reform aspects of family law that disproportionately affect families of color, such as the government's response to child abuse and neglect. This guidance shows us where we need to go and one way to get there. But we are a long way off.

Conclusion

Persistent inequality, especially along racial lines, is an appalling if all-too-familiar aspect of US family life. Redressing these inequalities, which are rooted in deliberate governmental policies, will require intentional and sustained effort. Notwithstanding profound polarization in the United States, government officials at all levels of government are adopting policies and programs that make a difference in the lives of low-income families. These efforts fall far short of the support that is needed. And they are decidedly not an effort to redress intentional racial discrimination. But they should not be dismissed either, as they may begin to lay the groundwork for future efforts.

The pressing question is whether these kinds of programs build momentum for other, perhaps even more far-reaching, programs of state support or whether they sap political will. The growing support for the child tax credit is some evidence that the programs might help build momentum, but the United States is unlikely to develop a truly robust support system anytime soon. The most troubling aspect of these programs is that they erase race. The programs are not predicated on an understanding that structural racism is a root cause of racial inequities. And the programs do not force US society to grapple with this history or with the ongoing effects of structural racism. Reasonable minds can disagree about whether this is an acceptable political calculus or a Faustian bargain. But there is no doubt that something significant is lost in the ongoing inability of the United States to reckon with its history of racial inequity—to the profound detriment of children, families, and all of society.

NOTES

1 Clare Huntington, *Failure to Flourish: How Law Undermines Family Relationships* (Oxford University Press, 2014); Clare Huntington, "Mutual Dependency in Child Welfare," *Notre Dame Law Review* 82 (2007): 1485–1536.

2 Huntington, *Failure to Flourish*, 55–80.

3 Huntington, *Failure to Flourish*, 113–202.

4 Huntington, *Failure to Flourish*, 5–25.

5 Richard Rothstein, *The Color of Law: A Forgotten History of How Our Government Segregated America* (Norton, 2017).

6 Nazgol Ghandnoosh and Celeste Barry, "One in Five: Racial Disparity in Imprisonment—Causes and Remedies," Sentencing Project, December 7, 2023, www.sentencingproject.org.

7 Clare Huntington, "Postmarital Family Law: A Legal Structure for Nonmarital Families," *Stanford Law Review* 67 (2015): 167–240.

8 Huntington, *Failure to Flourish*, 165–67, 187–90.

9 Huntington, *Failure to Flourish*, 165–202.

10 Dolores Acevedo-Garcia, Abigail N. Walters, Leah Shafer, Elizabeth Wong, and Pamela Joshi, *A Policy Equity Analysis of the Earned Income Tax Credit: Fully Including Children in Immigrant Families and Hispanic Children in this Key Anti-Poverty Program* (diversitydatakids.org, April 20, 2022), www.diversitydatakids.org.

11 Clare Huntington, "Pragmatic Family Law," *Harvard Law Review* 136 (2023): 1501–83. The remainder of this chapter is based on that article.

12 Pew Research Center, *In a Politically Polarized Era, Sharp Divides in Both Partisan Coalitions: Partisanship Remains Biggest Factor in Public's Political Values* (Pew Research Center, December 17, 2019), appendix, 111–12, www.pewresearch.org (reporting results of polling on issues dividing Democrats and Republicans, with the seven most divisive being, in descending order, "gun policy," "racial attitudes," "climate & environment," "social safety net," "immigration," "role of government," and "gender & sexuality").

13 Naomi Cahn and June Carbone, *Red Families v. Blue Families: Legal Polarization and the Creation of Culture* (Oxford University Press, 2011).

14 Alan I. Abramowitz, *The Great Alignment: Race, Party Transformation, and the Rise of Donald Trump* (Yale University Press, 2018), 27.

15 Abramowitz, *Great Alignment*, 10–11, 14–16.

16 Jacob Grumbach, *Laboratories Against Democracy: How National Parties Transformed State Politics* (Princeton University Press, 2022), 9–13, 81–84.

17 Jamal Greene, *How Rights Went Wrong: Why Our Obsession with Rights Is Tearing America Apart* (Mariner Books, 2021), 89–90; David E. Pozen, Eric L. Talley, and

Julian Nyarko, "A Computational Analysis of Constitutional Polarization," *Cornell Law Review* 105 (2019): 37–48.

18 Nicholas O. Stephanopoulos, "The Anti-Carolene Court," *Supreme Court Review* 2019 (2020): 123–26; Miriam Seifter, "Countermajoritarian Legislatures," *Columbia Law Review* 121 (2020): 1756, 1762–68.

19 Gene Demby, "The Truth Behind the Lies of the Original 'Welfare Queen,'" *All Things Considered*, NPR, December 20, 2013, www.npr.org.

20 Allison H. Friedman-Krauss, W. Steven Barnett, Karin Garver, Kate Hodges, G. G. Weisenfeld, and Beth Ann Gardiner, *The State of Preschool 2020* (National Institute for Early Education Research, 2021), 30, table 4 (providing enrollment figures). For an in-depth discussion, see Clare Huntington, "Early Childhood Development and the Replication of Poverty," in *Holes in the Safety Net*, ed. Ezra Rosser (Cambridge University Press, 2019), 144–46. For more details about Oklahoma, see David L. Kirp, *The Sandbox Investment: The Preschool Movement and Kids-First Politics* (Harvard University Press, 2007), 180–86.

21 Friedman-Krauss et al., *State of Preschool*, 32, table 6 (noting spending variations, which closely reflect the traditional red-blue divide with some exceptions, such as West Virginia).

22 Friedman-Krauss et al., *State of Preschool*, 31, table 5.

23 Timothy J. Bartik and Brad Hershbein, "Pre-K in the Public Schools: Evidence from Within U.S. States" (Working Paper No. 18-285, Upjohn Institute, 2018), 9–10, 31–32, 34–35, 37 (reporting results of large-scale prekindergarten programs).

24 IRS, "Earned Income and Earned Income Tax Credit (EITC) Tables," January 26, 2023, www.irs.gov (setting forth graduated credit amounts, which are tied to earned income).

25 IRS, "Earned Income."

26 IRS, "Earned Income."

27 ACF, "FY 2021 Federal TANF and State MOE Financial Data," table A.2 (2022), www.acf.hhs.gov; ACF, "Temporary Assistance for Needy Families (TANF) Caseload Data—Fiscal Year (FY) 2021" (2022), www.acf.hhs.gov.

28 IRS, "Statistics for Tax Returns with the Earned Income Tax Credit (EITC)," January 20, 2023, www.eitc.irs.gov.

29 Cecile Murray and Elizabeth Kneebone, *The Earned Income Tax Credit and the White Working Class* (Brookings Institute, April 18, 2017), www.brookings.edu.

30 Anne L. Alstott, "Why the EITC Doesn't Make Work Pay," *Law and Contemporary Problems* 73, no. 1 (2010): 285–86.

31 National Conference of State Legislatures (NCSL), "Child Tax Credit Overview," January 26, 2024, www.ncsl.org.

32 Patient Protection and Affordable Care Act, Pub. L. No. 111-148.

33 Abbe R. Gluck and Thomas Scott-Railton, "Affordable Care Act Entrenchment," *Georgetown Law Journal* 108 (2020): 495, 531, 545.

34 Gluck and Scott-Railton, "Affordable Care Act Entrenchment," 531, 546 (describing this opposition and these losses, including Democratic loss of "twenty-two state legislative chambers and six governorships").

35 Gluck and Scott-Railton, "Affordable Care Act Entrenchment," 495.

36 National Federation of Independent Business v. Sebelius, 567 U.S. 519 (2012); Carter C. Price and Christine Eibner, "For States That Opt Out of Medicaid Expansion: 3.6 Million Fewer Insured and $8.4 Billion Less in Federal Payments," *Health Affairs* 32 (2013): 1030–36.

37 Abbe R. Gluck and Nicole Huberfeld, "What Is Federalism in Healthcare For?," *Stanford Law Review* 70 (2018): 1752–53.

38 Kaiser Family Foundation, "Status of State Medicaid Expansion Decisions: Interactive Map," May 8, 2024, www.kff.org.

39 A Better Balance, "State Pregnant Workers Fairness Laws," November 4, 2016 (updated January 10, 2024), www.abetterbalance.org (listing these states).

40 A Better Balance, "Pregnancy Accommodation Laws"; Pregnant Workers Fairness Act, Pub. L. No. 117-328, div. II (2022); Deborah A. Widiss, "Pregnant Workers Fairness Acts: Advancing a Progressive Policy in Both Red and Blue America," *Nevada Law Journal* 22 (2022): 1131, 1136–43, 1153 (explaining the gaps left by federal law).

41 Widiss, "Pregnant Workers Fairness Acts," 1133.

42 Louis Menand, *The Metaphysical Club: A Story of Ideas in America* (Farrar, Straus and Giroux, 2001), 201–3, 221–26.

43 Menand, *Metaphysical Club*.

44 Cornel West, *The American Evasion of Philosophy: A Genealogy of Pragmatism* (University of Wisconsin Press, 1989), 148.

45 West, *American Evasion*, 141; W. E. B. Du Bois, *The Autobiography of W. E. B. Du Bois: A Soliloquy on Viewing My Life from the Last Decade of Its First Century* (International, 1968), 222; Robert Gooding-Williams, "W. E. B. Du Bois," in *Stanford Encyclopedia of Philosophy*, ed. Edward N. Zalta (Stanford University, Spring 2020), § 2, https://plato.stanford.edu/archives/spr2020/entries/dubois.

46 West, *American Invasion*, 4–5.

47 Patricia Hill Collins, *Fighting Words: Black Women and the Search for Justice* (University of Minnesota Press, 1998), 188 ("The Black women on my block possessed a visionary pragmatism that emphasized the necessity of linking caring, theoretical vision with informed, practical struggle"; internal quotations and citation omitted).

48 V. Denise James, "Theorizing Black Feminist Pragmatism: Forethoughts on the Practice and Purpose of Philosophy as Envisioned by Black Feminists and John Dewey," *Journal of Speculative Philosophy* 23 (2009): 92–93.

49 James, "Theorizing Black Feminist Pragmatism," 93 (noting that Dewey offers "a social hope reduced to a working program of action, a prophecy of the future, but one disciplined by serious thought and knowledge"; quoting John Dewey,

Philosophy and Democracy, in *The Essential Dewey*, vol. 1, *Pragmatism, Education, Democracy*, ed. Larry A. Hickman and Thomas M. Alexander [Indiana University Press, 1998], 72).

50 Deva R. Woodly, *Reckoning: Black Lives Matter and the Democratic Necessity of Social Movements* (Oxford University Press, 2021), 51–52.

51 Linda C. McClain, "Experimental Meets Intersectional: Visionary Black Feminist Pragmatism and Practicing Constitutional Democracy," *Drake Law Review* 69 (2021): 852–77.

52 Kirp, *Sandbox Investment*, 4–5, 50–73, 78–91, 160–61.

53 Kirp, *Sandbox Investment*; Christina Weiland and Hirokazu Yoshikawa, "Impacts of a Prekindergarten Program on Children's Mathematics, Language, Literacy, Executive Function, and Emotional Skills," *Child Development* 84, no. 6 (2013): 2125–27.

54 Kirp, *Sandbox Investment*, 152, 158, 163–64.

55 Kirp, *Sandbox Investment*, 182–83.

56 Kirp, *Sandbox Investment*, 183–84.

57 For a detailed account, see Gluck and Scott-Railton, "Affordable Care Act Entrenchment," 539–42.

58 Gluck and Huberfeld, "What Is Federalism in Healthcare For?," 1752–53.

59 Gluck and Huberfeld, "What Is Federalism in Healthcare For?," 1740.

60 Gluck and Scott-Railton, "Affordable Care Act Entrenchment," 540–42.

61 Gluck and Scott-Railton, "Affordable Care Act Entrenchment," 558–59.

62 Christopher Brown, "Medicaid Expansion Ballot Measures Brewing in Three More States," *Bloomberg Law*, January 26, 2021, https://news.bloomberglaw.com (describing the successful ballot initiatives in Idaho, Maine, Missouri, Nebraska, Oklahoma, and Utah; noting that supporters are also pushing for ballot initiatives in Florida, Mississippi, and South Dakota).

63 Dana Thomson, Renee Ryberg, Kristen Harper, James Fuller, Katherine Paschall, Jody Franklin, and Lina Guzman, "The Role of the Social Safety Net in Protecting Children from Poverty," chap. 3 in *Lessons from a Historic Decline in Child Poverty* (Child Trends, September 11, 2022), 55, table 3.4 (documenting this decrease and noting that the poverty rate for Black children declined at approximately the same rate as for children in other racial groups).

64 Thomson et al., "Role of the Social Safety Net," 55 (calculating the contribution of different social welfare programs in reducing child poverty and finding that the EITC has the greatest impact, reducing child poverty by 22 percent in 2019).

65 Martha Ross and Nicole Bateman, *Meet the Low-Wage Workforce* (Metropolitan Policy Program, Brookings, November 2019), 9, www.brookings.edu ("Both Latino or Hispanic and Black workers are overrepresented [in the low-wage workforce] relative to their share of the total workforce, while whites and Asian Americans are under-represented."); Chuck Marr and Yixuan

Huang, *Women of Color Especially Benefit from Working Family Tax Credits* (Center on Budget and Policy Priorities, September 9, 2019), 1, www.cbpp. org (noting that "[21 percent] of Black women receive the EITC, more than double the [9 percent] share of white women who receive it" and that, further, the average benefit is higher for Black women than for white women); Nora Cahill and William G. Gale, "Narrowing the Racial Wealth Gap Using the EITC and CTC," Brookings, February 2, 2022, www.brookings.edu (noting that "the EITC lowers income inequality between Black and white households by roughly 5 to 10% each year" but also noting that it may not reduce the racial wealth gap).

66 US Bureau Labor Statistics, "Labor Force Statistics from the Current Population Survey," January 26, 2024, www.bls.gov/cps/cpsaat11.htm (indicating that 87 percent of home health aides are women, and 32 percent are Black).

67 Kenneth Finegold, Ann Conmy, Rose C. Chu, Arielle Bosworth, and Benjamin D. Sommers, "Trends in the U.S. Uninsured Population, 2010–2020," Issue Brief HP-2021-02 (Assistant Secretary Planning and Evaluation, Office of Health Policy, US Department of Health and Human Services, February 11, 2021), 6, https://aspe.hhs.gov.

68 Jesse Cross-Call, *Medicaid Expansion Has Helped Narrow Racial Disparities in Health Coverage and Access to Care* (Center on Budget and Policy Priorities, 2020), 1, www.cbpp.org.

69 Bartik and Hershbein, "Pre-K in the Public Schools," 34–35, 37.

70 Maxine Eichner, *The Free-Market Family: How the Market Crushed the American Dream (And How It Can Be Restored)* (Oxford University Press, 2020), 19–42.

71 Thomson et al., "Role of the Social Safety Net," 52, table 3.3 (noting that on average, the EITC and related programs lift children from somewhat below the supplemental poverty measure [SPM] to 130 percent of the SPM).

72 Alstott, "Why the EITC Doesn't Make Work Pay," 287 ("The EITC—in anything like its present form—does not, and cannot, 'make work pay,' because it operates in a legal context that creates deep disadvantage for low-wage workers and their children."), 289 ("The EITC is part and parcel of the harsh and meager U.S. welfare state. It pays a wage subsidy that is too small to lift workers to a decent living standard, and it conditions payments on continuous employment—an aspiration that is unrealistic for many in the low-wage workforce.").

73 Aiden Lee, Rose C. Chu, Christie Peters, and Benjamin D. Sommers, "Health Coverage Changes Under the Affordable Care Act: End of 2021 Update," Issue Brief HP-2022-17 (US Department of Health and Human Services, 2022), 7 figure 6, https://aspe.hhs.gov; Latoya Hill, Nambi Ndugga, Samantha Artiga, and Anthony Damico, "Health Coverage by Race and Ethnicity," Kaiser Family Foundation, January 11, 2024, www.kff.org.

74 Kaiser Family Foundation, "Status of State Medicaid Expansion Decisions" (identifying nonexpanders: Alabama, Florida, Georgia, Kansas, Mississippi, South Carolina, Tennessee, Texas, Wisconsin, and Wyoming).

75 Jared Sharpe, "UMass Amherst/WCVB Poll Finds Nearly Half of Americans Say the Federal Government Definitely Should Not Pay Reparations to the Descendants of Slaves," University of Massachusetts Amherst, April 29, 2021, www.umass.edu.

76 There is, however, a compelling case for reparations. See, e.g., Katherine M. Franke, *Repair: Redeeming the Promise of Abolition* (Haymarket Books, 2019), 101–13; Ta-Nehisi Coates, "The Case for Reparations," *The Atlantic*, June 2014, www.theatlantic.com.

Conclusion

So Now What? Setting the Frame

R. A. LENHARDT AND NANCY E. DOWD

We invite and implore listening to stories of parenting, work, poverty, and more as a means to inform policy and measure the successful implementation of policy responsive to the needs of parents, families, and children who are Black and Brown. Many people, especially those who are Black and Brown, are invisible and ignored. This chapter will be the first in what we hope will be an ongoing effort to hear, understand, and support women, men, children, families, and communities by elevating and paying attention to their stories, which illuminate affirmative strategies to deal with broad issues and structures that disproportionately impact families of color. These stories offer dynamic models of the process and means for radical change that serves all families, individual by individual.

Invisibility is starkly evident in the District of Columbia. Each year, people around the globe visit the US capital in Washington, DC. Visitors get a window on the District and the experiences of many communities. They rarely, however, experience the life of many people, especially those who are Black and Brown, many of whom reside in areas referred to as "Chocolate City," which is not part of tours or the Washington experience. As with many other cities and parts of states, the marginalized, racialized pattern of our geography is walled off, separated, avoided. Yet this is precisely what our focus must include and exactly where we must listen.

The stories at the heart of this chapter are a beginning of that process, the stories of two community workers who care for families. They sat for extended interviews in the summer and fall of 2024 at Georgetown University Law with R. A. Lenhardt, assisted by Peter Lees. In the first part of this chapter, we introduce Gail Avent and Randall Baylor. We then explore two themes that emerged in the interviews that are particularly critical to a way forward of honoring Black and Brown families and their unique leadership as well as needs. First, we discuss the framework of leadership, strategy, collaboration, and process exposed by their work, which we argue is an essential part of policy making and implementation. Second, we detail how their extraordinary work exposes the breadth and depth of the structural needs that must be addressed to achieve equity and equality of Black and Brown families. The very success of their work ironically exposes the comprehensive need for change beyond existing Band-Aids that replicate hierarchies.

Two Stories

Lenhardt came to Georgetown after living many years in New York City. And when she decided to come to Washington, DC, she wanted to revisit issues of race and family that she had been thinking about for many years of her work. This is why she came to this work and to this text. She sought people who shared her concerns and interest in race and family. She had an initial conversation with a person who was leading a Georgetown program that was focused on Washington, DC, community engagement. That person introduced her to Gail Avent and Randall Baylor.

Gail Avent is the executive director of the Family Care Coalition based in Southeast Washington, DC. An attorney, Gail is a former teacher and works directly with families of color as they navigate the public school system. Gail also tries to assist families of color on how best to help their children, including finding strategies that the families can use to assert themselves.

Randall Baylor is project lead at Children's National Hospital based in Washington, DC. Randall works with Washington, DC, parents to ensure that local families obtain any funding or social services that families of color may need. Randall is an intermediary between the local families and the resources that they may need.

Washington, DC, government does not provide local families enough resources and applies a "cookie-cutter" approach to solving problems, with services that are separated and siloed. Gail and Randall outlined how they engage the families they serve and provide support based on the needs of each family. They do not apply a cookie-cutter approach because each family is unique. They try to provide the core support for Black and Brown families.

A Model of Leadership and Strategy: Centering Parents' and Community Voices

The model of community work of these two community care workers is one of listening, engaging, and supporting parents and community voices. They listen. The model is one of "engagement" and "totality" that is engaged in "wholeheartedly" (Randall). It involves genuine giving to others. "We make families feel comfortable," says Gail, identifying the components of that relationship as mutual respect, acceptance, and an acknowledgment that they have value. The focus is on needs and communicating, "We hear you" (Gail). They embrace the families they serve; there is identification with families. We are "inheriting the concern of families when working with them" (Randall).

One story that epitomizes this approach is Randall's story of helping a new father. He first met the father, an older man, before his girlfriend's baby was born, even before he knew his girlfriend was pregnant. After the baby's birth, the girlfriend was arrested, convicted, and sent to Texas to serve her sentence, all without his knowledge. The baby was born while she was incarcerated, and she listed this man as the father on the birth certificate. The authorities contacted him to tell him he had just ten days to take custody of the baby before the baby boy would be placed in foster care. He reached out to Randall, desperate for help. Randall not only guided the father in the intricacies of gaining custody but sustained his connection to the father as he helped him navigate housing, a job, and health care, putting together the pieces of creating a life as a parent. Randall's connection did not end. He continued to check in with the father to see how he was doing, and Randall was therefore still connected and supporting him when the mother returned after serving her sentence and delivered the bombshell that the man who had parented this baby was not in fact the biological father. This man was every bit this child's father, and Randall helped him to retain custodial rights. Randall continues to remain in contact with father and son, recounting a recent interaction that included a big hug and smile from this young boy. This is a story of the depth of the services and connections that are a hallmark of this method, strategy, and heart-centered way of connecting and supporting parents, just as much as it is a story of the power of love and care in this father-son relationship.

Randall and Gail link parents and community voices to services, not by patronizing or directing or expecting parents to follow their lead but by engaging with parents as equals, as valued human beings. They both expressed that the vast majority of families and parents suffer in silence. Parents are acutely aware of the negative perception of them as incompetent, deficient, unworthy. Randall and Gail aim to empower and give respect, and in that process, they urge service providers to see parents in a different light, as needing links to services and providers but as having value, as "dependent but independent." Randall and Gail do not separate or differentiate themselves; to the contrary, they sometimes connect to their clients with their own stories, communicating that they struggle as well or have in the past. Gail shares her life story and experience frequently, as part of her process. She sees as part of her success the reaction of parents that they can hear and recognize themselves in her story. Sharing the personal is to connect and collaborate. As Gail notes, "condescending is the usual" experienced by Black and Brown parents, but she works to make parents' voice heard, not to speak to them or at them or for them but to support them in the value and worth of their voices and to encourage them to keep persisting to get what they need for their families.

"We want to be seen like everybody else. But we're not" (Gail). This observation about the desires of Black parents captures the value given by the process and approach used by Gail and Randall. The parents and families they serve have unmet needs. They are like every other parent and family: They want the best for their children and families. But they are challenged—by inadequate income, substandard housing, children's needs for health care, inadequate education, and unmet special needs. So they are not like everybody else. In addition to those unmet needs, they are not like everyone else because they are Black or Brown. "People will not look at you equally, and you will get a label" (Gail). Their clients' difference and lack of value and competency is assumed, a norm, and therefore the ability to deal with unmet needs includes not only how to connect with services and providers but also how to deal with the inhumanity that pervades the systems that provide services and those who hold the power in those systems.

The process engaged in and described by these two community carers is critical to understanding what is essential to implement positive outcomes on the ground as systems currently stand. It is a critical implementation model for imperfect systems as well as a critical source of obtaining knowledge for system change. Their goal is empowerment, to continue to have parents' voices heard, and to lower their stress by achieving success.

Gail and Randall did not see their method or strategy as unique to them. Rather, this critical approach to parents and family, to elevating their voices and partnering, collaborating in change, is a method they saw replicated among their contacts. Indeed, they envisioned what a "think tank" of such family care workers could create with regard to structural and policy change. Most importantly, such a think tank for them would not be populated solely by those like themselves who work with families and communities; rather, it would be a think tank that includes, searches out, and listens respectfully to families and communities and empowers them to succeed. Relationships, and the quality of the relationships, are thus central to framing Black and Brown families at the heart of policy and structural change to address the issues of those families and, by extension, all families.

Systemic Comprehensive Needs

The very success of Gail and Randall is painfully ironic. They work within systems to achieve the best results they can for individual families and parents. They bend rules but do not break them. Yet they are acutely aware of the broad systemic imperfections, negativity, and bad outcomes that are particularly evident in Black and Brown communities. They are pragmatic realists, but at the same time, they are deep analysts of the interlocking failings and inadequacies of systems and the grounding of those failures in cultural bias and discrimination. If we are to engage in system analysis and policy change, their voices and the voices of the parents and families they serve must be at the core. If we want to understand how systemic injustice operates on the ground, then we should listen to them and to the parents they serve. If we want to change, radically change, systems, then both the shape of a new system and its implementation should be informed by their voices.

Efforts to help parents and families are confounded by the inadequacy of supports and their limitation to particular profiles that reinforce inadequacy and lack of well-being. The context of DC is a panoply of adverse situations without enough resources. These include the lack of opportunity for education and health, low incomes, poor housing, and violence. Families are marginalized and diminished, and the context of extremely negative community is normalized (Randall). The city creates dependency, in part by providing services but not enough; there is a lack of inclusion of all city citizens in its vision and support, in effect "pilfering from impoverished communities" (Randall).

Randall's response to where to begin systemically is guaranteeing to all a "living wage." The high cost of rent and the impossibility of home ownership for most impose unbelievable stress that plays out in a host of other psychosocial issues. "Forced resilience can show up," he says; it can look good, like a superhero, but people do not want to feel that way, as it requires being in "survival mode all the time." While the resilience of Black and Brown families should be celebrated, it should not be required; its very presence indicates structural flaws and failure. "Families don't always want to be resilient; they just want peace" (Randall).

Gail notes that while services have increased over time, they are in silos and function only to serve narrow, extreme needs rather than to proactively and universally address needs. Services are difficult to navigate. Randall echoed this critique of a pattern of limited, insufficient support. As an example, lottery programs or development incentives to create low-income housing only serve a limited number of members of the community. Those who are outside the scope of these Band-Aid solutions have unaddressed needs, and the needs related to housing are especially pervasive.

When services are provided, those who provide them are not held accountable. Parents seeking services must be persistent and calm, despite the stress this places on parents to conform to how the systems want them to behave (Gail). Instead of blaming parents, structures need to evaluate what parents grew up with (or not) and what skills are needed, and support the value of parents as they are while supporting them. The goal should be energizing parents and supporting them to have their voices heard, not structuring a system to require an advocate. Instead of the least that can be provided, what is needed is a commitment to do more and do better to serve needs (Gail). The current interactions of inadequate structures generate hopelessness and helplessness. They are "an abyss," negatives that lead to negatives. "DC is comfortable with insanity," the insanity of doing the same thing and not changing (Randall).

The shape of the existing structure and its impact are clear and known. This is the harsh reality of structure and policy on the ground that is inescapable from the concrete, daily experiences of Gail and Randall. Their voices are vital to our critique, analysis, and movement for change. They put real faces and situations before us.

One such story is Gail's interaction with a ten-year-old boy whom she encountered. Her approach with parents and families is often to ask, "What do you need?" When she asked that question of this ten-year-old, he responded, "A mask and a BB gun." Startled by his response, she asked him why. He explained that he had been caught recently in violent crossfire in his neighborhood; he wanted to be able to protect himself. She then asked him, "What is your dream?" He immediately responded, "I want to be a football player." That a ten-year-old faces a reality that requires him to literally defend his own life to reach a boyhood dream is a tragedy. It exposes the failure of every support that he needs and deserves to thrive. He is a symbol of the negative interlocking systems that plague Black and Brown families; he is the guide to what is needed.

The scope of problems is overwhelming for individual parents and families, but it is only by seeing them and listening to them that we can identify where we are and see where we need to go. The work of Gail and Randall is amazing and wonderful, but it is limited. Imagine what they could do with real reforms. In this volume as a whole, we have elevated the extraordinary and unknown models, leadership, and power of Black and Brown families. We also have exposed the needs of Black and Brown families. Paying attention to individuals like Gail and Randall, and the families they serve, is a critical means to envision and identify where we need to go by following their process of engagement and listening to parents and families. It is a fitting reminder of all the stories in this volume that are the beginning of real change, if we listen and act.

Note: The video and audio tapes of the interviews with Gail and Randall are on file with R. A. Lenhardt at Georgetown Law.

ABOUT THE CONTRIBUTORS

AZIZA AHMED is Professor of Law, N. Neal Pike Scholar, and Codirector, BU Law Program on Reproductive Justice, at Boston University School of Law.

MARKETA BURNETT is Assistant Professor of Human Development and Family Sciences & Africana Studies at the University of Connecticut.

YAEL ZAKAI CANNON is Associate Professor at Georgetown University Law Center and directs the Health Justice Alliance Law Clinic, a medical-legal partnership training the next generation of leaders in law and medicine to advance health equity.

NANCY E. DOWD is Emeritus Professor of Law, University Professor, and Director of the Center on Children and Families, at the University of Florida College of Law.

MAXINE EICHNER is the Graham Kenan Distinguished Professor of Law at University of North Carolina School of Law.

ANITA GONZALEZ is Professor of Performing Arts and African American Studies at Georgetown University and Founding Codirector of its Racial Justice Institute.

DEREK M. GRIFFITH is Professor at the School of Nursing, and at the Perelman School of Medicine, at the University of Pennsylvania.

CLARE HUNTINGTON is the Barbara Aronstein Black Professor of Law at Columbia Law School.

JASON JACKSON is Associate Professor of Political Economy at Massachusetts Institute of Technology.

MICHELLE S. JACOBS is Emeritus Professor of Law at the University of Florida College of Law.

EMILY C. JAEGER is Project Manager/Research Support Specialist in the Department of Health Management & Policy in the School of Health at Georgetown University.

R. A. LENHARDT is Associate Dean of Diversity, Equity, and Inclusion and Agnes Williams Sesquicentennial Professor of Race, Law, and Justice at Georgetown University Law Center and the Codirector of the Georgetown University Racial Justice Institute.

SERENA MAYERI is the Arlin M. Adams Professor of Constitutional Law and Professor of History at the University of Pennsylvania Carey Law School.

SOLANGEL MALDONADO is the Eleanor Bontecou Professor of Law at Seton Hall University School of Law.

PRISCILLA ALOYO OCEN is Professor of Law at Loyola Law School of Los Angeles.

PERRI PEPPERMAN is Research Manager and Clinical Trials Nurse at Prometheus Federal Services.

TRISTAN PORTER is a public health and religious studies researcher at Fifth Ward Church of Christ in Houston, Texas.

JESSICA DIXON WEAVER is Associate Dean for Research and Professor of Law at SMU Dedman School of Law.

ERIKA WICHMANN works in project management and research support in Washington, DC.

INDEX

Page numbers in italics indicate Figures.

PRWOA. *See* Personal Responsibility and Work Opportunity Act of 1996
public accommodation, 10, 13–14
public health workers. *See* essential workers

racial bias academic socialization, 75–76
racial identity, 104–9, 174–77
racism, 6; absence of family support system relation to, 164–79, 239–42; COVID-19 pandemic and, 124–25, 156–57; mental health impacts from, 73; in schools, 71–73, 75–76, 106, 134; segregation and, 13, 14, 67, 110; structural/systemic, 160–63, 174, 179; valorization of family and, 1–2
Randolph, Sherie, 43
rape: Memphis Massacre in 1866 and, 16; slavery and, 26–27; women in prison and, 220, 222–23
Reconstruction Era, 2, 9–14, 16–33
Recruiting Families Using Data Act (2023), 114–15
Reeves, Ricard, 85
reframing. *See* framing and reframing
Relf, Minnie and Alice, 44
Report on Memphis Riots and Massacres, 29
reproductive rights and justice: Black feminist leadership on, 43–49; pregnancy in prison and, 222–25; prison family law and, 204–6
resilience, 70–79
Rittich, Kerry, 153, 154
Roberts, Dorothy, 109, 191, 202
Rodriguez-Trias, Helen, 43
Roe v. Wade, 32, 43, 48, 234
Rosenthal, Caitlin, 11

Santosky v. Kramer, 202
schools, 47, 48; *Brown v. Board of Education* and, 2, 40, 57; Head Start programs and, 165, 168, 176; partnering with Black caregivers, 77; racism in, 71–73, 75–76, 106, 134; transportation to and from, 134–35. *See also* education
segregation, 13, 14, 67, 110
sexual violence. *See* domestic violence; rape
Skinner v. Oklahoma, 204
slavery, 18, 19; antislavery and, 9–14; human dignity and, 9, 10, 13–14, 28; rape and, 26–27
Smith, Mrs. Slyvester, 45–46
SNAP. *See* Supplemental Nutrition Assistance Program
social determinants of health. *See* healthcare, children and
state support of families. *See* family support system, absence of
storytelling, 57, 258–59
structural/systemic inequality, 5, 6, 160–79
Students for Fair Admissions Inc. v. President and Fellows of Harvard College, 109
Sufrin, Carolyn, 206, 224
summary, of chapters, 4–7
Supplemental Nutrition Assistance Program (SNAP), 93, 136
Supreme Court. *See* court cases
Survived and Punished Project, 218
Sutton, Percy, 43

TANF. *See* Temporary Assistance for Needy Families
tax credits: Child Tax Credit, 164, 170–71; Earned Income Tax Credit, 164, 242, 244, 248, 249
Taylor, Keeanga-Yamahtta, 44
Temporary Assistance for Needy Families (TANF), 112, 161, 164, 244
Tennessee, 16–33
Terrell, Mary Church, 195
Thirteenth Amendment, 11, 12, 16
Tillman, Johnnie, 49–50

transportation needs, 134–35
trauma: Adverse Childhood Experiences and, 129–30, 177–78, 215–16; mental health and, 26, 130; Reconstruction Era experiences of, 26–29; for survivors of domestic violence, 218–19
Turner v. Safley, 190, 191, 196, 197, 198, 205

violence, 17, 32, 66, 73; domestic, 125, 129, 155, 177, 218–19; Memphis Race Massacre, 23–31; Southern "outrages" against Black communities, 21–22, 24, 27; trauma and survivors of, 218–19. *See also* rape
vision, 61–66, 125, 191–92, 229–32
vote, women's right to, 13

Waldron, Jeremy, 13
Walter, Mildred, 50
Washington, DC, 57–68, 257–63
Wattleton, Faye, 43
Weinberger v. Wiesenfeld, 42

welfare: Black feminist leadership around, 45–51; child welfare system, 102–17, 127, 139–40; Medicaid, 136, 245, 247; rights, 49–51; SNAP, 93, 136; TANF, 112, 161, 164, 244; WIC, 93. *See also* foster care
West, Cornell, 246
White, Gardenia, 39
"white savior," 58–59
White v. Crook, 40, 42
WIC. *See* Nutrition Program for Women, Infants and Children
Williams, Patricia, 9
Willis, Lillie, 40
women: maternal health and, 88–89; voting rights and, 13. *See also* Black feminist leadership; Black women; feminism; prison, women in
Woodly, Deva, 246

Zora on My Mind (Gonzalez and Lawrence), 57–58, 61–66